# WEIRD & WONDERFUL

# WEIRD & WONDERFUL

## The Dime Museum in America

ANDREA STULMAN DENNETT

NEW YORK UNIVERSITY PRESS

New York and London

NEW YORK UNIVERSITY PRESS
New York and London

Library of Congress Cataloging-in-Publication Data
Dennett, Andrea Stulman, 1958–
Weird and Wonderful : the dime museum in America / Andrea Stulman Dennett.
p. cm.
Includes bibliographical references and index.
ISBN 0-8147-1855-X (clothbound : alk. paper).—ISBN 0-8147-1886-8 (paperbound :
alk. paper)
1. Museums—United States—History.  2. Dime museums—United States—History.
3. Curiosities and wonders—Museums—United States—History.  4. Eccentrics and
eccentricity—Museums—United States—History.  5. Popular culture—United States—
History.  6. Barnum, P. T. (Phineas Taylor), 1810–1891.  7. Barnum's American
Museum.  I. Title.
AM11.D46 1997
069'.0973—dc21      97–4880
                         CIP

Manufactured in the United States of America
10 9 8 7 6 5 4 3 2 1

*For Alex and Jonathan*

# Contents

# Illustrations

# Preface and Acknowledgments

The dime museum has been nearly forgotten, but during its heyday in the latter half of the nineteenth century, it was as popular an institution in the United States as the movies are today. Phineas Taylor Barnum made the dime museum a fixture of the American cultural landscape. Although he is famous for his circus career, he did not become involved with the circus until 1870, at the age of sixty. By that time he had made and lost several fortunes and was famous on two continents. Audiences loved Barnum's brand of amusement, and his museum in New York had made him rich years before he brought Jenny Lind, the "Swedish Nightingale," to America in 1850, and decades before he entered into the famous partnership with James Bailey. In fact, it was through his American Museum in New York that Barnum earned his reputation as the father of American show business. His museum was the prototype—all later museums followed his pattern.

*Weird and Wonderful* chronicles the evolution of the dime museum from its inception as a cabinet of curiosities to its demise as a victim of competition from newer amusements. Although I devote an entire chapter to Barnum, I concentrate mainly on his museum activities, from 1841 to 1868, and have left accounts of his personal, political, and circus life to his biographers.

The dime museum was a unique institution. It integrated many types of entertainment under one roof and for a single price. In addition, it was a safe environment for women and children and was open from early morning to late at night. Dime museums flourished until the turn of the century, but by World War I there were hardly any left in America.

There were dime museums throughout the United States, but most of the earlier and more important ones were concentrated on the eastern seaboard and in the Midwest. I am reluctant to say outright that the dime museum was an East Coast/Midwest phenomenon—there was, for example, the Pacific Museum of Anatomy and Natural Science, which can be dated as early as 1869—but resources are scarce. It is clear, however, that the dime museum concept began and flourished in the Northeast and that the existence of the museum circuit was one of the reasons there was a high concentration of museums in New York, Boston, and Philadelphia. Museum managers were constantly seeking new exhibits; after all, variation was what made patrons return again and again to the same museum.

Consequently, freaks, magicians, and other variety artists shuttled back and forth between museums, hardly ever staying at one institution longer than six weeks.

After establishing profitable museums in the East, many managers sought to create additional museums in the Midwest. George Middleton, who operated the Globe Dime Museum in New York, ventured west and created his own museum circuit. The tremendous success of the New York Eden Musée led to similar museums in Boston and Chicago. Southern cities like Richmond, Norfolk, and Atlanta, however, were out of the main dime museum loop. Although they may have cultivated the same types of itinerant amusements as Baltimore and Philadelphia, these cities were smaller. And since they were part of a slave-oriented culture, they did not have the thriving working-class population needed to support the dime museum industry.[1] The early dime museums prospered in industrialized urban cities where it was acceptable and theoretically profitable to have an entertainment environment that catered to all classes.

As a result, the dime museum material that I have detailed comes largely from the industrialized eastern seaboard cities and the Midwest. As with most ephemeral amusements of this period, documentation is sparse. For example, the name of a dime museum might be mentioned in a nineteenth-century newspaper, but when I went to do research on the institution, there were no documents. No archive has a file labeled "Dime Museum." Much of the information I found was in the theater section of file catalogs and newspapers, and most references were to the big museums, those with reputable theaters. Many of my examples are of New York City institutions, since they were widely imitated, and because New York was home to many types of museums. I tried to include detailed descriptions of a variety of museums in order to give the reader an exact idea of what they looked like and felt like; included in this project are descriptions of both the elite and the smaller, more colorful institutions. Luck had a lot to do with this research, and many times I found dime museum programs in files titled "Waxworks," "Freaks," or "Circus." The museums discussed are generally ones that were popular with nineteenth-century patrons. As a result, their popularity or their longevity left us a legacy, however scattered.

Competition was fierce among the big city museums, and managers had to advertise their exhibits prominently in the newspapers. Although this sort of documentation was valuable, it is difficult to tell what is fact and what is fiction when one is dealing with propaganda. Museum managers routinely lied to the public in order to make their exhibits sound more exciting. In addition, many of the articles I discovered on dime museum attractions were undated, which leads to confusion about what was taking place at any given time. I have done my best to sift through many strange sources of information and piece together in a logical way some descriptions of these museums. Throughout my research I found numerous contradictions in both primary and secondary sources; all discrepancies have been mentioned in the notes. Often I was disappointed by the lack of primary materials and found gathering information a difficult struggle. At length, however, the project began to come into focus. The end result is, I hope, a clear presentation of what a dime museum was, how important it was to nineteenth-century Americans, and how this institution, which lasted little more than half a century, affected the twentieth-century amusement industry. Because of the ephemeral nature of the dime museum, however, there will always remain questions that cannot be answered.

Live performances were the major draw of the dime museums. Many theater historians mention the dime museum as contributing to the development of vaudeville, but few have explored the theatrical productions, variety sketches, and freak shows that entertained thousands in the mid-nineteenth century. In my investigation, I found that the quality of plays performed at the dime museums was often very high; great actors and actresses of both the legitimate stage and vaudeville got their start in such productions. In fact, some dime museums, such as the Boston Museum and Wood's Museum and Metropolitan Theatre in New York, were eventually transformed into highly reputable playhouses. The larger dime museums even had their own resident stock companies. In the main, the plays produced by these companies were either original works or adaptations of popular melodramas. (The year in parentheses after the title of a play corresponds to the dime museum production date.)

When I started on this topic in 1990, Brooks McNamara's 1974 article on the dime museum was the only piece written on the subject. With the exception of Bruce McConachie, most scholars currently writing about late nineteenth-century culture and amusements recognize the historical importance of the dime museum but have been at a loss to fully describe this entertainment phenomenon. Hopefully, my research will fill that void.

• • •

This project has consumed most of my energies for the past six years and would not have been possible without the assistance of many people and institutions. I would like to thank all those who have seemed genuinely excited by the project and who helped me with their expertise. In particular I am grateful to Robert Bogdan, John Frick, and Ted Barber, who shared their research with me, and to Janet Boulton, whose editorial skills were indispensable. I owe thanks to the New York Public Library for the Performing Arts, the Museum of the City of New York, the New-York Historical Society, the Cincinnati Historical Society, the Harvard Theatre Collection, the Chicago Historical Society, the Philadelphia Free Library, the San Francisco Performing Arts Library and Museum, the San Francisco Historical Society, the Mütter Museum at Philadelphia's College of Physicians, the Barnum Collection located at the Bridgeport Public Library, and the Baltimore City Life Museum. Thanks also are due to Steve Kantrowitz, Nancy Levitan Kelly, Laura Stulman, Lisa Schwartz, Rosemarie Garland Thomson, and Kim Fritschi for all their help and to Peggy Phelan for all her encouragement. I am grateful to Eric Zinner, my editor at New York University Press, for truly believing in the merits of this project and making the transition from manuscript to book an easy one. A special word of appreciation goes to my dear friend the late Peter Arnott, whose intellect, talent, and humanity I deeply respected and sorely miss.

Special thanks are due to Brooks McNamara, who would never let me give up on this project even when it got tough. His enthusiasm for the topic and his belief in me were an inspiration; I thank him for his years of guidance and friendship. Finally, it's no secret that without the love and support of my family, my parents, Elga and Stephen Stulman, my in-laws, Lissy and Leonard Dennett, my children, Alexandra and Jonathan, and my husband, Rick, I would never have completed this book.

# 1. The Origins of the Dime Museum, 1782–1840

Come hither, come hither by night or by day,
There's plenty to look at and little to pay;
You may stroll through the rooms and at every turn
There's something to please you and something to learn.
If weary and heated, rest here at your ease,
There's a fountain to cool you and music to please.
                    —Advertisement for the Western Museum of Cincinnati, 1834

The earliest museums in this country, unlike dime museums, were created in the spirit of the Enlightenment and were meant to be centers of scientific study.[1] Private collections—often called "cabinets of wonders and curiosities"—were generally owned by wealthy citizens or by organizations such as libraries or so-called philosophical societies.[2] Most of the objects in these cabinets were labeled and displayed according to the Linnaean system of classification, which related each object to another in the so-called great chain of being.[3] Cabinets also included paintings and books, and many functioned as libraries.

Postrevolutionary America, however, was not a wealthy country, and philanthropy did not abound. But patriotism and a sense of democracy, coupled with the hope of disseminating knowledge and preserving New World culture, caused many eighteenth-century Americans who had amassed collections of books and objects to invite the public to view their assemblages, sometimes for a small fee. Some began gathering and displaying their collections as a way to earn a livelihood, or at least to supplement a meager income. Unlike the wealthy private cabinet owners, this new breed of museum proprietor depended on ticket sales to maintain his collection. Many museum managers who prided themselves on exhibiting only high-quality items, however, were soon compelled to display sensational novelties to attract crowds and remain solvent. As museums began to compete with one another for patrons, proprietors were driven to

1

concoct gimmicks and create phony relics. The "associated-value items" (artifacts that achieved importance by virtue of their association with a famous person, for example George Washington's shaving brush and night-cap or the bedroom curtains of Mary Queen of Scots) became essential displays. Obtaining the most novel and unusual exhibits, in fact, eventually became more important than maintaining a museum's pedagogical goals.

By the early nineteenth century, such live performers as musicians, hypnotists, and freaks had penetrated scientific museums.[4] Managers justified this innovation by claiming that their museums were repositories of rational amusements, establishments that helped divert pleasure seekers from such vices as gambling, drinking, and prostitution. These managers clearly expected live performers to attract rather than repel the bourgeois public. It was difficult, however, for them to strike the right balance between high-brow scientific exhibits and popular theatrical displays. Some collections, once reputed to be rational amusements, transformed themselves into exhibitions that pointedly favored the amusing over the rational.[5] This shift in emphasis paved the way for a totally new genre of popular entertainment, the dime museum. The raison d'être of the dime museum was the one-of-a-kind live exhibit, and a museum's reputation, popularity, and longevity resided in its diversified program of live performance.

•   •   •

The rise of the dime museum in the middle of the nineteenth century was a by-product of the enormous expansion of the American urban landscape. Rural migration and European immigration created cities filled with diverse peoples who desperately needed new and respectable forms of cheap entertainment. The clash of nationalities, religions, and classes created feelings of displacement and anxiety in city dwellers. Immigrants had to adjust to a new and alien culture, farm laborers were transformed into factory workers, and white-collar employees like shop assistants, clerks, and sales and office personnel surfaced as the new middle class, uprooting older notions of class and social status. Although heterogeneity gave the modern city its distinctly American character, there was, as Lawrence Levine wrote, a "sense of anarchic change, of looming chaos, and of fragmentation."[6] Traditional forms of culture began to erode and new cultural expressions developed in response to the dynamics of city life.

Demographic growth and industrialization destroyed local communities, produced slums, and threatened to change the structure of the nuclear family. While democratic capitalism promoted faith in the idea that an individual could achieve comfort and success, the realities of life in crowded cities and dingy factories perpetually challenged the validity of this belief. People had to make fundamental changes in their lives, thoughts, and culture.[7] Life became less home-centered, because for many, home was no longer a private house. Quiet family gatherings, where people exchanged stories, songs, and jokes, were no longer possible in the boardinghouses or the dark, airless, and overcrowded tenements of the period, where strangers were forced to live together and disease was rampant. Boardinghouse and tenement life played an important role in the emergence of a new mass culture.

While the domestic chores of tenement apartments—washing clothes, dishes, and floors and preparing meals—kept both employed and unemployed women busy at home, working-class men found many diversions that allowed them to escape appalling residential and working conditions— the most common lure being the saloon. Drink, food, shelter, and companionship could all be found there. Madelon Powers has written that "the primary function of the saloon was to offer the basic amenities of home in a public space." The saloon, Powers claimed, "offered the emerging working class a wide array of facilities, services, and contacts often available nowhere else."[8] Neighborhood saloons with regular patrons fostered a camaraderie, a group identity among working-class men that provided solace during this period of economic and social upheaval. But many families needed several incomes to survive, and working women and children, who had no claim to their own wages, watched helplessly as their husbands and fathers sometimes drank up their pay. Money for food, clothing, and shelter was squandered at the saloon, and women were often beaten or abandoned by their drunken husbands. Alcoholism became a formidable problem for many urban families.

Between 1840 and 1850 numerous antiliquor organizations were formed. They included people from all classes, both sexes, and various ethnic groups. The temperance crusade was by no means monolithic or even roughly unified; advocates looked at the growth of cities and the connection to drink from many different perspectives. They had distinct agendas, but most agreed that intemperance was the great destroyer of the American family.[9] "There seems to be little doubt," wrote Ruth Bordin, "that the Temperance movement developed in response to a social evil that was both real and widespread."[10] While some reformers believed that the abuse of alcohol was fostered by the social forces of industrial capitalism and the problems created by burgeoning cities, historian John Frick has

postulated that the hatred of drunkenness and the dread of its consequences for the next generation and the country's future "became a 'sym-
bolic expression of deeper fears about the direction of American Society.' "[11] The drunken husband thus came to epitomize the evils of a
fragmented modern society, and, as head of the household, he was often
seen as an oppressor of his wife and family.

In the midst of the social and economic chaos of antebellum America,
new forms of culture emerged in response to the problems created by the
modern city. The working and middle classes needed to form a common
urban identity, a shared culture that minimized the housing and labor
inequities caused by urbanization and industrialization. One of the functions of the new commercial amusements that got their start before the
Civil War was to knit, momentarily, a heterogeneous audience into a cohe-
sive whole by promoting assimilation, patriotism, and temperance, and by
diminishing the contrast between the wonders of the machine age and
the impoverishment, injustice, and human degradation that accompanied
them.[12]

At the beginning of the nineteenth century the theater catered to a wide
range of social and economic classes, which were distinguished—within
the theater—by where they were seated. According to Robert Toll, each
section of a theater formed a society of its own.[13] Box and orchestra seats
were reserved for the upper classes and genteel women, while the pit was
for mechanics and artisans and the gallery for the lower classes. The third
tier, with its separate entrance and bar, was reserved for "unescorted
women." Prostitutes did not attend the theater to see a play; their primary
business was to make arrangements for the evening, and they either took
their clients to a brothel or conducted their trade right in the theater.[14]

An evening's entertainment was not restricted to a five-act play. Between
the acts of a full-length drama were variety numbers: jugglers, acrobats,
dancers, trained animals, and human anomalies. The heterogeneous theater
audience often drank, ate, and smoked during the performance, and it was
not unusual for audience members to swear at performers they did not care
for. If they enjoyed a performance, they yelled, cheered, and insisted on an
encore. American theater had a reputation for condoning prostitution,
liquor consumption, and rude behavior and was not considered a respectable form of entertainment. New York's bloody Astor Place Riot of May
1849 confirmed that a single theater could not house culturally and economically different people. Some may argue that the riot spurred the
division between what is commonly referred to as high culture and popular

culture and marked the moment when the theater divorced itself from variety performers. The boundary between the two cultures, however, is permeable and fluctuating. Lawrence Levine argues that the term "popular" has been used to describe creations that not only command large audiences but also display questionable artistic merit. The use of such imprecise cultural categories, says Levine, has helped obscure the dynamic complexity of American society in the nineteenth century, where for a long time there existed a shared public culture.[15] While the theater no longer functioned as an amusement that embraced all classes, new forms of culture surfaced that had both a respectable reputation and mass appeal.

5

· · ·

In the middle of the nineteenth century, the dime museum—a distinctly American form of popular entertainment—emerged as a novel form of recreation that could divert a heterogeneous audience while supporting the new industrial morality of hard work, temperance, and perseverance. The exhibits displayed in dime museums affirmed the common person's worth and restored his dignity while perpetuating the dream of a better life. Dime museums attempted to bridge the ever growing gap between elite and popular audiences. The museums offered a democratic and ostensibly "educational" form of entertainment in which neither language, literacy, sex, nor the size of one's wallet was an issue.

The dime museum flourished throughout the late nineteenth century. As an entertainment venue it peaked between 1880 and 1900 and was in decline by the following decade. For a low, onetime admission charge, the dime museum dazzled men, women, and children with its dioramas, panoramas, georamas, cosmoramas, paintings, relics, freaks, stuffed animals, menageries, waxworks, and theatrical performances. Nothing quite like it had existed before.[16] No previous amusement had ever appealed to such a diversified audience or integrated so many diversions under one roof.

The process of uniting individual amusements and marketing them as a single, "walk-through" entertainment, suitable for the entire family, was what made the dime museum novel. In a sense it was a so-called environmental entertainment, among whose fixed exhibits mobile spectators could organize their own journey. The arrangement of space within a dime museum, with its display cabinets set around the periphery and grouped in the center of a room, created an environment in which customers were compelled to see each other as well as the exhibits themselves. In such a space the crowd became part of the performance, an important aspect of the experience.

The atmosphere of respectability—in the larger museums, at least—revitalized many ailing entertainments and introduced new ones to a mass audience. The theater, which by midcentury had become associated with prostitution and decadence, was revived in the family atmosphere of the dime museums, which offered "cheap and comprehensible entertainment that was seemingly accepted on moral and religious grounds."[17] The production of biblical and temperance plays helped the museums establish a reputation for morality and attract patrons with an antitheater bias. Freak shows, once thought to be simply a low form of itinerant amusement, gained a certain respectability and an undoubted popularity in the museums. Ventriloquists, magicians, musicians, and actors could find work opportunities in dime museums, and performers contracted with them for weeks at a time. Many late nineteenth-century spectators were introduced to their first vaudeville shows at a dime museum; others saw their first films there.

Significantly for the evolution of the dime museums, many Victorian Americans believed that leisure time should not be spent in idleness and frivolity but in edifying and constructive activities.[18] Conservative cultural reformers believed that "under enlightened municipal auspices, recreation could serve as a powerfully constructive force in social integration and moral development."[19] The success of the lyceum movement and the public education crusade, whose goals were to improve schools, academies, seminaries, and libraries and to promote the diffusion of useful knowledge, prompted managers to highlight their museums' pedagogical function. Stressing the educational benefits of a visit to a dime museum, however, was largely a simple marketing device. Popular impresarios of the age, such as P. T. Barnum and Moses Kimball, "mastered the rhetoric of moral elevation, scientific instruction, and cultural refinement in presenting their attractions."[20] Whatever learning did in fact take place was almost accidental, for the dime museums were established as family recreation centers, not as temples of learning. Artifacts were purchased not because of their educational merit but for their drawing power. In addition, many of the items on display had been faked, so that what patrons "learned" was often bogus as well.

The historical wax tableaux, for example, were created not to edify but to entertain and to foster nationalism; history was commodified, distorted, and freely falsified to please the public. The retelling of events in these tableaux suffered from a "historical amnesia" that avoided issues of racism, sexism, and class struggle.[21] In Civil War displays, depictions of the inhumanity of slavery or the horrors of bloody combat were rare. Most Northern museums, for example, simply highlighted the triumph of General Ulysses S. Grant over General Robert E. Lee.[22] The American Revolution was simply recalled by the tableau of "George Washington Crossing the Delaware River." The tragic side of war was almost never illustrated; unthinking patriotism was at the heart of such exhibits, and displays of blood were reserved for the chamber of horrors. Yet while blood was pervasive there, museums' displays of human primitivism promoted egalitarian ideals of modernization: all members of a civilized society, regardless of class or race, were equal in terms of measured progress from the state of barbarism.

Nevertheless, the tableaux functioned like popular newspapers of a sort: celebrities, well-known actors, famous musicians, and local murderers—the headliners of their day—were presented as important stories. Seldom was there anything controversial (except an item's authenticity) or potentially offensive about a dime museum display. Museums avoided such topics as women's suffrage and the plight of immigrants. Dime museums in fact were commercial enterprises, and the ultimate goal of every museum owner was to attract customers and make money.

Amid the formidable challenges of modernization, the dime museum was a safe haven, presenting unthreatening, comprehensible images of the wonders of the human and natural worlds. For those anxious about their own status, exotic freaks and wax displays of barbarism reaffirmed their self-worth and the civility of urban life. Historical wax tableaux and paintings promoted patriotism, and temperance melodramas, presented in the chaste theaters of the dime museums, offered optimistic solutions to the personal anxieties brought about by a rapidly changing society. These dramas promoted the genteel virtues of sobriety, diligence, and frugality and promised good fortune to those who adhered to these principles.

A consequence of industrial capitalism was the promotion of an unequal distribution of wealth. The dime museum, however, was a great economic equalizer. All who could afford the price of admission were treated the same, and for several years, some museum theaters did not charge extra for the better seats. The theaters in the larger museums were quite luxurious. Magic lanterns shows and, later, films offered visions of faraway places to those who could never afford to travel. Unthreatening exhibits of technology and curiosities of human behavior and evolution awed even educated patrons. For little money a spectator could enjoy a variety of pleasures.

However, "the roots of sensationalism," wrote Gunther Barth, "lay not merely in the human craving for thrills, but in the nature of the modern city itself."[23] The city, with its chaotic and ever changing landscape, accustomed residents to the shocking dramas of political scandals, poverty, crime, and the tireless sound of fire alarms.

● ● ●

American dime museums came in all sizes and many types, from grand five-story buildings that contained theaters accommodating three thousand spectators and curio halls parading upwards of ten thousand curiosities to small storefronts that were converted into exhibition rooms displaying a few old coins, petrified wood, and some living anomalies. "Dime museum," however, is a term used to differentiate all these popular amusement centers from endowed public museums such as New York's American Museum of Natural History (1869) or Boston's Museum of Fine Arts (1876).

Ironically, not all dime museums cost a dime. (Bunnell's New York museum was supposedly the first to lower its price to ten cents in 1876.)[24] Admission generally ranged from ten to fifty cents: the average museum charged twenty-five cents for adults and half price for children under twelve. Usually they were named for their founder, as in the case of Huber's Museum in New York; their street location, such as Philadelphia's Ninth and Arch Museum; or their city, such as the Boston Museum. Very few dime museums actually used the word "dime" in their names: the ones that did came primarily from the post-Civil War era, among them Peck's Great Dime Museum (1881), located in Philadelphia, or the Globe Dime Museum (1885) of New York.

In response to the average worker's growing leisure time in the last quarter of the century, dime museums often were open for ten to twelve hours daily, Monday through Saturday, and most on Sunday as well. Their inexpensive and unrestricted admission policy made them accessible to the masses, and their popularity grew explosively from 1860 to 1900.

Only a small percentage of a major dime museum's collection was ever on permanent display; the majority of its contents were rotated, and managers changed exhibits weekly to encourage repeated visits by patrons. Managers focused much of their attention on seeking out new displays, and some set up a network for exchanging curiosities.[25] P. T. Barnum, the legendary New York museum proprietor, regularly traded exhibits with his friend Moses Kimball, a lesser-known museum impresario who was man-

FIGURE 1. Eden Musée, New York, 1899. (Museum of the City of New York, Byron Collection.)

ager of the Boston Museum. In 1843 Barnum wrote to Kimball, "I *must* have the fat boy or the other monster [or] something new *in the course of this week* so as t[o be] *sure* to put them in the General's place *next Monday,* [?so] *don't fail!*"[26]

But cooperation was less common than competition, which prompted proprietors to advertise heavily in local newspapers, touting their exhibits with a mix of exaggeration and outright lies. Marketing and promotion were essential tools for a museum's survival, and humbugging became standard practice in the dime museum industry.[27] The language of the advertisements was bombastic; each museum was heralded as the grandest, largest, or most marvelous.[28] The facades of museum buildings served as billboards and often flaunted huge canvas banners or posters announcing the latest attraction (see fig. 1). Frequently museum buildings were decorated with flags and festive banners, or painted like huge billboards. Museum managers, well aware of the financial rewards of catering to a mass audience, sent patrons home with illustrated brochures describing the contents of their museums.[29] Additionally, they marketed souvenirs, such as handblown glass, personalized silhouettes, and cheap jewelry. To a nineteenth-century American, museum business clearly meant show business, and throughout the last quarter of the century there was a profusion of proprietary museums, each trying to outdo the other in promoting and exhibiting—and making a profit from—that one special rarity.

10

The story of the evolution of the public museum out of the American dime museum cannot be told without mentioning the contributions of Pierre Eugène Du Simitière, Charles Willson Peale and his son Rubens, all of Philadelphia; Gardiner Baker and John Scudder of New York; and Daniel Drake and Joseph Dorfeuille of Cincinnati. These men were at the forefront of the emergence of dime museums in America and contributed greatly to the public museum movement.

• • •

In April 1782, a Geneva-born American named Pierre Eugène Du Simitière announced his intention of allowing the public to view his Philadelphia collection of scientific and natural history objects for an admission charge of fifty cents.[30] With this announcement, the first postrevolutionary museum, the American Museum, was established.[31] Du Simitière earned his living as a painter: he created profile portraits of famous Revolutionary leaders and designed official seals and medals. A respected member of the Philadelphia community, he was elected to the prestigious American Society for the Promotion of Useful Knowledge.[32]

Du Simitière was concerned with documenting American history and culture and became especially interested in the plight of the American Indian. In addition, for many years he tried to generate funding for a project chronicling the history of the western states. Du Simitière's intention in exhibiting his collection of flora and fauna, Indian and African artifacts, prints, drawings, and colonial newspapers and books to the public was to broaden the artistic taste and attitude of the average citizen.[33] Attendance at his new museum was initially poor, but in June 1782 he advertised the contents of his collection and requested donations of natural history objects. The response was generous.[34]

Charles Coleman Sellers, Charles Willson Peale's biographer, believes Du Simitière's so-called American Museum was not a "museum" so much as a "magpie's nest of historical and scientific rarities."[35] Many scholars dispute this statement and credit Du Simitière with being the first postrevolutionary American to transform a private cabinet into a public museum. They argue that not only did Du Simitière pioneer the creation of an institution that catered simultaneously to popular and elite audiences, a duality unknown in Europe, but he focused his museum on American artifacts. For many, he was the first to try to preserve American culture and history and American Indian ethnography.[36]

11

As for the criticism that the collection lacked organization, the historian and curator Dillon Ripley points out that it was not uncommon for early public museums to be mere assemblages of curiosities. In fact, some critics of London's British Museum complained that its random displays were unscientific.[37] Kenneth Hudson, in *A Social History of Museums,* supports this argument, noting that "old-fashioned chaos had a strong appeal for children and other unsophisticated people, for whom a museum was, more than anything else, a chamber of wonders, a romantic place which scientific arrangement could and did only spoil." He claimed that only in rare instances was the eighteenth- and nineteenth-century collector an "orderly, systematic person. The more he acquired, the better pleased he was, and since space was expensive, museums and art galleries tended to be crowded places."[38]

Du Simitière's museum was open only for two years (1782–84), but it maintained a high level of integrity, apparently never integrating popular amusements into the exhibitions, and never catering to cultural tastes at their lowest. Since postrevolutionary America had no museum history, it was natural for Du Simitière to look to Europe for his model. European museums, such as Spain's Prado and England's British Museum, were indeed for the elite, and entrance to them was seen as a privilege, not a right. Most European collections were originally the "cabinets" created by royalty, the nobility, or gentry, and many continued to operate under royal patronage or government subsidy and were open only to a select few.

The contents of the British Museum, for example, which opened in 1759, had belonged to Sir Hans Sloane, a prominent physician who died in 1753. He bequeathed his collection to the city of London. When the new museum opened, only a limited number of people were given access to it. The museum was open Monday through Thursday; Friday was reserved for especially select visitors. Tickets were obtained by written application, and it took anywhere from two weeks to several months for museum authorities to check references and issue tickets. The museum operated on the "tour system," which meant that only a limited number of people could visit the collection at a given time. Ticket holders were asked to arrive between eleven and noon, and only 120 people were allowed in at a time. Tours were rushed. Kenneth Hudson believes that financial problems created a shortage of museum personnel, which "made it necessary to hustle visitors through the galleries."[39]

12

Du Simitière supposedly wanted to do away with the elitism of private cabinets, but when he opened his American Museum to the public in 1782, he also was hoping to supplement his income. While an open admission policy made his collection theoretically accessible to all, the museum remained in fact elitist and was not, in practice, available to all citizens equally. The fifty-cent admission charge was extremely steep, and although entrance to the public museum was theoretically a citizen's right, it was a right he could exercise only if he could afford the admission price. There was no government sponsorship for public museums, so unless an owner was wealthy, ticket sales were the only means by which he could maintain and expand his collection.

Since the museum imitated the European tour system, Du Simitière's ticket sales were necessarily limited; no more than eight spectators were admitted at a time and the museum was open only on Tuesday, Thursday, Friday, and Saturday. Hourly tours were restricted and visitors were not allowed to wander or view the collection at their leisure. In fact, the receipts from the American Museum did not solve Du Simitière's financial problems. He died in October 1784, at the age of forty-seven, apparently of starvation.[40] His experiment had been a failure, and although his museum attracted many visitors, it did not appeal to a broad spectrum of people. The museum's receipts had been insignificant, and Du Simitière died a pauper. The administrators of his estate failed to prevent the collection from being scattered; and all the objects in Du Simitière's possession at the time of his death were sold at public auction.

• • •

Charles Willson Peale's Philadelphia museum, on the other hand, operated for nearly sixty years (1786–1845). During that time it was forced to incorporate elements of popular entertainment as part of a larger trend; its owner had to become a showman to survive. When Peale first requested donations, people sent all sorts of bizarre objects. Realizing that donors would come to the museum just to see their private curiosities on public display, he began to exhibit such items as "a chicken with four legs and four wings, an 80-pound turnip, the trigger-finger of a convicted murderer, and a tiny piece of wood from the Coronation chair in Westminster Abbey."[41] Peale, also an artist and Philadelphian, opened his American Museum in June 1786 at Third and Lombard Street.

In the pre-endowment era of museum history, the immensely patriotic Peale devoted his life to the promotion of cultural nationalism and popular education. His museum offered authentic scientific displays, experiments, and lectures to an audience comprising both scholars and ordinary citizens. He wanted his museum to appeal to all classes, the illiterate and the scholarly, adults as well as children, and both men and women. The motto of the museum, inscribed above the building's entrance, was "Whoso would learn Wisdom, let him enter here!"[42] As a painter he encouraged the merging of art with natural history. His artistic displays of stuffed animals, depicted in their natural habitats, with painted skies and backgrounds, paved the way for the dioramas of later nineteenth-century natural history museums: "By showing the nest, hollow, or cave," claimed Peale, "a particular view of the country from which they came, some instances of the habits may be given."[43]

13

Like Du Simitière, Peale began his museum in an attempt to supplement his income as a painter. He succeeded, and in the process changed the way proprietary museums functioned. One of Peale's sons, Rubens, persuaded his father to employ live entertainers in order to tap into a wider audience.[44] Live performers added an element of levity to the museum, and the elder Peale began to feel that there was nothing essentially wrong with a touch of diversion. For his part, Rubens believed that the museum's heavy didactic and moralistic tone repelled those Philadelphians who wanted to attend the place for relaxation and enjoyment. After his father's retirement from managing the museum in 1810, Rubens began shifting its emphasis from scientific instruction to popular amusement.[45] Although he tried to maintain the museum's scientific integrity, he introduced distorting mirrors, live animals, and human prodigies. Rubens Peale felt that scientific lecturing was an important function of the museum, but he interspersed his symposiums with acts by musicians and magicians. The public liked Rubens's alterations; in one year he doubled the American Museum's revenue. The struggle for Rubens was how to keep the museum's probity and its high-quality displays while attracting a large enough audience to keep profits up. This was a battle he fought throughout his museum career.

The popularity of live performers and light amusements was such that when Rubens opened Peale's New York Museum in 1825, it was closer in spirit to a late nineteenth-century dime museum than to his father's museum. According to an 1827 guidebook, the museum had four floors: the

first housed natural history objects; the second, paintings and miscellaneous curiosities; the third, wax figures, fossils, and cosmoramas; and the top
floor, a lecture room and a terrace. But Rubens knew that it was the
outrageous curiosities that brought visitors; in early May 1828, for example, Peale's New York Museum exhibited "a calf with two heads, six legs,
two tails, two distinct hearts and backbones."[46] Rubens also placed on
exhibition a boa constrictor, an anaconda, and a so-called diamond snake—
all together in a wire cage—and a "learned dog" named Romeo, who
entertained by barking answers to questions.[47]

14

To increase revenues further, Rubens Peale offered museum discounts to
schools and students, a policy already established at the Philadelphia museum. In 1830, however, he lost the New York museum to his creditors,
and in the early 1840s Barnum purchased it and turned it into a full-
fledged dime museum.[48] Although Rubens no longer was involved with
Peale's New York Museum, he did operate Peale's Baltimore Museum,
which he had inherited from his brother Rembrandt, who was not as skilled
a showman. By 1843, Rubens was trying to generate new excitement in
Baltimore; he wrote to his rival, Barnum, in the hopes of borrowing one of
his most famous prodigies, General Tom Thumb.[49]

It was clear that the average citizen wanted diversion, favoring fun over
education. The efforts of men like Charles Willson Peale were not in vain,
however; his legacy has in fact been a rich one. The elder Peale's vision of
attracting both scholars and ordinary citizens to a place of scientific learning, with authentic displays imaginatively presented, was later realized in
the Smithsonian Institution (1846).

•   •   •

Attempts to open a public museum in New York began in 1789, when the
Tammany Society formally opened a chapter of its organization in New
York. Tammany, which began in Philadelphia in 1772, was an outgrowth
of a seventeenth-century fishing club named after the celebrated Delaware
Indian chief Tamenend, who welcomed William Penn on his arrival in
America. John Pintard, a Tammany organizer and later a founding father
of the New York Historical Society (1804), wanted one of the society's
prime functions to be the establishment of a museum that would preserve
and display all types of American artifacts.

In May 1791, under the patronage of the Tammany Society, the leader-
ship of John Pintard, and the direction of Gardiner Baker, the Tammany
Museum, better known as the American Museum, opened to the public.[50]

In June the following statement of intent was published in a museum pamphlet: "The intention of the Tammany Society . . . in establishing an American Museum is for the sole purpose of collecting and preserving whatever may relate to the history of our country and serve to perpetuate the same, as also all American curiosities of nature and art."[51]

15

At first the museum was not especially egalitarian; only Tammany members and their families were admitted. There was no charge. This policy, however, was changed, and the museum's doors were opened to the general public on Tuesday and Friday afternoons with an entrance fee of two shillings (about twenty-five cents). To reduce the admission price further, the management offered nonmembers the option of buying a yearly pass for one dollar.[52]

The first home of Tammany's American Museum was in New York's City Hall. Since Congress was in the process of relocating to the nation's new capital in Philadelphia, the society petitioned to use one of the building's upper rooms. By 1793, however, the collection had greatly expanded, and the museum moved to a larger room on the second floor of the Exchange Building on Broad Street, a block from Battery Park. The thirty-by-sixty-foot room had a twenty-foot-high arched ceiling that "was elegantly painted a sky blue, and intermixed with various kinds of clouds," as well as a thunderstorm and flashes of lightning.[53] The walls were adorned with murals featuring trees from all over the world, as well as all sorts of animals, from flamingos to lions. Pintard had wanted to limit the collection to Americana, but Baker sought to diversify, and the museum now included wax figures, Indian, Chinese, and African relics, and preserved animals. There also were freakish curiosities: in 1793, Baker claimed to have in his possession "a perfect horn, . . . about 5 inches in length," allegedly taken from the head of a New York woman (see fig. 2).[54]

Baker was a good businessman; knowing the value of publicity, he often placed advertisements for the collection in the daily papers. On March 31, 1794, for example, he shrewdly announced in the *New York Columbian Gazette* that the museum was exhibiting two guillotines, one of which was to be displayed "complete with a wax figure perfectly representing a man beheaded!"[55] With news of the French Revolution occupying most of the paper's front page, the perfectly timed exhibition aroused the public's morbid curiosity. Baker continued to hunt for scintillating and novel exhibits, and in the same year the museum occupied a second room in the Exchange Building, which now housed its menagerie. This was one of New York's first permanent animal exhibitions; it included a mountain lion,

FIGURE 2. Broadside, American Museum, 1793. (New-York Historical Society.)

raccoons, groundhogs, birds, and snakes.[56] The museum was now open every day except Sunday, and the use of candlelight enabled the collection to remain open until 9 P.M. three nights a week.[57]

In the meantime, Pintard had begun to separate himself from the project. He had grown unhappy as he witnessed the transformation of his vision: the museum, he felt, was losing sight of its pedagogical function and becoming simply an assemblage of curiosities, a place of lowbrow amusement. In addition, Pintard was an avid Hamiltonian, and he severed his ties with the Tammany Society in part because of the society's strongly Jeffersonian views. Around this time also he lost most of his money in a stock speculation and was sent to debtor's prison for two years.[58]

After Pintard's departure the leaders of the Tammany Society realized that the museum was an expensive failure. It was neither a powerful nor a profitable institution, and the society was reluctant to continue to support it. In 1795 the Tammany Society relinquished the collection to Baker, with the proviso that society members could still attend the museum free.[59] Without Tammany's support, of course, Baker had to rely solely on ticket sales to fund his museum. He immediately extended its hours and increased the admission charge to fifty cents. To encourage patrons to return again and again, he continually added new curiosities to the collection. In addition, he began to manufacture automata, opened a print shop on the first floor, and over the years established one of the finest menageries in the world. In spite of the proprietor's efforts, however, the museum was not very profitable.

In 1798 Baker died of yellow fever. After his death, his wife attempted to run the museum, but she died in 1800, leaving four children and no will. The museum was bought intact by William I. Waldron, a grocer who tried unsuccessfully to sell the collection at auction. While awaiting a buyer, he temporarily set up his own museum at 69 Broadway. Eventually, in 1802, the Baker collection was sold to Edward Savage, a historical painter, inventor, and showman. Savage owned what was in essence an art gallery, known as the Columbian Gallery, located at 80 Greenwich Street.[60] He acquired the Baker collection with the aim of creating an institution similar to Peale's Philadelphia museum. He renamed his new combined institution, which opened May 11, 1802, the Columbian Gallery of Painting and City Museum.[61]

Shortly after Savage obtained the contents of the American Museum, he hired twenty-six-year-old John Scudder, a naturalist and amateur wildlife mounter, to curate the neglected collection. Several years of working for Savage proved tedious for Scudder, however; he was disappointed with his boss's apparent lack of interest in the collection and believed that Savage was more devoted to his picture making and machine designing than turning the museum into a first-rate institution.

Scudder devised a plan: he would leave Savage's employment and find a better job, save his money, and one day buy the Columbian Gallery. He found a job as a seaman aboard ships that traded along the northeastern coast. It is not known how long Scudder was a sailor, but by 1809 he had accumulated enough capital to purchase Savage's museum.[62]

In March 1810, Scudder opened his American Museum at 21 Chatham Street. His true-to-life displays of stuffed animals and collections of shells and fossils satisfied those devoted to natural history, and he often gave natural science lectures at his museum. But Scudder expanded the wax-works department to include "Sleeping Beauty with Her Baby" and "King Saul with the Witch of Endor and Samuel's Ghost."[63]

18

The War of 1812 and economic hard times took their toll on museum going. By a stroke of luck, however, in 1816 Scudder was given the opportunity to house his collection rent-free on the second floor of the old almshouse in City Hall Park, which had been renamed the New York Institute (see fig. 3). He was to pay the traditional annual peppercorn for his new quarters in this new civic center, which he shared with the New-York Historical Society, the New York Society Library, the American Academy of Fine Arts, the Deaf and Dumb Institution, the Literary and Philosophical Society, the Lyceum of Natural History, the Board of Health, and the Bank for Savings.[64] The prestige of being a part of the New York Institute helped Scudder lure many municipal leaders and prominent patrons to the American Museum.

With the help of his friend John Pintard, Scudder redesigned the space to accommodate the display of six hundred varieties of natural history specimens. All the items displayed were classified according to the Linnaean system and labeled in Latin as well as English. He hired lecturers, who illustrated their talks with items from the collection. Demonstrating a parallel flair for showmanship, he hired strolling musicians to entertain visitors as they wandered from case to case. In June 1819, Caroline and Edward Clarke, lilliputian singers, were engaged for almost three weeks to amuse the spectators.[65]

Scudder's collection continued to grow until the American Museum occupied four large rooms. It now displayed "live mud turtles, a Baltimore oriole, an iguana, various minerals, and the bed curtains belonging to Mary Queen of Scots."[66] Scudder died on August 7, 1821. According to his will, the museum trustees, all of whom were his close friends, were to continue to operate the establishment until his only son, John Jr., was old enough to manage the collection.

Initially, John Scudder Jr. was not interested in following in his father's footsteps; he wanted to be a doctor, or so he thought. After dropping out of medical school in 1825, however, he mortgaged his inheritance, rebelliously setting up his own place of entertainment, called Scudder's New York Spectaculum, on July 1, 1825. He was thus competing directly with Peale's New York Museum and the American Museum, which was

FIGURE 3. American Museum, City Hall Park, 1825. (New-York Historical Society.)

then under the direction of Cornelius Bogert, an attorney. His Spectaculum failed, however, probably not because of mismanagement but because even a metropolis like New York could not support three similar museums. Although John Scudder Jr.'s Spectaculum did not succeed, he did demonstrate a flair for showmanship; later he made his mark running his father's museum.

By 1826 the American Museum claimed to possess 150,000 natural and foreign curiosities. To attract more paying customers it began to provide variety acts and freak shows.[67] Four years later, the large and noisy crowds that paraded daily through the corridors of the New York Institute on their way to the museum forced the institute to evict the collection from its rent-free accommodations. On December 24, 1830, the museum moved into a five-story building on the corner of Broadway and Ann Street, opposite St. Paul's Church.[68]

The new American Museum earned an average of seven thousand dollars annually, a healthy sum for that time. Much of its success was due to the showmanship of John Scudder Jr., now the manager.[69] Scudder hoped to lure patrons away from Peale's establishment; under his direction the museum's daily program included variety acts, minstrel shows, and displays of freaks. The new American Museum managed to survive the crash of 1837, and the receipts for both the 1839 and 1840 seasons totaled more than eleven thousand dollars.[70] The museum was making a good profit. In 1841, it was purchased by a small-time showman named Phineas Taylor Barnum, and the great age of American dime museums began.

• • •

The Western Museum of Cincinnati (1820–67) was the first of its kind in the Midwest. Like its sister institutions in the East, it followed a pattern of transformation from a center for scientific study to a place of entertainment.[71] Daniel Drake, the museum's founder, was a physician and, like Du Simitière and Peale, a member of all the appropriate intellectual organizations. By 1815 he had amassed a sizable collection of minerals, metals, fossils, and organic remains. Between 1820 and 1840, he founded many of the cultural and educational institutions in Cincinnati and was known to his contemporaries as the "Ben Franklin of the West."[72]

During the summer of 1818, Drake announced that he and an associate, a Cincinnati merchant named William Steele, would open a public museum. The collection was to encompass all aspects of science from archaeology and geology to zoology and natural history. The two collaborated with Cincinnati College, hoping that the two institutions could form one of the most comprehensive science libraries in the United States.[73] On June 10, 1820, the museum was opened to the public. Dr. Robert Bets of Cincinnati College was hired as chief curator; one of his assistants was John James Audubon, who worked at the museum as a taxidermist for a year.

The Western Museum of Cincinnati was operated initially as a private stock company. Shareholders were allowed to view the collection free; the general public paid the standard twenty-five cents, half price for children. By 1823 the museum was doing poorly. Its large collection of birds, shells, coins, mummies, and prehistoric bones was not enough to engage the average citizen's curiosity. After a political battle during which Drake was fired and then rehired, he resigned in 1822. Interest in the museum continued to decline. In fact it was so minimal that the stockholders could not even sell the collection. Instead they gave it to Joseph Dorfeuille, the new curator, on the condition that stockholders still be admitted free.

Dorfeuille, who had contributed many items to the museum, realized that the truths of natural science were not as compelling to viewers as the "occasional errors of nature."[74] Although he apparently tried to maintain the museum's scientific credentials by giving lectures, his format was unusual: at the conclusion of his talks he sometimes offered his audience a sniff of laughing gas (nitrous oxide).[75] Dorfeuille's intention was to engage the emotions, not the intellect, and the Cincinnati museum quickly became a place of popular entertainment.

21

Dorfeuille was much drawn to the grotesque and sensational. On entering the museum, spectators were assaulted by moving skeletons; an organ grinder played appropriate atmospheric music. Dorfeuille also created a wax tableau of a local ax murderer named Cowan, who was convicted of killing his wife and two children. He preserved in a jar the head, right hand, and heart of another local murderer, Mathias Hoover. Rather feebly, Dorfeuille attempted to justify this horrifying display as righteous and instructive. In an advertisement in the *Liberty Hall and Cincinnati Gazette*, dated July 4, 1837, Dorfeuille claimed that before his execution, Hoover had willed his body to the museum "for the express purpose of its being exhibited publicly, as a warning to others of the awful risk, attending a departure from the paths of virtue."[76]

The museum was best known for its Chamber of Horrors and its elaborate depictions of Hell, better known as "The Infernal Regions" or "Dorfeuille's Hell." (This spectacle, which became one of the most talked-about exhibits of the pre–Civil War era, will be discussed in more detail in the chapter on waxworks.) After Hiram Powers, the sculptor who created the original mechanical wax figures in "The Infernal Regions," left Cincinnati in 1834, the museum began to deteriorate. Powers's successor was not as skillful an artist, and the museum had to struggle to maintain the quality of the wax collection. Dorfeuille eventually sold his share of the museum for $6,500, keeping "The Infernal Regions" exhibit, and left for New York in the hope of discovering a fresh audience for his spectacle. (A version of "The Infernal Regions" remained at the Western Museum for years, and there was some dispute about which was the original.) In 1839 Dorfeuille opened his new museum just a stone's throw away from Scudder's American Museum. Within a year, however, Dorfeuille's New York museum was destroyed by fire. Its owner died a few months later, on July 23, 1840.

•   •   •

In the early years of the nineteenth century, an American museum was typically a miscellaneous collection of curiosities, a development of the European notion of the "cabinet of wonders." Most museums attempted to be instructive civic institutions, exposing the public to a wide variety of historical artifacts, natural history specimens, and instructive paintings— "colleges for America's culturally neglected Everyman."[77] Since these establishments also operated as businesses in a democratic society, however, they needed to be cheap enough to attract a wide audience, as well as sufficiently diversified in terms of what they displayed. In appealing to a mass audience, museums came to incorporate different categories of amusements. By midcentury they had become venues for all sorts of popular entertainments, and their educational agenda virtually had vanished. The dime museum was the result.

# 2. Barnum and the Museum Revolution, 1841–1870

**Luck is in no sense the foundation of my fortune; from the beginning of my career I planned and worked for my success. To be sure, my schemes often amazed me with the affluence of their results.**

— P. T. Barnum

Phineas Taylor Barnum was the quintessential showman; by organizing individual amusements and placing them within the confines of a single environment, he afforded hours of pleasure to those with little in their pocketbooks. Barnum adopted the early nineteenth-century concept of the proprietary museum and transformed it into the dime museum.

Some might argue that Barnum's American Museum functioned chiefly as a place of popular education—his natural history exhibits were illuminating and his guidebooks informative. By virtue of his years of collecting artifacts and his global searches for novel freaks, Barnum did assemble spectacular geological, ornithological, zoological, and ethnographic displays. But it was not his underlying intention to be didactic. Although he was a temperance advocate and a local civic leader, Barnum was fundamentally a showman who devoted his life not to scientific accuracy but to entertainment.

Barnum's museum guidebooks were published chiefly as maps of his museum, as popular diversion, and for the purposes of publicity. Barnum wanted his museum to be respectable, and he attempted to reject anything that might be repugnant to a conservative Victorian audience, but his "operational aesthetic," to borrow a phrase coined by Neil Harris, was not to instruct but to amuse.[1] Even though the melodramas performed in his lecture room could be defined as moral, virtuous, and somewhat didactic, the theater's slogan was "We Study to Please," not "We Study to Teach."[2] Barnum himself claimed that his museum was "educational," but this was a buzzword designed to attract business from a variety of social classes and to placate puritan consciences. Barnum wrote in his autobiography that he wanted his patrons to "think, talk and wonder," and he used showmanship to achieve this goal.[3]

• • •

24

New York City, with its prosperous shipping, railroad, and real estate industries, soon became the dominant industrial center of the Northeast. This expanding commercial city provided many job opportunities for both the working class and the modern middle class. By 1834, New York had over a quarter of a million residents; by 1850 the figure hovered around one million. Nearly 60 percent of these residents had been born elsewhere, either in America or Europe.[4] Many midcentury New Yorkers lived in tenements or boardinghouses because they could not afford to either own or rent homes. Without the pleasures of the parlor entertainments and family gatherings of the traditional home, boarders were forced to seek amusement in public places. David Nasaw claimed that "recreation and play were not luxuries but necessities in the modern city."[5] The entertainment-seeking population was growing rapidly, and entrepreneurs were spurred to find new enterprises. While restaurants, hotels, churches, concert and lecture halls, pleasure gardens, and saloons provided a certain amount of recreation and entertainment, none could offer the range of amusements of the dime museums. These establishments, where, for a onetime admission, pleasure seekers could be amused for hours by a variety of organized popular entertainments, were slowly becoming New York institutions.

P. T. Barnum purchased Scudder's American Museum in 1841. At the time, the proprietors of already established proprietary museums, in a desperate attempt to remain solvent, had already begun to embrace the idea of developing entertainment centers, jettisoning their loftier goal of the dissemination of scientific and historical knowledge. During the 1840s, Peale's New York Museum (Rubens Peale lost the museum to creditors in 1830, and the museum was now owned by a showman named Harry Bennett) advertised a "magician, a mind-reader and an anaconda that swallowed live fowl twice a week in front of a crowd of gaping patrons."[6] Under Bennett the museum even began opening its doors to the performances of "Ethiopian melodists and serenaders."[7]

It did not make much difference, however, who or what appeared at Peale's New York Museum, or for that matter at any similar New York establishment; Barnum's American Museum was to eclipse them all. By 1843, its proprietor had forced Peale's New York Museum out of business and had purchased its collection for $7,000.[8] But, believing that any competition was good for business, Barnum kept his acquisition quiet and continued to run the Peale museum as a separate enterprise. Through his expert showmanship, his adroit business sense, and his unequivocal gall, Barnum turned the American Museum into a national attraction for all showmen to emulate. By the 1850s it was already considered unthinkable to visit New York without seeing it, and by 1860 the museum was on the itinerary of the well-publicized visit of the Prince of Wales to New York.[9]

The five-story white building (see fig. 4), located on Ann Street and Broadway, opposite the prestigious Astor House hotel, contained the remains of John Scudder's collection, once valued at $25,000. Barnum, however, had purchased the building and the collection in 1841 for less than half that amount. The story is truly Barnumesque in its complexity. Then an impoverished showman with only extraordinary dreams, Barnum required considerable financial backing. He sought the help of Francis W. Olmsted, the building's owner, who agreed to buy the collection for him and then issue him a ten-year lease, charging him an annual rent of $3,000.[10]

Ironically, while Barnum was making the financial arrangements that would enable him to purchase Scudder's American Museum, its board of trustees sold the collection to the Peale Museum Company for $15,000. The museum company paid a $1,000 down and agreed to provide the remainder by December 26, 1841. Barnum was convinced that the museum company was purchasing the Scudder collection on speculation, in order to manipulate its stock value, and he wrote to various newspapers, hoping "to blow that speculation sky-high."[11] Angered by all the adverse publicity, the Peale Museum Company, in an attempt to subdue him, hired Barnum to manage the soon-to-be-acquired Scudder collection at an annual salary of $3,000.

Barnum wrote in his autobiography that he was convinced that the Peale Museum Company was in effect buying his silence in order to keep its stock value high. As straight-faced as ever, he agreed to their terms and consented to begin his tenure after the first of the year. Barnum then went back to the Scudder trustees and negotiated an agreement whereby, if the Peale Museum Company failed to pay the $14,000 balance by December 26, he would be permitted to buy the collection on December 27 for his original $12,000 offer. After hiring Barnum, the museum company, unaware of any other bidders, decided to wait until all the notoriety had subsided before actually purchasing the collection—as Barnum had imag-

25

26

FIGURE 4. P. T. Barnum's American Museum, Broadway and Ann Street, 1851. (New-York Historical Society.)

ined they would. As a result, they failed to make their promised payment on December 26, and on the next day Barnum acquired the museum for himself.

With his business ability, his talent for collecting a dazzling array of attractions, and his "devotion to . . . gigantic posters and colored inks," Barnum was able to pay back Olmsted's loan in fifteen months.[12] He buttressed the neglected Scudder collection with freak shows and novelty performers, and he changed exhibits constantly. Three years after he took over the museum, Barnum claimed to possess thirty thousand exhibits. He featured Siamese twins, fat boys, bearded ladies, rubber men, legless wonders, and an array of midgets. In addition, he held baby shows in which he awarded cash prizes to the fattest, smallest, tallest, and prettiest babies. He held flower, dog, bird, and poultry shows. Barnum enlarged the museum's lecture room and eventually turned it into a full-fledged and "thoroughly reputable" theater for the production of "moral" dramas.[13] His 1849 production of William H. Smith's play *The Drunkard*, in fact, was the first play to run for a hundred uninterrupted performances in New York.

The showman proudly described his American Museum as an "encyclopedic synopsis of everything worth seeing in this curious world." [14] An 1849 program claimed that the museum housed 600,000 curiosities. By 1864 the American Museum boasted a collection of over 850,000 items. Barnum's acumen for show business proved extremely profitable. As early as 1842, the American Museum earned $28,000, which was $17,000 more than the previous year, when the museum had been operated by the Scudder Museum board of trustees. [15]

27

Sensational exhibits and spectacular freak shows, as well as Barnum's penchant for business, all aided in the success of his establishment. Beyond that, the proprietor understood and respected his paying patrons, believing that he never really cheated them, since he offered so many diverse entertainments. If a patron felt disappointed by one exhibit, there was always another in the museum that would make the admission price worthwhile. Through massive advertising campaigns, which inflamed the potential customer's expectations, topped off by a little controversial "humbug," he discovered the combination needed to lure paying patrons back to his museum for a third and fourth time. Barnum did not discover most of his most famous curiosities. He merely acquired exhibits and marketed them in such a powerful way as to devise sensational crowdpleasing exhibitions. He created a place where one could exchange money for wonder, and "he knew that it is the story above all else that makes the object interesting." [16] In the twenty-three years that Barnum operated his first American Museum, from 1842 to 1865, he sold more than thirty million tickets. [17]

In 1843, for example, Barnum carefully manipulated the publicity for his infamous Fejee Mermaid exhibit in order to attract a huge viewership. The Fejee Mermaid was a manufactured curiosity. It had once belonged to a Boston sea captain who, in 1817, anticipating that the curiosity would someday make him a fortune, stole $6,000 of his ship's money to buy the creature. The mermaid failed to excite much interest, however, and it passed into the possession of the captain's son. Moses Kimball, the proprietor of the Boston Museum, bought the mermaid from the son and immediately contacted Barnum. [18] The two men entered into an agreement to share in the expenses and profits of the mermaid, which was to remain the permanent property of Kimball, although it was Barnum's task to create the notoriety. Without Barnum's imagination, the Fejee Mermaid might just have been a minor exhibit stashed away on a shelf in the Boston Museum.

In fact, Barnum did not display the mermaid at once but engineered a publicity campaign to insure that people would have to see his latest acquisition. He printed enticing stories about the discovery of the mermaid near the Fejee Islands (Hawaii) by the fictitious Dr. J. Griffin from London's "Lyceum of Natural History." (Griffin was, in fact, a longtime Barnum collaborator named Levi Lyman.)

**28**

The stories claimed, however, that the fictitious English scientist was to be in the United States with the Fejee Mermaid only a short while before sailing for Europe. For weeks the press was filled with Fejee Mermaid anecdotes, and New Yorkers anxiously awaited the fake scientist's visit as he supposedly ventured north from Montgomery, Alabama, to New York. As Dr. Griffin's visit drew near, Barnum circulated pamphlets about the mermaid and duped three local papers into printing engravings of the curiosity. The tension mounted until finally the Fejee Mermaid arrived in New York and was exhibited for a week in early August at the Concert Hall, 404 Broadway. When the week ended, Barnum took possession of the mermaid and exhibited it at his American Museum. Controversy and word of mouth enhanced the public's curiosity, and he pulled in a thousand dollars during that week, three times his normal revenue.[19]

Many viewers were disappointed. The mermaid was described as small (only eighteen inches long), black, and extremely shriveled. The upper part of its body was hairy, tapering off twelve inches below the head to scales and the sort of tail generally associated with a mermaid. The manufactured curiosity was so cleverly constructed, however, that it was difficult for anyone not to believe that it was real. And the public came in droves. Barnum later admitted to Kimball in an 1848 letter that even he felt a little guilty about becoming rich off this particular "humbugging" of the public.[20]

From Barnum's point of view, however, good publicity, controversial publicity, negative publicity—all of it helped generate customers. When Barnum received word that President Abraham Lincoln was to visit his establishment on February 19, 1861, he quickly sent a note to an editor urging him to "notice this fact & oblige."[21] During his exhibition of Joice Heth, George Washington's supposed nurse, Barnum himself sent anonymous letters to various newspapers denouncing Heth as a fraud. He even went so far as to claim that she was an automaton and that he was the ventriloquist. This brought people flying to his exhibit to find out whether the attraction was in fact real or mechanical.

When he exhibited Mme. Josephine Fortune Clofullia, his Swiss bearded lady, in the early 1850s, Barnum planted statements in the papers claiming that "she" was really a "he." In order to heighten the dramatic conflict and provoke his audience, he paid a spectator to publicly challenge Josephine Clofullia's true sexuality. The matter ultimately landed in court, where the allegation that Clofullia was a man masquerading as a woman was refuted, not only by her husband but by several doctors as well. The case was dismissed, and Barnum made a huge profit from all the publicity.

29

Several years later, Barnum capitalized on the publicity a second time by exhibiting Clofullia with her two-year-old child, the "Infant Esau," whose body was covered with hair. Once again Barnum had been successful in encouraging scores of people to visit his museum. Press agentry of this inflammatory sort made people want to see for themselves what all the controversy was about. Barnum found that if, on their first visit, pleasure seekers were under the impression that an exhibit was real, but later became inclined to believe that it was a fraud, they would return to appease their curiosity and try to determine how the deception had been achieved.[22] Thus, he made deceit a game and an integral part of his museum exhibits, and he used the press as bait.

In spite of—or because of—dubious management and promotional practices, millions of people visited the American Museum. But as Arthur Saxon has suggested, "Barnum was not the only entrepreneur to fool Americans in the nineteenth century."[23] Humbugging, Barnum wrote in 1866, was "an astonishingly wide-spread phenomenon—in fact universal." In particular, "the most stupendous scientific imposition upon the public that the generation with which we are numbered has known," Barnum wrote in *The Humbugs of the World,* had been the so-called Moon Hoax, which had nothing to do with him.[24] It was conceived by Richard Adams Locke and was published in the *Sun,* a nineteenth-century penny tabloid that specialized in human interest stories, in August and September 1835. Locke's tales described how astronomer John Herschel was able to view life on the moon through a high-powered telescope. The paper printed detailed descriptions of moon vegetation, lunar animals, and winged inhabitants. So spectacular was the story that the *Sun* soon found itself with a fifty-thousand-reader increase in circulation.[25]

The increasing pace of nineteenth-century technological development had created an atmosphere in which people could reasonably believe almost anything. Modernization taught that the unimaginable was possible, and technology made material reality of ideas that had existed only in the realm of the imagination. In his biography of Barnum, Neil Harris noted that nineteenth-century hoaxing was a kind of intellectual exercise. For those who delighted in learning, there were many challenging and delightful aspects to a hoax. The discovery of the deception and of how it had been accomplished was sometimes even more enjoyable than the trick itself.[26] Barnum was the first showman who understood this innate attraction to the hoax and was able to turn it into a profit-making venture. "Everyone is open to deception," he wrote, "people like to be led in the region of mystery."[27]

"The Great Model of Niagara Falls, with Real Water," was a Barnum banner headline sure to entice anyone who had heard of this natural wonder but had not seen it. The scale model of the falls, complete with rocks, trees, and neighboring buildings, was only eighteen inches high. Yet those enticing words on the banner, as Barnum wrote them, were threatening to the Board of the Croton Water Commissioners, who felt that Barnum's exhibit might dry up the city's water supply. Real water was indeed used, but it was recycled; a mechanical pump enabled Barnum to reuse the same pool endlessly. He had not blatantly lied in his advertisement, but he had manipulated the language in order to make it attractively ambiguous.

Similarly, Barnum's famous "To The Egress" sign was put up not to show the customer where to view an "egress," whatever that might be, but rather to control the crowds that poured into his museum. Barnum's autobiography is filled with similar anecdotes about how he humbugged his customers by using provocative language, theatrics, and creative marketing. His "What Is It?" for example, became the quintessential "Is It Real or Is It Not?" exhibit (see fig. 5). Capitalizing on the ever growing interest in theories of evolution and the origin of man, Barnum exhibited several versions of this "missing link," or half-man–half-monkey attraction. His earliest missing link was Mlle. Fanny, an orangutan that he exhibited in the 1840s.

Perhaps his most successful "What Is It?" was William Henry Johnson, a small, retarded black man (he stood between four and five feet tall), with a large nose, protruding eyes, and no hair except for a little tuft at the center of his pointed head. This tuft soon became a trademark.[28] Johnson was first displayed in 1860 and most later exhibits of the "What Is It?" genre looked strikingly like Johnson: they were generally endowed with only a single tuft of hair, costumed in a monkey or other animal coverall, and positioned in front of a jungle background. Barnum marketed his contrived curiosity with his usual creativity. Because of the ambiguous exhibit title "What Is It?" Barnum was able to set the spectator up, placing all alleged "misrepresentations" squarely in the lap of the viewer, who was forced to form his

FIGURE 5. Barnum's "What Is It?" exhibit, c. 1860. (Harvard Theatre Collection, Houghton Library.)

own opinion as to whether the exhibit was a man, an animal, or a combination. In addition, by connecting this freak with "scientific" theories of evolution, Barnum avoided making a racial statement about blacks in 1860 America. While a Northern white audience surely was curious about slavery, Barnum masterfully averted the politically charged discourse of the status of African Americans with the ambiguity of the "What Is It?" title.

During the early years of his career, Barnum had been proud to be called the "prince of humbugs," and he rationalized his perpetual trickery by insisting that he gave the paying patron more curiosities for his twenty-five-cent admission charge than any other amusement institution. It was customary for Barnum to offer an opening address at the beginning of each season. In 1861, he supposedly gave the following rhymed speech in his lecture room, defending his penchant for humbugging. It began,

32

> That Prince of Humbugs, BARNUM, so it appears
> Some folks have designated me for several years—
> Well, I don't murmur; indeed, when they embellish it,
> To tell the truth, my friends I rather relish it.[29]

•   •   •

In the 1850s Barnum made renovations costing fifty thousand dollars. At the entrance to the high white building, decorated with banners announcing prize exhibits, panels depicting animals and birds, and posters illustrating scenes from moral dramas, visitors were now confronted by a grand staircase that led to the second floor. If they chose to continue rearward, however, they would find the First Saloon, better known as the Cosmorama Department.[30] The walls in this room were fitted with peepholes with lenses, through which could be seen brilliantly colored views of "St. Marks Church, Venice," the "Crystal Palace, London," a "General View of Naples," and the "Tuilleries, Paris." Before going upstairs, spectators could choose to descend to the basement to a rifle and pistol gallery.[31]

The grand staircase led spectators up into a large hall known as the Second Saloon (see fig. 6). Scattered throughout the room were glass cases housing natural history specimens such as "Red-headed Ducks of North America," and the "African Ostrich and Ant Eater." The Third Saloon, located next to the second, contained specimens of bows and arrows, a variety of stuffed birds, wax figures, and such miscellaneous paraphernalia as "the court dress Tom Thumb wore when he was presented before Queen Victoria," a machine for testing strength, and a collection of famous autographs.

The Aquaria Department was located in Saloon Four, to the right of the Second Saloon. The first public aquarium had been displayed in London at the Regent's Park zoo, and after visiting the zoo in the late 1850s, Barnum immediately launched his own imitation. In addition to the fish tanks, the Aquaria Department also had cases displaying varieties of shells, oysters,

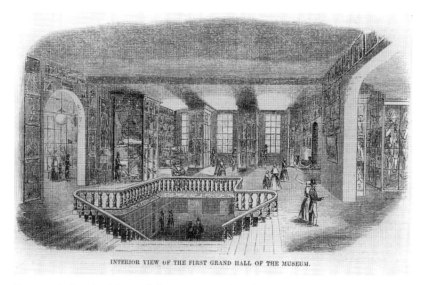

33

FIGURE 6. Interior View of the First Grand Hall, known as the Second Saloon, Barnum's American Museum, 1853. (New-York Historical Society.)


and stuffed fish. Barnum's catalog provided the visitor with historical information on aquatic exhibits; a pike on exhibition, for example, was said to be the largest and oldest ever discovered. It had been caught in Mannheim, Germany, in 1497, Barnum claimed, was nineteen feet long, and weighed 350 pounds.[32]

The Fifth Saloon, occupying the third floor, contained paintings, including landscapes, portraits of famous people, and engravings of flags from around the world. Stuffed animals, among them a bear, a kangaroo, and a giraffe, were also housed in this saloon. Directly above was the Sixth Saloon, a large chamber where one could find such curiosities as snowshoes from Norway, a three-thousand-year-old Egyptian mummy from Thebes enclosed in a case of sycamore wood, a ball of hair found in the stomach of a sow, and a collection of shoes and slippers.

One more flight up was the Seventh Saloon, where visitors could see not only more paintings but also the museum's fantastic skeleton collection and live animals. It was also in this chamber that Barnum housed his famous exhibit called "The Happy Family," in which sixty or more different animal species lived "harmoniously" in one cage. A guidebook claimed that each was "the mortal enemy of every other," and that the miracle was that in this cage, all were found to be "contentedly playing and frolicking together without injury or discord." [33]

34    Entrances to the museum's Lecture Room were located on the third, fourth, and fifth floors. In the eighteenth century, so-called lecture rooms hosted natural history lectures and science demonstrations. Later these spaces had gradually become the home of more popular presentations, such as magic lantern shows and musical acts. Choosing to maintain the Lecture Room title was presumably a deliberate attempt on the part of Barnum (and later museum showmen) to entice puritanical visitors who would not willingly attend a performance in a conventional theater. "My plan," wrote Barnum in 1850, "is to introduce into the lecture room highly moral and instructive domestic dramas, written expressly for my establishment and so constructed as to please and edify while they possess a powerful *reformatory* tendency." [34] Barnum, who was a reformed drinker and a temperance advocate, used his Lecture Room as a pulpit. After each performance of *The Drunkard* (1847), a popular temperance melodrama, audience members were urged to go to the box office and sign a pledge against drinking.

The Lecture Room was expanded and renovated several times. "Originally narrow, ill-contrived and inconvenient," by 1850 it was enlarged to a seating capacity of three thousand, and, wrote Barnum, was "to remind us of the like erections in the palaces of European sovereigns and nobles." [35] Spectators could be seated in the gallery, the first balcony, the parterre, or the proscenium boxes. The parterre and the stage were on the same level as the second floor of the building. Admission to the Lecture Room was included in the museum entrance fee, with the exception of the better seats, which cost extra. At first, performances were given in the evenings and on Wednesday and Saturday afternoons. Soon, however, these hours were expanded to include a daily matinee schedule, although performances never took place on Sundays.

The proscenium arch contained stage doors and boxes situated between white and gold Corinthian columns, and the auditorium was furnished with rich crimson wallpaper and velvet-covered seats. Sixteen "medallion compartments" on the ceiling contained portraits of famous Americans, from General Lafayette to President Andrew Jackson. Lamps fitted with glass globes were positioned all around the balcony and gallery fronts to provide light, and two magnificent chandeliers were placed on either side of the proscenium. The theater's motto, "We Study to Please," was emblazoned across the arch. Barnum hired a stage manager, Francis Courtney

Wemyss, to help select plays and to commission original works and adaptations of popular novels. Spectacle and fantasy abounded in Barnum's Lecture Room, but the museum was known mainly for its moral dramas, among them William H. Smith's work *The Drunkard* (1847), T. P. Taylor's play *The Bottle* (1847), and Royall Tyler's *Joseph and His Brethren* (c. 1859). Over the years, Barnum presented no fewer than half a dozen productions of *Uncle Tom's Cabin*.[36] Such moral dramas, together with melodramas, spectacles, novelty acts, and farce afterpieces, all provided family entertainment that conservative Christians could watch safely in the knowledge that no indecencies would affront them.

Before Barnum enlarged his Lecture Room, the auditorium had been the site of occasional freak displays. After 1849, however, when it was transformed into a workable theater, the museum began to employ a stock company to perform its dramas, comedies, and farces. Living curiosities were generally displayed only between acts or as an afterpiece. Freaks became primarily platform entertainers, shown in various saloons during the day and evening.[37]

Barnum provided his visitors with the opportunity to purchase souvenirs at concession stands located strategically throughout the building. They could take home a carte de visite photograph of a freak, with a biography printed on the back, or they could buy a trinket from the Bohemian glassblowers who sold their wares in the museum. Spectators also could drop off the remains of a departed pet at the resident taxidermist's shop and, after completing a tour of the museum, take home a nicely stuffed and mounted animal. Fish tanks in a variety of shapes and sizes were sold, at prices ranging from ten to thirty-five dollars.[38] Fortune-tellers, clairvoyants, and phrenologists offered their services to the public. If pleasure seekers worked up an appetite, there were various food concessions, including an oyster saloon and "aerial garden" on the roof, where visitors could eat a homemade picnic or buy such snacks as cake and ice cream.

Merchandizing was a by-product of industrialization, and the female spectator played an important role in the evolution of urban culture and the dime museum. Transatlantic immigration separated many families, and young women were often sent to America to find work. Many of them found jobs as domestic servants, seamstresses, or factory workers; they lived with relatives or alongside other working men and women in tenements or boardinghouses. With the breakdown of the traditional home and without their fathers' control over their time and earnings, single women were free to enjoy whatever diversions pleased them.[39] The collapse of familial and communal influences, the hard working and ugly living conditions, and bouts of homesickness intensified their need for escapist entertainment. After work or during a free afternoon, single women needed pleasant and appropriate places to go. Although there were a host of amusements that catered to an all-male clientele, there were few deemed respectable enough for unchaperoned women. Barnum's museum represented a new concept in chaste entertainment, and it provided women with a safe and easily accessible meeting place for lunch, conversation, and amusement, free of rowdy or drunken men. To further insure the safety of his female patrons, Barnum hired undercover detectives who escorted back to the street all patrons whose behavior was unacceptable. As customers, women were "icons of decency," and as an audience, they guaranteed respectability; "a mixed audience was by definition a respectable one, a male-only one, indecent."[40] Women flocked to Barnum's, and soon his museum theater began presenting matinees for its female audience. The American Museum was both affordable and fashionable, and women of all classes were attracted to the wholesome atmosphere stressed by the pedagogical rhetoric of Barnum's museum.

This was also a period of upheaval for the middle-class American woman. New ideas about womanhood, sexuality, and leisure were being debated, and modern technological advances such as running water and interior plumbing provided middle-class women with more personal freedom. They soon became involved in philanthropy, reform, and politics.[41] In addition, the advent of department stores in the 1850s brought many women of moderate means into downtown areas during the daytime. As Gunther Barth wrote, clean and orderly sidewalks became an extension of the department store, and "women came downtown purposely to see and be seen."[42] Broadway soon became the most fashionable street in New York. Even wealthy women, driven in private carriages, came not only to "see and be seen" but to shop for the latest fashions, home furnishings, and jewelry in downtown Broadway, known as "Ladies Mile."[43]

Barnum strove to maintain his respectability and shied away from the tableaux vivants that were common in New York in the 1840s. But he substituted his slightly titillating Gallery of Beauty, filled with displays of "female pulchritude." This exhibit had sexual undertones, but because the scantily clothed women were fat, they were seen as freaks and could thus be displayed not as erotic but as scientific objects.

There were many transgressive elements that slipped through, especially in the freak displays, but incongruity, elements of surprise, and the erotic and exotic were all skillfully manipulated to attract without repulsing. There was, in fact, something for everyone at the dime museum. Barnum had invented a type of democratic popular culture that was to be very much in demand. He allowed his guests to become exhibits themselves, in a way, and he made his patrons feel they personally were a vital part of his museum environment.

37

During the summer of 1855, Barnum sold the contents of the museum to his assistant manager, John Greenwood Jr., and his partner Henry D. Butler for $24,000 plus an annual rental fee of $29,000.[44] More successful than he ever imagined, Barnum had sought an early retirement from the museum business in order to pursue other ventures, and even to dabble a bit in local politics. He became passionately involved in the development of the East Bridgeport community.[45] In an effort to enhance the new community's commerce, he became embroiled in a scheme to convince a New Haven–based clock manufacturing company to relocate to East Bridgeport. The Jerome Manufacturing Company agreed to move, and Barnum promised to lend it up to $110,000 to finance the move and take care of any outstanding debt.

Because of faulty accounting and blatant incompetence on Barnum's part, he eventually signed half a million dollars' worth of promissory notes. In the end, the clock company never moved to East Bridgeport and Barnum was ruined financially.[46] As a result, he was forced back into show business to recoup his losses. He began a series of lectures on the art of making money, and after a highly successful European tour with Tom Thumb, he was back on his feet again. It was no coincidence that the American Museum did not prosper during Barnum's absence, and in March 1860, after all his debts had been paid, Barnum repurchased his museum.

Five years later, on July 13, 1865, the American Museum burned to the ground. The fire started in the building's engine room and spread quickly. Luckily, no one was killed. All the visitors escaped easily, but the freaks and the animals had a more difficult time since most were lodged on the upper floors. Anna Swan, the "Nova Scotia Giantess," who stood seven feet eleven inches tall, had the most dramatic escape. She could not fit through the damaged doors inside the building, and firemen had to create an escape hatch by breaking through the outer walls on either side of a window. In all, eighteen firemen were needed to lower her to the ground. Many animals died, and those that were able to flee the building created havoc in the nearby streets.[47]

Barnum had only $40,000 worth of insurance, and the estimated total damage to his collection was some $400,000. Once again he was ruined, but he did not give up. During the spring of 1865 he took over an entire institution, the Great Chinese Museum, located on Broadway between Spring and Prince Streets, and by the fall of that year he had transformed the collection into Barnum's New Museum. This was never as successful as its predecessor, however. In 1866 Barnum entered into a partnership with the famous lion trainer Isaac Van Amburgh, the "Lion King," and the museum became known as the Barnum and Van Amburgh Museum and Menagerie. Van Amburgh owned 60 percent of the operation; Barnum owned 40 percent and was named president of the museum company. He was also general manager, though in name only, and he gradually withdrew from an active role in its day-to-day operations.[48]

The Barnum–Van Amburgh enterprise was very similar to the old American Museum, with a wax figure room, a picture gallery, three "cosmoramic rooms" with two hundred changing views, and a rifle and pistol gallery. The Lecture Room, with its parquet, balcony, and private boxes, was almost as opulent as that of the first museum. Reserved seats cost an extra thirty cents beyond admission to the museum, and private boxes cost sixty cents. The stage was large, measuring fifty by forty-six feet. The auditorium could hold some 2,500 spectators and was decorated in a patriotic motif, with an act-drop depicting the capitol beneath the ever present slogan "We Study to Please." There was also a bust of George Washington surrounded by American flags, as well as the flag of France, a tribute to that nation's aid during the American Revolution.[49]

In the new Sixth Saloon was a resident photographer who was available for portraits. An astrologer and a fortune-teller could be retained for consultations, and "artistically carved ornamental ivory jewelry" was for sale on the second floor.[50] On March 2, 1868, the new museum was in turn destroyed by fire. Barnum never owned and operated a museum of his own again.

Barnum did, however, lend his name, reputation, and expertise to help promote other dime museums, among them George Wood's Museum and Metropolitan Theatre, which opened on August 31, 1868, on the corner of Broadway and Thirtieth Street and which housed the surviving part of Barnum's collection (see fig. 7). In return for his aid and the drawing power of his name, Wood paid Barnum 3 percent of the museum's gross receipts.[51] In 1869 Wood changed the museum's name to Wood's Museum and Menagerie. Eventually it became known as Wood's Museum. The

FIGURE 7. George Wood's Museum and Metropolitan Theatre, New York, c. 1868. (Museum of the City of New York).

building operated as a dime museum until 1876, when John Banvard took possession and renamed it the Broadway Theatre. By 1879 it had been transformed into the famous Daly's Theatre.[52]

In November 1876 Barnum entered into yet another partnership, this time with George Bunnell, an itinerant showman who operated a traveling museum and circus. Barnum, who by now had a prosperous career as a circus operator, furnished half the capital Bunnell needed to establish a permanent museum. Bunnell opened his New American Museum at 103–105 Bowery in 1876 and later purchased the Wood collection for his establishment. Barnum remained a silent partner in the business venture, since his circus collaborators wanted his name associated with their operation alone.

In the 1880s Barnum attempted to establish a new museum in New York, which he planned to call simply Barnum's Museum. It was to be located on the former site of Madison Square Garden between Twenty-sixth and Twenty-seventh Streets and to cover the area between Madison

Avenue and Fourth Avenue. This five-story museum-to-end-all-museums was to be two hundred feet wide by four hundred feet long and was to sprawl over an entire city block. Its interior floor space was estimated at eleven acres.[53] Largely because of the enormous complexity of the concept, the museum never came to fruition. As the project began to slip away from Barnum, he returned his attention to his career as a circus showman.

As Barnum aged, he became uncomfortable about his reputation as the "prince of humbugs," and he began to be increasingly civic-minded, participating in local politics and, in the early 1880s, establishing a Museum of Natural History at Tufts University in Medford, Massachusetts. Obviously he/*did* understand the difference between a true museum of natural history, whose underlying principles are scientific accuracy and education, and a popular dime museum.

It is not enough merely to look at the artifacts housed in Barnum's museums, of course. One must also consider who produced the show, who created the special dime museum atmosphere, and who established its purpose. The answer is clear: Barnum conceived his extraordinary museum for the purpose of entertainment—not education—and with profit as his central concern. "I must confess," he wrote in his autobiography, "that I liked the Museum mainly for the opportunities it afforded for rapidly making money."[54]

# 3. The Peak Years: From the Civil War to 1900

I don't contend that it is intellectual, but I say that it is often clever
and charming at the ten-cent shows, just as it is less often clever and
charming in the ten-cent magazines.
—William Dean Howells, *Literature and Life*

To lure patrons who otherwise would not partake in such "popular"
amusements, managers promoted the educational value of their dime museums. For those citizens who yearned for middle-class status, rational
amusements were a symbol of respectability. There is no doubt that while
the quest for greater profit margins obscured the accuracy of much of the
education peddled by entertainment entrepreneurs, the veneer of sophistication sold tickets; immigrants wanted to learn about American culture,
while the middle class wanted to be associated with refined amusements.
Although dark or subversive exhibits appeared in many museums, most
having to do with freak shows, human anatomy, or the chamber of horrors,
managers made great efforts to maintain a museum's respectability. Moral
dramas, religious tableaux, patriotic displays, and art galleries were included
in many of the larger, more successful institutions. The imposing edifices of
the larger museums gave them an aura of refinement and respectability.
Titillating freak shows juxtaposed with high-minded dramas, historical wax
displays, and natural history objects made an appealing combination to a
wide variety of late nineteenth-century spectators, regardless of sex, age, or
education.

The public's fondness for dime museums increased throughout the
1880s and 1890s, and during this period permanent museums appeared in
such major cities as St. Louis (McGinley's), Baltimore (Herzog's), Boston
(Austin and Stone's, Keith and Batchelder's, B. F. Keith's, and the Grand),
and Providence (the Pleasant Street Museum and the Westminster). There
was also the extensive Kohl and Middleton Circuit, which established
museums in Midwestern cities, including Chicago, Milwaukee, Cincinnati,

Louisville, Cleveland, Minneapolis, and St. Paul, as well as the Sackett and Wiggins Circuit, with houses in Detroit, Grand Rapids, St. Joseph, Toledo, Kansas City, Omaha, Lincoln, and Denver.[1] Pennsylvania, probably due to its ability to attract major acts from New York and Philadelphia, became the home of many dime museums, including the Harry Davis Museum in Altoona, the Grand Museum in Allegheny, Anderson's Musée in Wilkes-Barre, and a sizable museum located in Johnstown. Philadelphia itself was host city to the important Ninth and Arch Museum, which remained in operation into the next century.

The northwest corner of Philadelphia's Ninth and Arch Streets originally was the home of Colonel Joseph H. Wood's Museum, which opened in 1869. The collection contained many curious objects as well as a menagerie. But Wood's museum was known primarily for its splendid dramatic productions, performed in its large auditorium. On September 3, 1883, the museum was bought by two showmen, W. D. Hagar and W. T. Campbell, who transformed it into a more distinctively Barnumesque institution, called Hagar and Campbell's New Dime Museum. But Hagar and Campbell's efforts were short-lived, and in 1885 the museum passed into the hands of Charles A. Brandenburgh and Company, and became the famous Ninth and Arch Museum.

The first floor of the museum was similar to the modern notion of a penny arcade, with distorting mirrors and various "trial and test" amusements, including a "lung tester," a "health lift," a "registering striking machine," and so on. The second floor housed the menagerie, which consisted of "Barbary Apes, Pig Tail Monkeys, Ocelots, Alligators, Kangaroos, Armadillos, Snakes, and Boa Constrictors." On the third floor were exhibited the "Minnesota Woolly Baby," the "Long Haired Venus," and other human anomalies. Performances, which featured sketch teams, impersonators, and singers, were presented hourly in the Theatorium.[2]

By 1911, however, business at the Ninth and Arch Museum had declined considerably, and T. F. Hopkins, the manager, and Norman Jeffries, the press agent, devised a Barnumesque publicity stunt to stimulate attendance. One midwinter Tuesday a Philadelphia daily paper ran the headline, "The Fabulous Leeds Devil Reappears after an Absence of Fifty Years."[3] Supposedly a farmer and his wife had been awakened by an "unearthly sound." They soon saw a monster with long hind legs, short forelegs, a tail, horns on its head, and short wings. The farmer alerted his neighbors, and the nearby town was soon on the lookout for the monster. By Saturday, Jeffries announced that the "devil" had been captured and was to be placed on exhibition at the Ninth and Arch Museum on the following Monday morning. For two weeks crowds poured in to see Hopkins and Jeffries's obviously fabricated monster. The stunt was all in vain, however; the museum closed a few weeks later.

Over the years, the Ninth and Arch Museum had several competitors. On September 20, 1884, the Chestnut Street Dime Museum was opened in the Old Masonic Temple at 713–721 Chestnut Street by John Burke and Michael Goodin, only to close five weeks later. The museum's lease was subsequently purchased by George C. Brotherton, who revamped the building and opened his Temple Theatre and Egyptian Musée in 1886. The building was destroyed by fire in December, only a few days after the newly "Egyptianized" structure opened. Theater manager John A. Forepaugh, who was a nephew of the circus czar Adam Forepaugh, opened a dime museum on September 15, 1884, on Eighth Street below Vine Street. The museum was unsuccessful, however, and closed a year later.[4]

Philadelphia, like any number of large cities, had its share of distinctly seedy establishments, including the Great European Museum, at 708 Chestnut Street, which boasted in its advertisements of its "magnificent temple of Nature and Art."[5] At first glance the establishment appeared to resemble a typical middle-of-the-road dime museum, featuring a life-size wax tableau of the Spanish Inquisition and the requisite freaks and curiosities. But it also supplied clearly provocative "medical museum exhibits" like "The Anatomical Venus," on view for male customers only.[6]

Post–Civil War dime museums in Chicago included the West Side Museum, Whit John's Museum, Arthur Putney's Museum, the Wonderland Compound, the Congress Museum, and the London Dime Museum. Most were small-time museums that either closed within a year of their openings or, in some cases, were destroyed by the Great Chicago Fire of 1871.

That conflagration demolished Colonel Joseph H. Wood's large and important Chicago museum, which contained more than "sixty cases of birds, reptiles, insects, and objects from around the world."[7] The collection, located at 111–117 Randolph Street, included ship models, a scale model of the Parthenon, Daniel Boone's supposed rifle, a pair of Egyptian mummies, and the ninety-six-foot skeleton of an alleged prehistoric whale known as the "Great Zeuglodon." In addition, when Wood took over proprietorship of the museum in January 1864, he had created an impressive theater department, expanded the museum's auditorium to a seating capacity of 1,500, enlarged the stage, and hired a stock company of actors.

Chicago never again had an institution on such a grand scale as Wood's

43

museum, but it did become the home to two other reputable museums. New York's Eden Musée was the model for the Chicago Eden Musée, which opened in 1891 on Wabash Avenue at Jackson Street. Paul Olah's Hungarian orchestra, which had debuted at the New York musée in 1884, also performed in Chicago, and popular wax tableaux, such as "Lee's Surrender to Grant" and "The Rulers of the World," were copied directly from the New York collection.[8] The large, handsome four-story building was open daily from 10 A.M. to 10 P.M. Its interior was divided into halls similar to those in the New York museum. There was the usual Historical Hall, along with the Scientific and Literary Hall, the Hall of Sovereigns, the Stereoscopic Hall, the Chamber of Horrors, and so on. Like the New York original, the Chicago musée's Chamber of Horrors featured a collection of death masks and an area that depicted the four stages of a crime.

Charles F. Gunther, the proprietor of the Libby Prison Museum, was born in Peru, Illinois, and made his fortune in the candy business. He became an amateur collector in the 1870s. Among other curiosities, Gunther bought an Egyptian mummy, which, he claimed, was the Pharaoh's daughter who had discovered Moses on the banks of the Nile. Gunther at first displayed the mummy on the second floor of his State Street candy store, along with other relics. But he found that his patrons appreciated his sideshow, and he decided to house his entire collection permanently in a single building.

In 1889 Gunther purchased Libby Prison in Richmond, Virginia, and moved it to Chicago. During the Civil War the famous prison had housed Northern prisoners and gained a "national reputation for the hardships endured by its inmates."[9] Gunther moved the structure to Wabash Avenue between Fourteenth and Sixteenth Streets, stone by stone, filling 132 railroad cars. He made the four-story building into what a journalist called "a sort of P. T. Barnum museum," filled "willy-nilly with a collection of fake antiques and Civil War memorabilia."[10] The Libby Prison Museum became an overnight sensation, and tourists came from miles around to see such exhibits as the beam from which Mrs. Surratt and the other Lincoln assassination conspirators were hanged, the boards used as headstones on their graves in the prison yard in Washington where they were buried, and the bloodstained towel placed under Lincoln's head as he lay dying.

Many of the items displayed in the Museum, including the skin of the serpent that, Gunther claimed, had tempted Eve in the Garden of Eden, were purchased in 1920 by the Chicago Historical Society. This eccentric artifact is maintained there today, along with an early document attesting to its authenticity. The Libby Prison Museum was replaced in 1900 by the Chicago Coliseum, and the old prison walls became the outer walls of the new structure.

45

•  •  •

Prior to the Civil War, concert saloons, panoramas, and lecture halls were probably the dominant forms of popular entertainment in New York. In particular, such lecture venues as Antique Hall, Croton Hall, Gothic Hall, Irving Hall, and Hope Chapel, in addition to booking musicians and humorists and housing grand balls, hosted many novelty entertainments similar to those seen later at dime museums. Thus, Artault's mechanical figures, Angus McKaskil, the "Scottish Giant Boy," Cornelius Vroman, the "Man Who Slept for Five Years," and the "Indian Rubber Man" all graced the stages of New York's lecture halls during the mid-nineteenth century.[11] General Tom Thumb, who brought throngs of spectators to Barnum's American Museum, became an independent agent early in his career and performed at several New York halls, including Croton Hall in 1845 and Hope Chapel in 1860.[12] In addition, in March 1863, he and his new bride, Lavinia Warren, adorned in their wedding attire, prompted thousands of spectators to attend their Irving Hall exhibition.

The museum, as an urban institution offering both permanent and itinerant displays, reached its apex during the 1880s and 1890s, when New York became America's dime museum capital. During these decades museums became some of the most influential and important forms of entertainment available to a mass audience. The passion for dime museums expressed by both city residents and tourists dissipated only toward the end of the nineteenth century, when vaudeville and movies began to provide more attractive forms of cheap amusement.

Not all New York dime museums were like Barnum's prototype or the many minor-league institutions charted in George C. D. Odell's famous *Annals of the New York Stage*. At the top of New York's museum hierarchy, for example, was the large and elegant Eden Musée, located on Twenty-third Street between Fifth and Sixth Avenues, which specialized in waxworks. At the bottom of the spectrum were the "medical" museums, known for their so-called pathology rooms, displaying the distinctive effects of untreated syphilis and gonorrhea on the human body. Most proprietary museums lay somewhere in between.

The Eden Musée American Company was incorporated on October 5,

1882. The cornerstone of its impressive "modern French Renaissance" building was laid on February 24, 1883, and the establishment remained open until 1915.[13] According to the managers, it was to have a higher purpose than mere profitability. A guidebook explained to visitors the museum's objectives: the founders, it claimed, had attempted to construct a "temple of art which . . . would afford to all, both young and old, an opportunity for instruction, amusement and recreation, without risk of coming into contact with anything vulgar or offensive."[14] The museum was considered conservative and slightly upscale because of its size, fancy decor, and lack of a "theater."

The Eden Musée supplied New York and its visitors with an assortment of family entertainments, from Paul Olah and his Hungarian band, which made its American debut the year the museum opened in 1884, to Japanese acrobats, Spanish dancers, and magicians.[15] Acknowledging that special exhibits and ephemeral entertainments reaped huge profits, the Eden Musée sponsored its share of "one-time-only shows." Billboards outside the building announced daily or weekly special exhibits. In 1887, for example, the museum promoted the exhibition of an orchid, a newly discovered flower at the time.[16] The orchid show was so successful that the museum routinely held exhibits of new plants for their audiences. The Eden Musée was also one of the first dime museums to show films. Its most impressive and distinctive exhibits, however, were its ever changing wax re-creations and its famous Chamber of Horrors.

The museum's waxworks collection was extensive. The figures, created from life or from pictures, were constructed on the museum's premises, in a vast workshop in the upper portion of the building. The museum required the use of a second building on Forty-sixth Street to store its figures and to house the properties required for displays. The waxworks curator seemingly paid meticulous attention to detail in an attempt to make every aspect of the tableaux authentic. Each wax figure, for example, had two sets of clothing, a winter and a summer outfit. Twice a year the figures were bathed, repainted, and dressed in their seasonal garments.[17] One observer wrote that he objected to the cleanliness and resulting lack of realism in the displays. Why, he asked, was the late Prince Imperial, Napoleon-Eugene-Louis, who had been brutally assassinated, garbed in a newly ironed uniform instead of one that was dirty and stained with blood?[18]

Since the Eden Musée's exhibits were changed constantly in an attempt to remain current, it is impossible to describe all the figures displayed at the museum over the years. The following section, however, provides a look at some of the attractions mounted at one time or another at the Eden Musée.[19]

On entering the museum's vestibule, patrons sometimes witnessed a pickpocketing scene. Although this tableau varied over the years, what remained constant was that the victim was always a tourist—sometimes an old country gentleman, or in another version, a visiting Englishman. Each tourist seemed to be reading an advertisement for the museum with his daughter or wife as he was being robbed. Advertisements warned the out-of-towner to "Beware of Pick Pockets." On other occasions the vestibule featured street activities, with wax figures of an organ grinder and monkey displayed alongside a pencil vendor. In other years a lady bicyclist in wax was displayed.

47

Also located in the vestibule, near the ticket office, was a wax police officer watching the entering spectators, as if to protect them or to guard the ticket booth. According to a guidebook, the "Bluecoat Guardian, or Doorkeeper"—as a similar figure was called at the Boston Eden Musée—was "a model officer, he never visits the corner saloons, flirts with the nursery maids, or jollies the cooks; but attends strictly to his duty every day, remaining on guard from early morning until late at night."[20] For several years a gypsy fortune-teller also stood in the vestibule, offering predictions to all who passed by. The gypsy woman, however, was not an effigy, but a performer. She stood beside a cage that contained a bird and a hundred or so envelopes stuffed with fortunes. For a small sum the bird would select the patron's fortune.

It is not surprising that patriotism, as a means of generating self-esteem and promoting assimilation, was at the heart of many of the tableaux. In 1884, for example, the museum proudly mounted a replica of Bartholdi's Statue of Liberty.[21] Its quintessential "Americana" display, however, was "America Enlightening the World," which cost the then very substantial sum of $10,000 to produce. The display consisted of twenty-two wax figures. Its intention, a guidebook claimed, was not to affirm American superiority, but to illustrate "the position America occupies among countries of the world, in Liberty and Civilization" and the "irresistible victory of civilization over barbarity."[22] Columbia, a figure representing America, stood on a giant pedestal overlooking the entire world. In her right hand was a banner proclaiming liberty and freedom, and her left hand raised the torch of civilization. Grouped about her were figures representing America's ethnic diversity. At Columbia's left was an Indian, crouched in "a half defiant attitude," and below the banner was a black woman gazing up in gratitude. Surrounding Columbia were three allegorical figures symboliz-ing the continent of Europe ("Diplomacy," "Art," and "Commerce"). Asia was represented by "Despotism," Africa by "Old Traces of Civilization," and Australia by a group of "Aborigines."

**48**

In honor of the Dewey celebration, held in New York in September 1899, the museum erected several special exhibits that paid homage to the admiral and the heroes of the recent war with Spain. In the museum's entrance hall stood models of warships. A tableau depicted life on board the *Olympia,* the flagship of Admiral Dewey's fleet, from which had been fired the first shot in the ensuing war with Spain.[23]

Standard displays such as "The Rulers of the World" generally consisted of some twenty emperors, czars, kings, queens, sultans, shahs, presidents, and popes (see figs. 8 and 9). The 1898 arrangement, for example, in-cluded President McKinley, who was seated across from Queen Victoria and Pope Leo XIII, seated in front of Prince Bismarck, who in turn was shaking hands with the emperor of Germany. Since the museum manage-ment worked to keep the display contemporary, the 1905 exhibit was altogether different. It included President Theodore Roosevelt, who was standing beside an empty chair, which perhaps represented the murdered President McKinley, and Pope Pius X, who replaced Pope Leo XIII. Prince Bismarck was absent. The emperor of Japan was now standing in the front, stage left, next to the emperor of China, who in 1898 had stood behind Queen Victoria. By 1905, of course, Queen Victoria had been replaced by King Edward VII.

The museum's other famous exhibit, "People Talked About," also changed repeatedly (see fig. 10). In 1905 the gallery of celebrities consisted of such figures as Booker T. Washington, General William Booth of the Salvation Army, and the theatrical personalities E. H. Southern (dressed in a pirate costume), Sir Henry Irving, Anna Held, and Lily Langtry. Histori-cal tableaux, such as "The Assassination of Julius Caesar" and "Queen Isabella Receiving Christopher Columbus," remained unchanged for many years.

The majority of these permanent and changing exhibits were located in a large room directly off the entrance hall, called the Center Hall, the dominant feature of which was a domed glass roof. "Rulers of the World" took up the entire left side of the hall; the literary and artistic tableaux generally were located near the entrance to the hall. On leaving the Center Hall, visitors were escorted directly into the Winter Garden or Concert

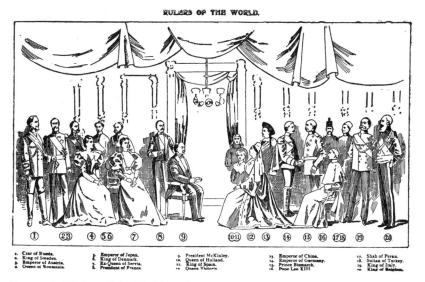

FIGURE 8. "Rulers of the World," Eden Musée catalog, 1898. (New-York Historical Society.)

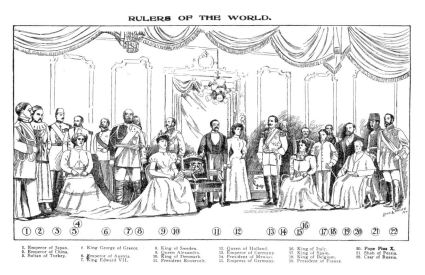

FIGURE 9. "Rulers of the World," Eden Musée catalog, 1905. (New-York Historical Society.)

50

PEOPLE TALKED ABOUT.

1. John Mitchell.    4. Marshal Oyama.    7. Governor Odell.    10. General Booth.    13. Judge Parker.    16. Booker T. Washington.
2. Anna Held.    5. Marshall P. Wilder.    8. Prince Henry.    11. Lord Roberts.    14. Mrs. Leslie Carter.    17. Lord Kitchener.
3. Wm. J. Bryan.    6. Sir Henry Irving.    9. Mrs. Langtry.    12. Joe Jefferson.    15. Adelina Patti.    18. E. H. Sothern.

FIGURE 10. "People Talked About," Eden Musée catalog, 1905. (New-York Historical Society.)

Hall, a large room occupying the full height of the building and extending through to Twenty-fourth Street.

The Concert Hall, decorated with French plate glass mirrors and tropical plants, could hold a thousand people comfortably (see fig. 11). On the south side was the stage, where the Eden Musée orchestra performed for visitors all day long. Scattered throughout the room were tables and chairs where fatigued patrons could sit and enjoy refreshments while being entertained by the orchestra. Wax figures of Japanese jugglers were mounted on pedestals around the walls, and fifteen wax acrobats were suspended from the ceiling trusses, among them a young woman on a trapeze and another balancing on a high wire. Also in the room were a Japanese warrior in armor and a bronze statue allegedly carved in 100 B.C.

Ajeeb, the famous chess and checkers automaton, was also displayed in the Concert Hall (see fig. 12). Ajeeb was a richly clothed, bearded Moor, seated cross-legged on a cushion, which in turn rested on a large box with open sides. In front of him lay a checkerboard on which he could be challenged by spectators to play chess or checkers. He was seldom defeated, and if any player attempted to cheat him, Ajeeb would immediately "sweep the chessmen from the board in apparent anger." [24]

Located in the gallery of the Winter Garden were stereopticons—views

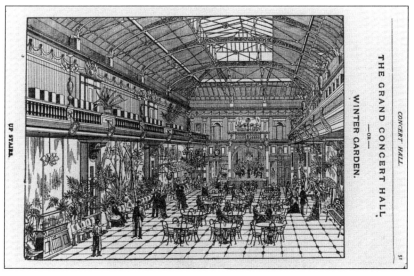

51

FIGURE 11. Eden Musée Winter Garden, Eden Musée catalog, 1887. (New-York Historical Society.)

enclosed in small walnut cases—where visitors could glimpse faraway places and famous artworks from foreign countries. At the far end of the gallery was a so-called Turkish smoking room—supposedly a reproduction of the Oriental smoking room at the Chateau de Blois. A brochure claimed that this room cost the museum more than $4,000 to re-create.

The Chamber of Horrors, the Sacred Chamber, and, in later years, the Historical Chamber, were all located in the basement of the museum. In 1883 the Chamber of Horrors was located in the center room of the crypt and consisted of nine displays, several of which would be recycled decades later. To the left of this room was the Sacred Chamber, which depicted the life of Christ in six tableaux. Three of these tableaux—"The Adoration," "The Entrance into Jerusalem," and "The Betrayal"—lined the left-hand wall. Opposite were "The Coronation," "The Crucifixion," and "The Resurrection." Apparently the Sacred Chamber was not a permanent exhibit, since references can be found only in catalogs before 1889.[25] At first it seems incongruous that it was located near the profane Chamber of Horrors. The Chamber of Horrors, however, was arguably the most popular exhibit at the Eden Musée, and it probably was a deliberate act of the managers to locate the Sacred Chamber where almost everyone was sure to

FIGURE 12. Ajeeb, c. 1889. (Museum of the City of New York, Byron Collection.)

go. This kind of subtle reinforcement of the museum's moral posture, of course, helped validate its educational claims.

In the Historical Chamber, which had replaced the Sacred Chamber by 1889, were scenes depicting people known either for their valiant deeds or for particular cruelty. Among the exhibits in the 1890s were "The Chicago Anarchists," "Washington Crossing the Delaware," and "The Storming of Constantinople by Mahomet II."[26] Also included in the collection were wax reproductions of famous death masks from the Pantheon Collection in

Paris. In France, visitors were provided only a glimpse of the masks; at the Eden Musée, on the other hand, spectators saw the complete figures of famous people dressed as they appeared shortly after their deaths.[27] Among the reproductions were Martin Luther, Napoleon I, Frederick II, Dante, Mary Queen of Scots, the Earl of Bothwell, Queen Elizabeth, Oliver Cromwell, Napoleon III, Thorwaldsen, Mendelssohn, Schiller, Goethe, and Beethoven.

A narrow passageway paneled in deceiving mirrors led visitors from the Historical Chamber to the Chamber of Horrors. This famous portion of the crypt was filled with crime-related material that subliminally forced spectators to acknowledge the importance of civilization: while day-to-day living might be strenuous, and the city's streets dirty and crowded, one should be thankful not to have been alive during the Spanish Inquisition. Torture instruments were displayed, such as an iron boot in which a victim's foot could be encased while torturers poured in boiling oil or melted lead, and the so-called iron maiden, which, when wrapped around a person, caused steel points to be thrust through his body. Illustrations of punishments and methods of public execution were mounted in the chambers, including "The Horrors of the Spanish Inquisition," an "Execution of a Burmese Criminal," and a "Beheading in Morocco." These exhibits tended to highlight the victim's agony. In "The Hindoo Woman's Sacrifice," for example, a young widow was shown "on a funeral pyre erected before the temple" in front of her dead husband's body. As the flames began to engulf her, spectators could see her body undulating, struggling, and writhing with pain.[28]

On August 6, 1890, convicted murderer William Kemmler became the first person in America to die in the electric chair.[29] Capitalizing on spectators' fascination with this new and modern method of execution, the museum created two alcoves in the Chamber of Horrors devoted to the "Execution of Criminals by Electricity." In 1898 the museum exhibited the death of Martha Place, the first woman to be electrocuted. In one room Place could be seen seated in the electric chair. Surrounding her were the warden, his assistant, and several witnesses. In a second alcove the executioner was standing at the switch, waiting to receive the signal that would permit the deadly current to flow. In 1899, the museum displayed the execution of Dr. Robert W. Buchanan, who was convicted of killing his wife on July 1, 1895. By the early twentieth century this display had been replaced with the electrocution of Leo F. Czolgosz, President McKinley's assassin.[30]

Toward the far right of the crypt were four more alcoves, depicting "The Story of a Crime." A young man, caught in the act of robbing a wealthy man's safe, was shown plunging a dagger into the owner's heart. The scenes also re-created his arrest, trial, and imprisonment, his subsequent parting with his mother before the gallows, and a small tableau of his children, a homeless boy and girl, seated on the steps of a mansion. According to an 1899 guidebook, "all the pathos and pity of a lifetime are shown on their faces and the group is recognized as one of the most artistic ever."[31]

•  •  •

Early nineteenth-century reformers believed that poverty was a sign of personal weakness. Many citizens concluded that the poor were self-made victims of a "fatal preference for easy living"; thus there was a moral dimension to poverty.[32] While "poverty was a major presence in New York," wrote Edward Spann, "it was a presence which successful New Yorkers ignored whenever possible."[33] For natives and tourists the city represented wealth and power as epitomized by Wall Street and Broadway; despite such reminders as unsanitary slums and streets filled with garbage, carts, ragpickers, peddlers, and beggars, the poor were easily forgotten. However, during the 1890s beliefs began to change, and poverty was no longer viewed as a result of personal failings but was linked more closely to environmental causes. Susan Moeller has suggested that cultural entertainments at the turn of the century revealed this modern perspective: "Plays blaming poverty on the evils of drink," wrote Moeller, "became less common after contemporary attitudes shifted to reflect the new theory that poverty drove men to drink."[34] "The Story of Crime" sympathetically supports the argument that the pressures of poverty can turn even a good-hearted man into a criminal. Hunger forced a father to steal in order to feed his family. The starving children, the blameless victims, were purposefully included in the tableaux to add pathos. This display should be contrasted to an 1887 Eden Musée tableau, "The Fruits of Idleness," which clearly supports earlier nineteenth-century assessments of poverty, crime, and idleness.[35]

Although most dime museum impresarios shied away from politically controversial displays, some urban dime museums attempted to address civic and social problems, and most museums supported the temperance movement and vividly illustrated the evils of drinking in melodramas, magic lantern shows, and wax displays. At the Boston Eden Musée, for example, a tableau titled "The Home of Drunkenness" depicted a family living in misery and filth. The neighboring tableau was titled "The Home of Sobriety," which in contrast depicted a happier—and sober—family enjoying life. "The moral to be drawn from these tableaux," according to a guidebook, "cannot fail to impress the most casual observer."[36] All of them probably owe a debt to the tableaux in Barnum's American Museum in the early 1850s, which displayed "The Drunken Family," a wax representation of a family dressed in rags and living in squalor captured gazing upon the face of a dead little boy. "No person can look upon that family group," a guidebook claimed, "without deploring in his heart the crime of which it is a commentary."[37]

The most profound political issues in nineteenth-century America were slavery and the Civil War. Slavery first became a major subject in the legitimate theater in 1852 with the production of *Uncle Tom's Cabin*. But some proprietors of museums had taken a political stand on the issue before Mrs. Stowe. In 1850, for example, Moses Kimball made public his abolitionist point of view by creating a seven-figure display representing the "Horrors of Slavery" at his Boston Museum. In doing so, he clearly reflected the abolitionist views so common in his city.[38]

The abolition of slavery—and the war, in fact—remained controversial subjects long after the Northern victory. Indeed, depictions of the Civil War were found in many museums throughout the remainder of the century. In the Eden Musée's American Gallery, for example, just to the left of the entrance hall, there were several Civil War–related groupings, including "The Surrender of General Robert E. Lee's Army at Appomattox Court House," "A Scene from Gettysburg," "Lincoln Freeing the Slaves," and a tribute to Ulysses S. Grant titled "Our Dead Hero," which was erected in 1885.[39]

The Eden Musée housed a spectacular collection of paintings in its Art Gallery and also became a pioneer in film exhibition. In 1898 the museum exhibited a film version of the Oberammergau Passion play, which ran for nine months in its Winter Garden. The film was projected on a mammoth screen, which measured twenty-two by twenty-six feet. The film was 2,200 feet in length, remarkably long for the time, since most were no more than 500 feet.[40] But as film historian Charles Musser has suggested, "*The Passion Play* was not in fact a single *film* but a *program* composed of as many as twenty-three discrete scenes (each of which was its own film) and an unknown quantity of slides."[41]

*The Passion Play,* written by Salmi Morse, originally was to have been

56

produced on the stage in 1885 by Henry E. Abbey at Booth's Theatre on Twenty-third Street. However, because of its then controversial subject matter, the production, never opened. Many conservative Christians considered it sacrilegious to portray Christ in the theater. Thirteen years later, however, the costumes and scenery were purchased with the intention of making the play into a film. The filming took six weeks on the rooftop of the Grand Central Palace.[42] On Sunday, October 3, 1898, five thousand people paid fifty cents each to see the curiosity at the Eden Musée's Winter Garden. It became a tremendous success and gained in popularity throughout the year.

The Eden Musée operated long enough to celebrate its thirtieth birthday in 1914, but its revenues waned as department stores and entertainment venues moved uptown above Twenty-third Street at the turn of the century. The museum's last business season was 1915. In later years the major wax figures from the collection were displayed at two Coney Island establishments, Gumpertz's Eden Musée and Santangelo's World of Wax.[43] Many other imitations, known simply as musées, could be found throughout the country between 1890 and 1910, in places like Johnstown, Pennsylvania, and Youngstown, Ohio.[44]

•  •  •

The majority of New York's dime museums were more colorful and eclectic in their approach to entertainment than the Eden Musée. Bunnell's Museum, Huber's Palace Museum, Doris's Eighth Avenue Museum, and Doris's Harlem Museum, for example, were more typical late nineteenth-century middle-of-the-road dime museums catering to a working-class and lower-middle-class clientele.

As mentioned earlier, George B. Bunnell opened his first permanent museum in 1876 with Barnum as a semi-silent partner. Bunnell's museum was located initially at 103–105 Bowery and, with Barnum's permission, called the New American Museum. Bunnell went to great lengths to imitate his mentor, even appropriating Barnum's lecture room slogan of "We Study to Please" and placing it in a prominent position on the front of the building. Bunnell's museum was one of the first large post–Civil War establishments to open in New York. During the 1870s there were smaller museums along the Bowery, but they were not respectable establishments.

A special feature of Bunnell's museum was "Dante's Inferno," a representation of Hell where "wax figures of sinners were menaced by red-and-green-shaded gaslight."[45] Bunnell infused his version of Hell with effigies of such unpopular living people as Boss Tweed, Henry Ward Beecher (after his sensational fall from grace), and Jay Gould, all of whom suffered amid the Inferno.

The building's facade was reminiscent of Barnum's American Museum, with its flags and giant posters announcing the current attractions.[46] Three of the building's four stories housed Bunnell's collections, and each floor was subdivided into two rooms. The ground floor contained the "theatorium" and the main hall; the second story housed both curiosities and Bunnell's menagerie; the third floor was entirely devoted to freaks. Three years after its founding, Bunnell moved his museum to larger quarters at 298 Bowery.[47] He maintained his operation there for only a short time, however; on June 2, 1879, a fire destroyed the museum. Determined not to be defeated, Bunnell opened a third museum at 711 Broadway, near Ninth Street.[48]

This large museum, which opened on December 8, 1880, was nicknamed the Hub and attracted not only many visitors but several curiosities from other museums. Among them were "Chang, the Chinese Giant" and Admiral Dot and Major Atom, two well-known midgets of the time. The "Wild Men of Borneo" made an appearance in September 1881, and the "largest living couple," Captain Bates and his wife (the former Anna Swan), were exhibited in December of that year.[49]

Bunnell also sponsored several special exhibitions and contests. He held a cat show, a bird show, a baby show, and a pigeon show. Many of Bunnell's exhibits focused on topical issues, such as his wax display on the Ford brothers, labeled "Slayers of Jesse James and the Annihilators of Bandits." Along with such waxworks Bunnell offered the standard museum fare of bizarre attractions: rubber men, fat men, tattooed ladies, two-headed girls, and Zulu princesses. He kept his museum open during the summer months, a novel practice for the time, and staged performances six times daily. In 1883 Bunnell moved his museum yet again, this time to Broadway near Eighth Street. According to an advertisement, he renamed this "Great Family Resort" Bunnell's Old London Museum. He remained in the dime museum business until around 1887, when he officially retired and moved to Connecticut.[50]

George H. Huber's museum opened the next year and remained in operation far longer than Bunnell's had; it closed only after the 1909–10 season, when the property was sold to Albert Luchow, who used it to expand his famous restaurant.[51] In 1888 Huber and his partner, E. M. Worth, a long-established showman, bought three adjacent buildings on East Thirteenth Street (running through to Fourteenth Street), knocked down all the connecting walls, and created an L-shaped complex five stories high and occupying five city lots. When the reconstruction was completed, five thousand square feet of glass-fronted cases (in eight rooms known collectively as the Curio Hall) were provided for oddities.[52]

When the museum opened on August 13, 1888, at 106–108 East Fourteenth Street, the partners called their establishment Worth's Museum. They advertised in the *New York Herald* that it was "the resort of ladies and children for wholesome entertainment," and that it contained a million rare curiosities, provided "continuous stage performances by a carefully selected company from 1 P.M. to 10 P.M.," and charged only a dime admission.[53] Early in 1890, the museum was renamed Worth and Huber's Palace Museum.

Within months of its opening, a popular assortment of live prodigies was on exhibition, including "Jo-Jo, the Dog-Faced Boy," "Big Eliza, the Fat Negress," "Baby Bunting, the Smallest Living Horse," and "I-Am," billed as the "Mastodon, the Largest Hog in the World." Ajeeb, a mechanical chess player, also was put on display—no doubt an imitation of the one at the Eden Musée. At the top of the building, above the floors occupied by the museum's exhibits, Huber and Worth provided lodgings for their freaks, many of whom were married and lived settled and domestic lives.

On April 12, 1890, the *Clipper* announced that Worth and Huber were dissolving their partnership. Huber now became the sole proprietor of the Fourteenth Street establishment (called Huber's Palace Museum from 1890 to 1901 and simply Huber's Museum from 1901 to 1910). Worth subsequently moved to Sixth Avenue and Thirtieth Street, where he established E. M. Worth's Model Museum and Family Theatre, with a theater hall that seated seven hundred.[54] Although he had spent $18,000 remodeling the old Haymarket Theatre on Thirtieth Street and Sixth Avenue into a dime museum, he had trouble obtaining a license. Finally he was able to open his new museum in January 1891. Worth's Museum gained a reputation of having an amazing and eclectic selection of freaks. Famous attractions, among them Charles Tripp, the armless man, and Jonathan Bass, the "Ossified Man," shared billing with such bizarre freaks as Nichodemus Senoj. Senoj was twenty-three years old, twenty-seven inches tall and weighed a hundred pounds. His head and right arm were normal, but his left arm was half the appropriate length and terminated in a horn. Senoj had no legs, and one of his feet was webbed, while the other was hairy and resembled the hoof of a hog.[55]

Huber's Museum also was successful and went on to become one of the most popular New York tourist attractions until it closed in 1910. The proprietor's slogan was "a dollar show for ten cents," and a large colorful sign over the entrance expanded on the entertainment bargain: "Admission 10 cents. One Million Natural, Historical, Oriental, National, Antique Curiosities, One Million. Admission 10 cents."[56] After Huber remodeled his museum and reopened it on August 17, 1891, George C. D. Odell points out, it was "greater and grander than ever. Every hall was fitted with iron ceilings, the floors were fire-proof and broad, easy stairways provided comfort and safety."[57]

Huber catered to the public's penchant for contests and exhibitions. During the week of October 5, 1892, for example, he held his famous fasting contest, which offered a five-thousand-dollar purse to the winner. This "absurd spectacle," wrote Odell, "of course drew vast throngs of morbid sensation seekers."[58] Six contestants entered, including one from England and another from Germany. After six days of fasting, the field was narrowed to four. By October 25 only Henry Stratton, of Courtland, New York, remained. A portly man, and "hungry for fame," Stratton continued to attempt to beat the fasting record of forty-five days set by a Mr. Succi at Koster and Bial's Music Hall sometime earlier. He did it, but disaster struck on November 19 (46 days into the fast): Stratton died, apparently of "heart failure superinduced by fasting."[59]

This was not the sort of publicity Huber needed. In the nineties many dime museum exhibits were being protested against as demoralizing. Although museums claimed to be family-oriented recreation centers, a number of them provided amusements that now were considered inappropriate for women and children. As a result, the Society for the Prevention of Cruelty to Children, for example, lodged an official complaint against museum exhibition rooms in January 1891.[60] A year later, on February 1, 1892, the licenses for stage performances at a number of museums and concert halls officially expired. Twenty-five establishments requested a renewed permit, but only twenty-one were issued. Four major establishments, including Huber's, the two Doris museums, and the popular Grand Museum located at 345 and 347 Grand Street, were cited for poor management.[61] The charges rested heavily on the fact that these museums allowed unaccompanied minors into their "theatoriums." After these negative citations, the Grand Museum, which had opened only in December 1888, could not remain solvent and closed at the end of the 1892 season.

• • •

John B. Doris had operated two dime museums during the late 1880s and early 1890s. His uptown Harlem Museum, located between 124th and 125th Streets on Third Avenue, opened on September 23, 1889. Originally founded as the Mt. Morris Museum, its collection was leased to Doris because its managers needed cash to pay off their debts.[62] When Doris acquired his downtown location at 351 Eighth Avenue is not known, but the establishment first appears in Odell's *Annals of the New York Stage* on October 29, 1889.[63] His museums were highly topical; like the proprietors of the Eden Musée, Doris had an up-to-date waxworks department, displaying models of celebrities within days of their deaths. Doris became especially well known for his sensational Jack the Ripper displays, first mounted during the week of May 4, 1891, only days after the famous murder of Carrie Brown.[64] The museum also engaged the usual freaks, among them Maury, a human pin cushion, Congo, a leopard man, Kamchaka, a cannibal princess, and young Chauncey Morlan, a fat boy. In addition, Doris staged many novelty acts, including Professor Queen, who was known for performances in which he hanged himself. Doris also conducted beauty contests and fat shows, and his hallways were lined with cases of bizarre artifacts.

By 1891 Doris's Eighth Avenue Museum had three theaters on its premises. One housed his resident acting company and presented plays. In another theater the manager provided variety entertainment, and in the third he presented such miscellaneous entertainments as puppet shows and comedians. Fanny Herring, whose career blossomed well before the Civil War, had performed with Edwin Booth, as well as with other noted Shakespearean actors. After her theatrical prime, she continued performing leading roles, mostly in dime museums, and ultimately became a resident actress in Doris's theater company. During the 1891–92 season she starred in such forgotten melodramas as *Ireland's Oppressors, Little Buckshot, The Sailor's Return, The Bandit Merchant of Greece, Knights of the Road,* and *Denver Dan.* Many critics and fans were distraught at the idea of such a fine actress performing to dime museum crowds, but Herring, who became known as the Sarah Bernhardt of the Bowery, seemed to enjoy the notoriety.[65]

• • •

The Bowery, in fact, was a kind of dime museum center. In the first half of the century, the street had gained its reputation for housing colorful and boisterous places of amusement, from shooting galleries to saloons, gambling dens, and boxing arenas. At the middle of the century, after the Astor Place Riot of 1849, many of the more pretentious shops in the area moved uptown, and increasingly the Bowery became known for its cheap trade and inexpensive amusements. Many of its venues, such as the Sultan's Private Divan at 241 Bowery, which featured dancing barmaids, were open only to men.[66] The countless saloons and brothels made the Bowery a likely neighborhood for small-time showmen to open low-end dime museums (see fig. 13).

The best-known museums in the area in the last quarter of the nineteenth century were the Gaiety Museum, the Globe Dime Museum, Alexander's Museum, the Chatham Square Museum, the Berlin Academy of Waxworks, Morris and Hickman's East Side Museum, The European Museum, the New York Museum, and the New Natural Museum. Gradually these museums began to acquire bad reputations, especially for cheating their customers by charging a "blow off"—an additional admission to certain exhibits. In particular, spectators were lured into believing that for a supplemental dime they could see views of "the unclad female form in all its loveliness."[67] Those who paid were taken into a small room and shown nothing but pictures of actresses in burlesque poses. It then cost another ten cents to be able to enter the "real sanctum" where, through a curtain, they viewed the promised unclothed bodies. What the pleasure seekers actually saw were stripped mannequins.

In many of the so-called medicine or anatomical museums on the Bowery, gullible patrons were lured into the office of the "doctor" or "professor" for blood pressure or lung tests, a phrenological examination, or a palm reading. But it was well known that the fear of a painful death by some incurable disease—especially syphilis, or "paresis" as it was then called—prompted most of the visits to these seedy museums and requests for treatment. Of course, nothing about an additional fee for treatment was ever mentioned in most museums until, in the middle of a procedure, a flap on the wall would fall, exposing a sign that read, "Professor so-and-so's fee is $2.00."[68]

Although Dr. Kahn's Museum of Anatomy, at 713 Broadway, and the

FIGURE 13. Barker at entrance to a Bowery dime museum, 1881. (New-York Historical Society.)

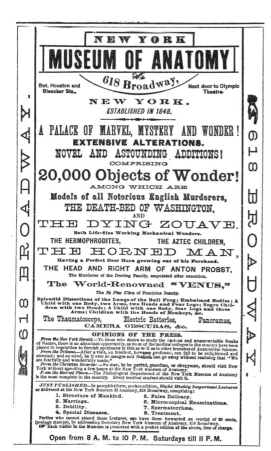

FIGURE 14. Program, New York Museum of Anatomy, c. 1863. (Billy Rose Theatre Collection, New York Public Library for the Performing Arts, Astor, Lenox and Tilden Foundations.)

New York Museum of Anatomy, at 618 Broadway, were not on the Bowery per se, they were among the better known medical museums that marketed the medical advice of their managing doctors—a number of whom were either disbarred physicians or completely untrained confidence men. Little is known about Kahn's establishment, but the New York Museum of Anatomy is better documented (see fig. 14). It was founded in 1848 by Dr. H. J. Jordan and a Dr. Beck, whose practice was located at 40 Bond Street, two blocks away. Typical of medical museums, the venue was open only to men; the fee, in this case, was twenty-five cents. The primary object of the museum, according to an 1863 guidebook, was "to enable the thinking mind [of nonmedical personnel] to fully comprehend the wonders of the human structure."[69] In a way, that was so. One of the most frequently described exhibits was the so-called embryology section, where fetal gestation was depicted in a display that featured various stages, from an eight-day embryo down to a full-term fetus.[70]

The embryology exhibit was preceded by displays of the uterus and vagina. Thus, the boundaries between graphic sex education and pornography were blurred. According to the 1863 guidebook, these exhibits "excited great interest, for their perfect illustration of the scientific anatomy of the subject." Because of the sexual slant of the museum's displays, women were not allowed to enter the premises. For their all-male audience, however, the proprietors took great care to offer a "selection of subjects which bear on the beauties of the human form . . . the perfection of the feminine beauty is exquisitely portrayed in the large figure of Venus, and the great and world-renowned Gertu, 'the Ne Plus Ultra of Feminine Beauty!'"[71]

The New York Museum of Anatomy also exhibited the skulls or skeletons of famous people, including—it was claimed—the skull of Will Somers, the jester to King Henry VIII, and the full skeleton of a Frenchman named Henri Jacques, who was sentenced to death for the murder of his wife and three children. Also included in this eclectic display were bones of animals, including the skull of a seal and the remains of a chicken with four legs and three wings. Among the human anomalies were the head of a Hungarian who supposedly had grown horns, and the skeleton of a child born with two heads and four arms and legs. Healthy and unhealthy specimens of semen—the latter, according to the museum doctors, usually caused by that "direful habit, self abuse"—were magnified 500 to 1,500 times.[72]

An entire exhibit was dedicated to the human heart, and one section of the museum was devoted entirely to diseases. There were displays illustrating scarlet fever, "cancer of the back and thigh," smallpox, and an ovarian tumor—most made from papier-mâché or wax and painted to resemble the decaying organ. The museum's main attraction was the Sepulchre or Pathological Room, entered beneath a sign that noted, "The Wages of Sin is Death." The room was, the guidebook explained, for the use of medical men and students only. (Presumably, though, any visitor could be considered a student.)[73] The museum's proprietors claimed that all models in this section were bona fide specimens, real examples of what today would be called sexually transmitted diseases. Here, in this dimly lit room, were displayed the supposed effects on the human body of untreated venereal diseases and nightly sessions of self-abuse.

Elongation of the testicles was described as a direct result of masturbation, while penises infected with warts and gangrene illustrated the devastating effects of gonorrhea. Syphilis, in its most malignant form, was shown in the completely distorted face of a victim whose eyes and facial features had become disfigured. By contrast, healthy organs were displayed, all of which were a testament to the cures provided by Jordan and Beck. This, in fact, was the whole point of the museum. The alleged physicians, who also gave lectures at the museum, were available for daily consultations. On the last page of the museum's guidebook the doctors made a final pitch for their services (a consultation cost five dollars):

65

### *Diseases*
### *Contracted In An Unguarded Moment*
### And Other Ills Inflicted Upon Mankind By The
### Social Evil—How Such Unpleasant Diseases May Be
### Effectually Cured, Without The Use Of Mercury, Injury
### To Constitution, Or Fear Of Secondary Symptoms.
### No. 40 Bond Street Drs. Jordan and Beck

If patrons so desired, they also could write for the doctors' published lectures on such topics as "The Philosophy of Marriage," "Special Diseases," "Spermatorrhoea," and "False Delicacy." Most similar medical museums sold such books, as well as worthless potions, to their gullible clients on the premises. A "floorman" might convince an already terrified spectator that he was in need of medical attention. The victim was then ushered upstairs to the "medical institute" run by a so-called specialist and encouraged to purchase a bottle of some mysterious cure-all.[74]

•   •   •

The marriage of popular entertainments with quasi-educational artifacts had proved successful. By the 1880s proprietary dime museums were providing entertainment to millions of patrons daily, and had become an important feature of American culture. Although the post–Civil War years brought about the incorporation of public museums dedicated to "high culture," such as the American Museum of Natural History (1869), the Metropolitan Museum of Art (1870), and the Boston Museum of Fine Arts (1876), these establishments did not compete directly with traditional dime museums.

# 4. Freaks and Platform Performers

Freaks are what you make them. Take any peculiar looking person whose familiarity to those around him makes for acceptance, play up that peculiarity and add a good spiel, and you have a good attraction.
—Attributed to showman Clyde Ingalls

One feature that distinguished most dime museums from genuine historical or art museums was live performance. In addition to providing melodramas, strolling musicians, and lecturers, most museums exhibited an array of freaks, who were displayed on platforms, either together or throughout the various curio halls. To be considered fit for exhibition as a museum oddity, a person did not have to be taller or shorter than average or fatter or thinner or even deformed. Many other criteria came into play.

In general, five classes of human anomalies were displayed in dime museums: natural freaks, who were born with physical or mental deformities, such as midgets and "pinheads"; self-made freaks, who cultivated freakdom, such as tattooed people; novelty artists, who were freaks because of their "freakish" performances, among them snake charmers, mesmerists, hypnotists, and fire-eaters; non-Western freaks, who could be promoted as exotic curiosities such as "savages" and "cannibals," usually billed as being from Africa; the fake freaks, or "gaffed freaks," who faked freakishness, such as "Siamese twins" who were not attached or the "Armless Wonder" whose arms were hidden under his costume.[1]

The first recorded freak shows for profit were held in England during the thirteenth century and established a durable tradition.[2] According to historian Richard Altick, the display of freaks became so popular during the sixteenth century that the "demand was well abreast of the supply."[3] Shakespeare, who was aware of the prevalence of freak shows, made a reference to the profitability of displaying freaks in *The Tempest*. When Trinculo first meets the bestial Caliban, he wishes he had a booth at

Bartholomew Fair in which to exhibit this wondrous "monster." He would be rich if he had such an opportunity, for in England, Trinculo claims, "there would this monster make a man; any strange beast there makes a man: when they will not give a doit to relieve a lame beggar, they will lay out ten to see a dead Indian."[4]

67

The greatest human freak show in London, however, was the open door policy at Bedlam asylum, which was established in 1609. At Bedlam, "the cells were arranged in galleries, in the manner of cages in a menagerie . . . in each cage was a chained lunatic, whose behavior, if it were not sufficiently entertaining to begin with was made so by the spectators prodding him or her with their sticks or encouraging further wildness by ridicule, gesture and imitations."[5] Eventually, such spectacles were discontinued due to humanitarian legislation. The public's attraction to freak shows, however, continued to grow and, according to the *London Spy,* freaks were exhibited throughout England in the eighteenth century. "Wild beasts, learned pigs, dwarfs, giants, prodigious monsters having one head and two distinct bodies, and an admirable work of nature in the form of a woman having three breasts could [all] be viewed by a pleasure seeker."[6] In the back rooms of taverns and inns, at marketplaces and fairs, wherever there were itinerant performers, inevitably there were freaks.

Before the emergence of dime museums in the mid-nineteenth century, the majority of human oddities in the United States were also itinerant performers, their careers handled (or mishandled) by managers who usually booked them into taverns, rented storefronts, or concert and lecture halls. With the advent of dime museums, the luckier freaks became at least somewhat more active participants in the American popular entertainment industry. Performing in an organized freak show was a relatively respectable, if not stable, way to earn a living, and many performers—the tattoo artists, the sword swallowers, and the snake charmers—billed themselves as freaks in order to become part of the industry.

• • •

The dime museum freak show, or "platform entertainment" as it was known, was a huge crowd-pleaser and a solid moneymaker, and proprietors had a powerful incentive to treat their freaks well. Successful museum managers like George Huber and P. T. Barnum understood this point, and cherished their freaks as they would any other profitable investment. Huber's Museum, as mentioned in chapter 3, and Barnum's American Museum provided lodgings for many of their freaks on the top floors of their museums. Although the accommodations were far from glamorous, they were cheap, and there was always plenty of food, heat, and companionship. Out-of-town actors often shared lodgings with these platform entertainers. As young performers, for example, Weber and Fields worked at many museums on the East Coast. While at Keith and Batchelder's museum in Boston during the early 1880s, they slept in the attic along with other museum employees, paying six dollars a week to "Mom Keith" for room and board. According to their biographer, Felix Isman, the large attic room was divided into individual cubicles: "Eight-by-ten partitions [sic] in which the actors both dressed and slept lined the walls and opened upon the dining-room, occupying the center of the attic floor."[7]

Although the dime museum business provided a certain opportunity for otherwise impoverished and lonely freaks, the conditions endured by most were far from glamorous. Many were abused by small-time museum operators, kept to grueling schedules, and given only a small percentage of their total earnings. Individual exhibits were hired for one to six weeks by the proprietors of dime museums; the average freak performed in ten to fifteen shows a day and was shuttled week after week from one museum to another. Some, however, like "George, the Turtle Boy," were privileged enough to have long-term contracts; George was displayed at Huber's Museum for three consecutive years.[8]

Many freaks in fact were lucky (and gifted) enough to earn a good livelihood through exhibitions, and some became celebrities, commanding high salaries and earning far more than acrobats, novelty performers, and actors. The salaries of dime museum freaks varied from twenty-five to five hundred dollars a week, on the whole substantially more than lecture room variety performers were paid. Lecture room performers received twenty-five to thirty-five dollars a week for a so-called single act and fifty to seventy-five dollars for a double.[9] Late nineteenth-century stage actors were paid only thirty-five to eighty dollars a week.[10]

George Middleton, who operated several Midwestern dime museums with C. E. Kohl, wrote in his memoirs that he hired fat women for twenty-five and fifty dollars a week; yet when a very special curiosity came along he could be persuaded to pay much more. Such was the case with "Winny, the Fat Negress," to whom he paid the considerable salary of three hundred dollars a week. "Everyone wanted to see Big Winny," Middelton recalled. "They lined up in front of the box office and across the sidewalk, and were going in just as fast as they could. They looked like soldiers going to the war. That business kept up for weeks, and it surely opened up our eyes."[11]

Charles Stratton, "General Tom Thumb," probably the most famous freak of all time, eventually split his weekly profits with Barnum. Stratton owned a house in Bridgeport, Connecticut, several pedigreed horses, and a yacht. And he was not unique. A number of freaks were able to afford real estate and to retire comfortably: Chang and Eng, the original Siamese twins, owned a farm, a business, and several slaves in North Carolina; Millie-Christine, Siamese twin singers, earned five hundred dollars a week and owned a plantation in North Carolina; Zip the "What Is It?" owned property in New Jersey and lived in an elegant house in Connecticut, a gift from Barnum; Chauncey Morlan, the famous fat man, owned an estate in Indiana; diminutive Admiral Dot owned and operated a hotel in White Plains, New York. Commodore Nutt, a midcentury midget, was heralded as the thirty-thousand-dollar Nutt because he had a three-year contract worth that sum, an extraordinary amount of money at the time.[12]

Although many freaks were paid handsomely, museum managers were often insensitive about performance schedules; profit margins were their main concern. This was especially true of their top attractions, since the more shows these freaks performed, the more tickets were sold. When Theodor Jeftichew, "Jo-Jo, the Dog-Faced Boy," appeared at the Globe Dime Museum in New York, its managers arranged to have him perform twenty-three shows during a twelve-to-fourteen-hour day.[13]

In fact, at worst, a freak was simply a commodity packaged by museum operators and showmen in such a way as to bring in business. Novelty, variety, and humbugging, the trademarks of the successful dime museum, all figured in the exhibiting of human oddities. The display of phony freaks occurred regularly, especially among the smaller dime museums, which needed the drawing power of fabulous attractions to lure customers away from the larger establishments. Not only did managers manufacture freaks, but they also lied to the public about the exhibition of celebrity attractions. Once in the 1880s, for example, when Jo-Jo was performing in Europe, his name appeared on the bill of a Jersey City museum. Usually Jo-Jo only growled onstage; a fellow performer, however, believing the New Jersey Jo-Jo to be an impostor, attempted to discredit him by trying to make him laugh or fight during his performance. After a week of such antics, the Jersey City Jo-Jo pulled his wig off to reveal that he was indeed a fake.[14]

• • •

Showmen also fabricated the biographies of freaks to make their oddities more fascinating. For example, when Barnum first exhibited Charles Strat-

69

ton as General Tom Thumb in 1843, he told the public that the prodigy was eleven years old instead of five, fearing some would think Tom Thumb an unusually short child instead of an anomaly. In addition to giving Stratton a new name, Barnum provided him with British ancestry, believing that it added class.

70

The original "Wild Men of Borneo" were two brothers, Hiram and Barney Davis (Waino and Plutano were their stage names). Their published biography, a supposedly "true life" pamphlet, claimed they were captured off the coast of Borneo in 1848; in reality, however, Hiram had been born in 1825 in England and Barney two years later in New York City. They grew up on their family farm in Ohio with their parents and three other siblings. But their biography described them as literally "wild animals full of monkey antics, ugly in temper and hard to manage."[15]

Inches were added to the height of giants and subtracted from that of midgets; fat ladies gained pounds and skeletal men lost them. Superlatives abounded; every display was billed as the tallest, smallest, fattest, ugliest, or hairiest—and of course the most extraordinary or original. Vivid and provocative epithets often followed the names of performers. Lizzie Harris, who weighed 676 pounds, was heralded as the "Largest Mountain of Flesh Ever Seen." Captain and Mrs. Bates were billed as "Extraordinary Specimens of Magnified Humanity." The captain was 7 feet 11.5 inches tall and weighed 478 pounds. His wife was the same height and weighed only 65 pounds less.[16]

Midgets were given exotic new names, usually with titles: General Mite, Admiral Dot, Baron Littlefingers, Prince Ludwig, Duchess Leona, and Baroness Simone. They appeared with normal-sized people or sometimes with giants to emphasize their tiny stature. Several freaks had routine partners or alter egos: the diminutive Admiral Dot often shared a platform with the seven-foot giant Anna Swan, and Mrs. Tom Thumb stood in the spotlight with Noah Orr, who was a trifle over seven feet tall and tipped the scales at 516 pounds.[17] Lucia Zarate, probably the smallest midget ever displayed, measured only twenty-eight inches as an adult and weighed no more than five pounds. Managers routinely did whatever they could to capitalize on the freakishness of their freaks. In 1890, for example, the managers of one museum, while exhibiting Zarate, offered a diamond ring to any baby who could match her ring size.

A common promotional device was the juxtaposing of odd combinations of freaks such as "Me and Him," an exhibit of a fat boy and a skeleton dude on the same platform. The Clare Sisters' (or "Twins," as they were also billed) act was built around the fact that one sister was of "mammoth proportions and the other a Lilliputian" (one weighed five hundred pounds and the other fifty).[18] In the dime museum freak show, names meant less than labels. Siamese twins, for example, don't have to come from the country we now call Thailand to be genuine, they just have to be joined. The term was codified after the successful exhibition of actual Siamese joined twins, Chang and Eng. A hirsute boy was commonly called the "Dog-Faced Boy" or the "Lion-Faced Boy," and the term "Living Picture-Gallery" was the standard label for human tattooed exhibits.[19] The original routine of two boys (the Davis brothers) chained together and grunting and groaning was called the "Wild Men of Borneo." It was so successful that all its imitations were also billed as "Wild Men of Borneo," and the imitators copied the sound and movements of the original "Wild Men."[20]

The performances of freak show characters generally became codified, and even sets and costumes rarely deviated from the formula: the tuft of hair on Zip's head became a feature of all other "What Is It?" freaks. Bushy hair (later called an Afro) was the trademark of all "Circassian Beauties." Bearded ladies appeared with their spouses to establish their feminine authenticity; midgets were given status-enhancing titles and paraded around in grandiose costumes to exaggerate their shortness; armless men and women drank tea, played instruments, and wrote letters with their feet. Sometimes, however, to add intrigue, the more-or-less routine freak might perform a novelty act. Warrimeh Boseth, the armless Indian boy, would lie on his back, shoot a bow and arrow with his feet and impale a flying pigeon in front of a crowd of spectators.

•   •   •

Although physical anomaly was the only real drawing power of most freaks, some were truly talented. General Tom Thumb sang and danced for appreciative audiences in the United States and Europe. The following is an example of a song he sang for Queen Victoria in 1844. The lyrics were written by James Morgan of Liverpool, supposedly at the general's request, and were set to the tune of "Yankee Doodle":

> I'm General Thumb, just come to town,
> Yankee Doodle Dandy,
> I've paid a visit to the Crown,
> Dressed like any grandee:
> *The Queen* has made me presents rare;

*Court ladies* did salute me;
*First rate* I am, they all declare,
And all my dresses suit me.
Yankee Doodle loves you all,
Yankee Doodle Dandy,
Both Young and old, and short and tall,
Declare that I'm the Dandy.

*The Prince of Wales*—dear little boy
Yankee Doodle Dandy,
When First we met, was rather shy
And could not understand me.
But since, we've been the best of friends,
And play'd at romps together:
I wonder when he next intends
To mount another feather.
Yankee Doodle loves you all,
Yankee Doodle Dandy,
Both Young and old, and short and tall,
Yankee Doodle Dandy.

*Prince Albert* speaks so kind and free
Yankee Doodle Dandy;
He's taller *very much,* than me,
Although I'm neat and handy;
He loves the Queen, and so do I—
They both say I'm a beauty;
I'm much obliged to all—goodbye—
Today I've done my duty.

Yankee Doodle loves you all
Yankee Doodle Dandy,
Some other day, I guess, you'll call,
To see your little Dandy.[21]

The general's repertoire also included several "Negro songs," as well as dances such as the polka and a "highland jig" (see fig. 15). He also did impersonations of Napoleon Bonaparte and Frederick the Great. Sometimes Stratton would appear adorned with jewels and surrounded by the gifts he had received from Queen Victoria and other European dignitaries.

73

FIGURE 15. General Tom Thumb in a Scottish costume, c. 1855. (New-York Historical Society.)

Millie-Christine—or Christine-Millie—known as the "Two-Headed Nightingale," were also talented performers. Unlike the original Siamese twins, Chang and Eng, who were attached at the chest, these sisters were joined at the spine. Although they had separate bladders, they shared a single vagina, uterus, and anus. Above the point of their union, each had her own nervous system; below that point, they shared a single system. One sister was said to resemble their father and the other, their mother.

Christine was a soprano and Millie a contralto; they entertained the public by singing popular duets while accompanying themselves on guitars.[22]

A prodigy's performance was not necessarily limited to the singing and dancing he or she—or they—could manage on a mere platform. Some freaks also performed in museum lecture rooms or in legitimate theaters in scripted plays and afterpieces. Charles Stratton made his American stage acting debut on December 4, 1848, when he was ten years old, in a play especially written for him called *Hop o' My Thumb*. Adapted by Albert Smith from the French extravaganza *Le Petit Pounce*, the play was about a miniature—and precocious—child who outwitted a giant who had been terrorizing the kingdom of Old King Cole. During the course of the play, Stratton could be seen running under the legs of adults, being dragged in a shoe, and getting served up in a pie. The play was the perfect vehicle to illustrate the comic skills of a talented midget. After Stratton retired, the play was revived with Commodore Nutt playing the starring role. Another play, adapted by H. J. Conway and commissioned for Stratton, was a version of Harriet Beecher Stowe's novel *Dred*.[23]

Giants also were cast in specifically written or adapted plays. Monsieur E. Bihin, a famous French giant, played the ogre in *Hop o' My Thumb*, opposite Commodore Nutt, in 1862. Another popular giant, Colonel Roth Goshen, performed in *The Giant of Palestine* at Wood's Museum in 1868, as well as in Laura Keene's production of *Jack and the Beanstalk*, which for obvious reasons was a perfect vehicle for both giant and midget actors. Admiral Dot and Noah Orr costarred in another version of the fairy tale, called *Jack the Giant Killer*.[24]

Typically, there were no seats in the curio halls of dime museums, and as spectators poured into the room, they were ushered from platform to platform by a lecturer, whose role was that of master of ceremonies. During his performance, the lecturer, usually given the pretentious title of "professor," held the audience's attention by describing the freaks displayed on the various platforms. In addition to a strong voice, the lecturer needed to have some sort of magnetism and eloquence. His elocutionary style usually was filled with the traditional hyperbole of carnival barkers, and his recitations were filled with classical and biblical allusions. Professor Bumpus described Cherrie Burnham, a 610-pound woman, as "A mighty girl, fat, magnificent. Five chins! Cheeks like the sun-kissed melon! Arms like vats of luscious Falernian wine. . . . Few women of modern times have equaled you. Six hundred and ten pounds! Twice the weight of Queen Victoria, three times the weight of Boadicea, four times the weight of Delilah!"[25]

Not only did museum proprietors hire lecturers for the halls of the museum ("inside talkers"), they employed "outside talkers" as well. One spectator described the outside talker at Huber's Museum as looking like a "bankrupt count of the grand old school of pomp and wax," who sported "evening dress of the same epoch."[26] The outside talkers' job, in popular entertainment lingo, was to "turn the tip," or to persuade a group of people to buy tickets. His spiel advertised all the wonders of the museum. The verse recited by one of their number was a synopsis of the astonishing things spectators could see once they paid their money:

> Ladies and gents,
> for only ten cents
> you can see all the sights.
> And there on your right
> is the great fat lady;
> she's a healthy baby
> weighing three hundred pounds;
> she's six foot around.
> Her husband is the living
> skeleton—see him shivering.
> The dog-faced boy
> will give you all joy,
> and the tattooed man
> does the best he can.
> The human horse
> is wonderful, of course,
> and I'll show to you
> the boxing kangaroo.
> The lady lion tamer
> will please every stranger.[27]

Invariably there also was a "shill" to help the outside talker. An employee of the museum who pretended to be a paying customer would give the ticket-taker his money over and over again, enticing others to follow.

• • •

One premise of the dime museum freak show was that each of us has an innate desire to behold the misfortunes of others in order to build our own confidence and self-respect. The historian George C. D. Odell, after years of chronicling dime museum entertainments, came to believe that "the freaks of the dime museum served the purpose of raising dull persons from the throes of their inferiority complexes." He thought pleasure seekers could not look at such "monstrosities" without convincing themselves that, after all, their normal selves were "pretty good, if not beautiful."[28] As Odell saw it, not everyone could be a famous artist or a talented singer, but at least the spectator could be relieved that he or she was not a dog-faced boy or a Siamese twin. Watching freak performers, Odell believed, built self-esteem; people left freak shows feeling more at ease with their lot in life.

In part, the freak show also was rewarding for a Victorian audience because it encouraged a person to compare his life, his achievements, and his productivity with those of other human beings instead of with the capabilities of a machine. The typical mid-nineteenth-century individual was at odds with the increasingly fast-paced developments of industrial technology. As Stuart Ewen and Elizabeth Ewen write in *Channels of Desire,* the new machine age promised a world of plenty, "free from toil," but it also evoked "a world gone mad, out of control, the vision of Frankenstein."[29] The subtext of the freak show was fear of a mad world. Anxiety was relieved, however, by the audiences' collective viewing of nature out of control—of otherness. Savages, missing links, giants, and diminutive people were positioned on platforms to be admired, ridiculed, or laughed at by a unified crowd bonded by the collective act of looking and by their so-called normalcy. Modern medicine was still in its infancy, and the average person was afraid of being incurably different, unalterably abnormal. But the definition of "normal" was very narrow, and this very narrowness, a product of ignorance, was in its way comforting. In a sense, then, the deformed person was not necessarily born a freak but was transformed into a freak the first time he or she stood on the exhibition platform. Freaks were created by others out of fear. Thus, the freak show format gave everyone in the audience permission to gaze openly and to ask personal questions; in such a context the average person always came out ahead.

The onstage freak, of course, was someone else offstage. As performers, they were cast as the major, the general, the fat lady, or the skeleton dude. Once their freakishness was discovered and labeled, it was inescapable: they would always be branded the legless wonder, the bearded lady, or the What Is It? In the halls of the dime museum, deformed or diseased people were reinvented as freaks; the mise-en-scène of the freak show, the very atmosphere of the dime museum, incarcerated the individual in an inescapable, lifelong role. Some freaks led the semblance of a normal life, with a family and children, but it was still a freakish one, manipulated by showmen, whose normality was tainted by association with the freak show world. Even Chang and Eng's normal children were exhibited as freaks because their fathers were joined twins.

The "true life" pamphlets distributed to the spectator by the freaks as souvenirs were usually fabricated, highly engaging stories about how their subjects had been destined to be born as anomalies. Apart from his height, for example, Charles Stratton was a normal boy and physically well proportioned. His shortness was explained to the public through the very common "maternal impression" theory, which proposed that when something out of the ordinary happened to a pregnant woman, the circumstances affected the fetus. Thus, an expectant mother who saw dogs copulating was supposed to have reason to fear the birth of conjoined twins, and one who witnessed her husband mauled by a lion, the birth of a lion-faced boy.

Anna Leak Thompson, the "Armless Wonder," was said to be an example of this kind of causation. One day, as her father was returning home drunk, his pregnant wife saw him walking up the road with his overcoat thrown over his shoulders in such a way as to conceal both of his arms. This vision had its "logical" effect and their daughter was born armless. Similarly—in a less clearcut example—shortly before Charles Stratton's birth, the family's black-and-tan puppy was drowned in a river that flowed behind the house. Stratton's pregnant mother was so distraught that she placed a "mark" on her unborn child and doomed her son to be a midget.[30]

The popular fifteen to fifty-page life sketches, which were sold to the public from each platform, in effect formed part of the performer's "pitch."[31] In addition to providing biographical material, the pamphlets generally included printed statements by physicians who had examined the performer, declaring his or her malformations to be genuine. Usually the deformities were described in elaborately clinical terminology, adding to the publication's air of authenticity and erudition. In addition, the leaflets contained enthusiastic reviews of the performance by (mostly bogus) critics.

The financial success of freaks and of the dime museums that housed them was also promoted by photography. Two prominent photographers, Matthew Brady (famous for his Civil War pictures) and Charles Eisenmann (who became the world's leading photographer of unusual people and performers), had studios in the heart of New York's entertainment district.

At the height of the "photomania" frenzy, from about 1857 to 1900, these photographers were prominent among those who made cartes de visites for dime museum performers.[32] Cartes were very small picture postcards measuring 2.5 by 4 inches, approximately the size of a visiting card. Most cartes had a logo on the bottom or back of the card giving the photographer's or publisher's name and location, as well as the name of the person in the photo. Millions were sold annually; the profits were generally split between the museum and the performers. The average spectator purchased cartes as souvenirs and often used them as postcards. Many people became collectors, storing their cards in albums. Not only did the cartes de visites generate additional income for the performer and the museum, they also facilitated bookings in other cities, as they were sent to museum owners to give them an idea of a performer's abilities.

The backdrops used in these photographs of human oddities ranged from Victorian parlors to jungles. In their photos freaks often were presented in one of two codified styles, which Robert Bogdan describes as the "exotic" and the "aggrandized."[33] In the exotic photos, the freak appeared in a primitive, bestial, or at least non-Western environment, often in jungle backdrops or with papier-mâché boulders; the freak wore skins or loincloths and carried appropriate props, such as a spear or a hatchet, as in the photograph of Zip.

In so-called aggrandized photos, on the other hand, individuals appeared in parlor settings, wearing expensive-looking clothes and accessories. The aggrandized mode gave status to freaks, offsetting their disabilities. We have already seen one example of aggrandizement with the high-flown titles adopted by midgets, such as general, commodore, and so on. Another example may be seen in the staged performances of the freaks: armless men drew with their feet, midgets sang and danced, and a few played musical instruments.

Talented or educated freaks were a rare commodity and thus constituted an elite. Krao, the hirsute anomaly from Korea (see fig. 16), spoke five languages; General Tom Thumb and Millie-Christine sang; and Eli Bowen, the "Legless Acrobat," along with Charles Tripp, the "Armless Wonder," entertained with their wit and dexterity. Bowen and Tripp often performed together, each making the limbs he had perform those tasks ordinarily achieved by his missing extremities—in essence, overcoming their disabilities. When they performed together, the two dressed in business suits and rode a bicycle built for two, with Tripp peddling in the back and Bowen steering in front, amusing their audiences with comical exchanges: Tripp

FIGURE 16. Krao photographed in a dress, c. 1895. (Harvard Theatre Collection, Houghton Library.)

would say to the legless Bowen, "Watch your step!" and Bowen would retort, "Keep your hands off me!"[34]

Krao, or the "Missing Link," was intensely promoted during the heyday of the Darwin conflict. Basically she was no different from the other hairy freaks, such as "Jo-Jo, the Dog-Faced Boy" and "Lionel, the Lion-Faced Boy," but when she was labeled a missing link, she become part of a scientific, religious, social, and political debate, which elevated her status and transformed her into a more lucrative celebrity. Krao was displayed in both the exotic and the aggrandized modes: she could be seen wearing jewelry and a dress, or in a loincloth surrounded by jungle growth.

• • •

Dime museum managers were notorious for their manipulation of both the images and the personal lives of freak performers. Motivated by profit, managers fabricated love affairs between entertainers to lure patrons to their establishments.[35] While he was on display at Worth's Museum in May 1888, for example, J. W. Coffey, the elegant skeleton man, who dressed in a high hat, morning coat, wing collar, and bow tie and carried a walking stick, advertised in the *New York Herald* for a wife. Coffey, who was five feet six inches tall and weighed a mere seventy pounds, was looking for a "plump and pleasing person" to be his life's companion. He received numerous responses and selected a wife from among the applicants. Whether Worth knew about the advertisement is not known; however, he managed to make a profit from the publicity by exhibiting Coffey and his new wife through the end of the 1888 season.[36] For her part, when Mrs. Coffey married her husband, she was an ordinary, though overweight, woman. As the wife of a famous freak, however, because of her bizarre union and postnuptial exhibitions, she became a freak as well in the eyes of the public.

Marriages often were arranged—or claimed—between incongruous freaks, and most of these unions were exploited for profit. It is not known, for example, whether "Mr. and Mrs. Atherton," a bizarre couple, were really married. The "Original Aztec Children," Maximo and Bartola, who were publicized as brother and sister, in fact were married on January 1, 1867, while on tour in London.[37] Probably no one will ever know whether they were actually siblings and their marriage a publicity stunt or whether they were merely marketed as brother and sister and their marriage a true legal love match. Some marriages between freaks, of course, were undoubtedly genuine. Although Charles Stratton's love for Lavinia Warren was bona fide, Barnum milked the situation for all it was worth by exhibiting the engaged couple before their marriage. The exhibition was incredibly profitable; it was such a windfall, in fact, that Barnum begged Stratton and Warren to delay their wedding, offering them $15,000 if they would postpone the ceremony for a month.[38] The young lovers refused to reschedule for publicity purposes.

81

Stratton's marriage ceremony, however, did not want for publicity. He and Warren were united in Grace Church in New York on February 10, 1863, in front of two thousand distinguished spectators. This was the event of the season; it filled the front pages of the major New York newspapers and for a time eclipsed the Civil War. The wedding was "the grand marital event of the week, and one of a lifetime," recounted a journalist.[39] After they were married, the Strattons were exhibited for a time with a child alleged to be theirs. Their "daughter" supposedly was born on December 5, 1864, and died two and a half years later. In fact, the Strattons never had a child of their own; the promotion scheme was devised by Barnum.[40]

But marriages between freaks abounded, bringing fame and fortune to some couples. Anna Swan, the "Nova Scotia Giantess" (who almost lost her life when Barnum's American Museum burned), married another giant, Martin Van Buren Bates, billed as the "Kentucky Giant," in London on June 17, 1871. The day after their wedding, a reception was held in their honor with such guests as the Prince of Wales and other British dignitaries.[41] Chauncey Morlan and Annie Bell, the "Heaviest Couple Alive," whose combined weight was more than 1,400 pounds, were married on November 30, 1892, at Huber's Museum, and exhibited for six weeks to a capacity crowd.[42] For a time they traveled the country as man and wife, saved a small fortune, and soon were able to retire to an estate in Indiana.

Freaks married to nonfreaks were also routinely exhibited with their spouses. The Siamese twins Chang and Eng (see fig. 17) provided an even more titillating look at freak marriages. By the age of twenty-eight, these twins had accumulated a small fortune of about $60,000 and decided to retire to Wilkesboro, North Carolina. They filed to become American citizens and took the surname Bunker. They courted and married sisters in a double wedding ceremony in 1843; Eng married Sara Ann Yates and Chang married Adelaide Yates. Between them they fathered twenty-two children, all normal except for two who were deaf mutes. In 1850 they came out of retirement because they needed more money to provide for their families; they placed themselves in Barnum's hands once again and appeared in public with their wives and children.[43]

82

THE SIAMESE BROTHERS.
Aged.18.
Drawn on Stone & Published, by T.M.Baynes, 41, Burton Street, Burton Crescent. Printed, by C.Hullmandel.

FIGURE 17. Chang and Eng, the original Siamese twins, 1829. (Chang is on the right, Eng on the left.) (Harvard Theatre Collection, Houghton Library.)

Siamese twins posing with their normal spouses and offspring not only prompted questions about everyday privacy but also raised issues of sexual privacy. Sex, in fact, was a powerful component of the performance text of the freak show; spectators imagined sexual intercourse between incongruous partners—the fat woman and the thin man, the bearded woman (who may not after all be a woman) and her husband—and among couples like Chang and Eng and their wives. Such a performance readily inspired images of transgressive sex, ambiguous sex, homosexuality, bisexuality, and group sex, challenging the conventional boundaries between male, female, sex, self, and other. Tattooed women, fat women, and skeletal women were costumed in short, sleeveless dresses, the better to verify their freakishness.

Circassian Beauties with their wild and frizzy hair were outfitted in garments that accentuated their busts and hips. Snake charmers wore minimal clothing, exaggerating their wildness and exoticism. Sometimes patrons were allowed to touch the limbs of fat ladies or pull on the whiskers of bearded ladies. It was deeply arousing to Victorians to be able to touch a strange woman in a legitimate, respectable setting, and it was a tantalizing and disturbing sight for the other spectators, especially adolescents. A wondrously titillating dialectic emerged, in which performers were alluring as well as repulsive.

83

The subtexts of a freak show concerned sex, fear, power, and self-definition. Children saw themselves reflected in the midgets. They saw small people acting like adults—smoking, drinking, and marrying. When standing next to a midget, a child felt bigger, more like an adult, more powerful than the midget.[44] Women were able to challenge the dominance of men through images of bearded ladies, fat ladies, and female giants. Freak shows also provided relatively ordinary women with the opportunity to work, for such women could be found in every imaginable category of the self-made and novelty performer: Mlle. Agnes Charot (hypnotist), Flossie La Blanche (female Samson), Nettie Lytell (rifle queen), Miss Doddretta (comic mathematician), Dora S. Gerry (fire eater), Alice Lewis (snake charmer), Lillie Tobin (glass eater), Mattie Lee Price (magnetic girl), Lalande Fuller (human stepladder).[45]

Museums exploited the box office appeal of female sexuality by hosting all-women exhibitions, such as boxing matches and tug-of-war games. Some of the sleazier establishments produced tableaux vivants featuring women in flesh-toned tights. It was the female performer whose costume overtly suggested worldliness and even sexual promiscuity who fueled the strongest public criticism. Although many of the well-proportioned snake charmers and Circassians did not look so different from burlesque girls, museum managers wishing to project a clean, family-friendly image downplayed the sexual aspects of such performers. The top museums tried to emphasize their wholesome and refined atmosphere, but it is easy to understand why some critics called them immoral and deemed them inappropriate for family entertainment.

Spectators not only enjoyed watching the performances of human anomalies at the museums, but also received a thrill from the occasional opportunity to be "freaks" for a day. There were a host of museum-sponsored public contests, from standard beauty pageants and baby shows to unique forms of competition such as gum-chewing, quail-eating, smallest feet, walking, and typewriting contests. These events provided pleasure seekers with an opportunity for freedom of expression and a chance to show off; they could be exhibitionists for a few moments.

Meade's Midget Hall, at the corner of Fifth Avenue and Fourteenth Street, was a well-known establishment whose gimmick was to display only midgets and children. Among its exhibits were a fat baby who at five months weighed fifty pounds and an infant born weighing only three-quarters of a pound. Meade's was strictly an exhibit hall, and neither the infants nor the midgets performed in variety entertainments. But spectators did flock to Meade's famous "Great National Baby Show," an extravaganza held for two weeks in 1877. Parents and nannies sat with their adorable, fat, small, good-humored, supercilious, and pugnacious babies (temporarily turning their cherubs into freaks), hoping to win a gold chain or a diamond ring.

The babies, all under the age of five, were exhibited continuously from 10 A.M. to 10 P.M. in rooms decorated with flags and banners inscribed with such lofty messages as "The Boy Is Father of the Man" and "Suffer Little Children to Come unto Me, and Forbid Them Not, For of Such Is the Kingdom of Heaven!" The establishment provided cribs for the weary tots on the upper floor of the building, as well as a restaurant for the adults. In its thirst for novelty, Meade's even approached the Society for the Prevention of Cruelty to Children and asked whether the museum could display a baby in the SPCC's care, with two unsightly black eyes and a crimson bruise on one of its temples, as an example of a battered child.[46] Meade's Midget Hall did not change its novel exhibits often, however, and it did not present variety entertainments, so there was rarely any reason, except for the baby contests, for pleasure seekers to visit it more than once. As a result, the museum failed and was forced to close a year after it opened.

•  •  •

Most dime museums routinely closed for the summer. Many freaks found work during those months with circuses or with independent traveling museums such as Barnum's Great Asiatic Museum and Menagerie, organized in 1851 by Barnum, Seth B. Howes, and Tom Thumb's father, Sherwood Stratton. Barnum's traveling entertainment, with its 110-foot tent, toured the country for four years. Barnum also established another traveling museum later in his career, P. T. Barnum's Great Traveling World's Fair, Museum, Menagerie, Polytechnic Institute and International Zoological Garden. There were many other well-known traveling museums, such as Colonel Wood's Museum, which toured up and down the Mississippi in the late 1850s. Some would be set up in vacant storefronts or on the boardwalks of resort areas. Other traveling museums, which usually consisted of a few wax effigies, some animals, and a carload of freaks, attached themselves to circuses or equestrian shows. In 1869, Bunnell's traveling museum combined with Stone and Murray's Circus and in 1875 with Barnum's.

85

Most traveling museums did not operate on a very grand scale. The majority were small and somewhat shabby, cropping up on carnival midways and at other types of outdoor fairs. By the 1880s most were limiting their displays to human oddities, and gradually, around the turn of the century, the word "sideshow" replaced "museum."[47] With the advent of the sideshow the display of human oddities for profit began to become an especially seedy part of the outdoor amusement industry. During the early twentieth century, sideshows, often called "ten-in-ones" by fairground people, could routinely be found at carnivals, world's fairs, amusement parks, and seaside resorts. Many old-time dime museum attractions, including Krao, Zip, Eli Bowen, and Charles Tripp, performed in these establishments.

•   •   •

The era of P. T. Barnum and the first formally organized freak performances is long past, and modern science has demystified and cured many of the ailments that created the nineteenth-century freak. Today, freaks shows are thought to be dehumanizing and have been outlawed in many states. Ironically, however, freak shows provided independence to many disabled people. Freaks had marketable attributes, and those who were exhibited had an opportunity to become celebrities, sometimes to obtain fame and fortune. In support of this idea, in 1972 the Florida Supreme Court struck down a 1921 law banning freak shows, ruling that the state had no business preventing anyone from earning an honest living.[48] Thus the concept of the freak show is not quite dead; versions of the nineteenth-century entertainment still exist, reconfigured for contemporary society. In these shows, however, the once-prominent position of the physically deformed person has, for the most part, been filled by the novelty performer and the self-made freak. Today's version of the traditional platform freak show may include a fat lady and a "pickled punk" display, but the new kings and queens are the tattoo artists, snake charmers, fire artists, and human torture machines.

# 5. Lecture Room Entertainments

We confess that it is very difficult to make a distinction between the two, [theater and dime museums], when the same plays are performed, the same actors employed, and the same effort given.

—Anonymous

The lecture rooms in dime museums varied not only in size but also in quality and in the nature of the theatrical experiences they offered. Some rooms seated a thousand, were lavishly decorated, and mounted full-scale dramatic productions; others consisted of a small platform and perhaps a few rows of seats, were hardly embellished at all, and presented programs no better than the tawdry variety bills of the concert saloons. But canny selection and constant change were the major operating principles of the dime museum business and the strategies with which most proprietors enticed patrons back to their museums again and again. In the curio halls the attractions changed weekly or biweekly, but it was difficult for managers to keep outdoing themselves. A three-headed animal displayed one week could not be followed by a two-headed version the next week.[1] The appeal of a lecture room entertainment, on the other hand, was based not on uniqueness or strangeness but variety alone, and here it was easy for managers to change programs daily, even twice a day, if necessary. The success of these lecture room entertainments enabled many dime museums to survive through the 1890s in direct competition with vaudeville, and to make a profit.

It is not known when the first dime museum began to offer theatrical productions; however, Albany's Trowbridge Museum (sometimes called the New York State Museum), which opened in 1798, was certainly one of the first. The Trowbridge Museum, on the corner of Beaver and Green Streets, was open from 9 A.M. to 9 P.M. every day except Sunday. Aside from its assemblage of stuffed birds, live animals, and antique curiosities, the museum had a lecture room, a small auditorium on the third story of the building seating four hundred spectators. Its stage measured only seven by nine feet, yet it was large enough to accommodate the performances of magicians, ventriloquists, hypnotists, and actors in some melodramas. In fact, many aspiring actors made their professional debuts there. William Warren, who later became famous for his comic roles at the Boston Museum, was a member of the museum's stock company between 1834 and 1836, and Mr. and Mrs. John Drew also appeared on the museum's dramatic roster.[2]

Henry Trowbridge moved his museum to State Street in 1830. Roughly ten years later he remodeled extensively, at a cost of between $9,000 and $10,000.[3] In the process he enlarged his dramatic department and refurbished his theater, enabling it to seat an audience of 1,500. The new Museum Saloon, as it was called, consisted of a parquet, a family circle, and private boxes. On February 1, 1841, Charles Taylor, the museum's musical director, made a lengthy opening night speech outlining the objectives of the management. Among other points, he promised that there would be no offense "to the eye or the ear, to the most particular audience or the most sedate."[4] The proprietor of the museum would offer only amusements that were untarnished, pleasant, and chaste.

But Albany's Trowbridge Museum was far from the national spotlight, and Trowbridge's contribution to the popular entertainment industry was overshadowed by the showmanship of P. T. Barnum and his longtime friend, another museum impresario, Moses Kimball. It is Kimball, in fact, who has been acknowledged as the transformer of the dime museum lecture room into a respectable theater, the prototype of those of other dime museums.

•   •   •

Moses Kimball's Boston Museum and Gallery of Fine Arts (see fig. 18), on the corner of Tremont and Bromfield Streets, opened on June 14, 1841, six months before Barnum acquired the Scudder museum and four months after Trowbridge opened his Museum Saloon. As was typical, the Boston Museum maintained a collection of living curiosities, mechanical wonders, paintings, and stuffed animals, and kept a house taxidermist on staff. (Wax figures were not introduced into the museum until 1850.)[5] The Boston Museum's collection was an amalgamation of three others: the New England Museum, the New York Museum (Boston-based), and Nix's New Haven Museum.[6] In 1839, with the help of his brother David,

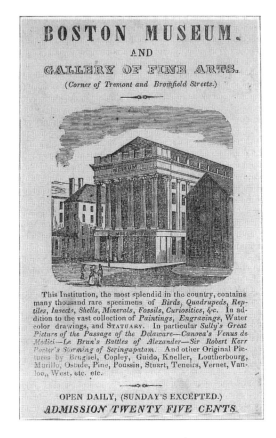

FIGURE 18. Boston Museum and Gallery of Fine Arts, 1844. (Harvard Theatre Collection, Houghton Library.)

Kimball purchased the collection and two years later moved it to Tremont Street.[7]

Most of the curiosities of the Boston Museum could be found throughout its lower levels. On the top floor was a spacious picture gallery that doubled as a "music saloon," where concerts, olios (a medley of songs, dances, and comic sketches), and other miscellaneous performances were given.[8] This large gallery, when used as a performance space, could accommodate about 1,200 spectators, who were forced to sit on crude wooden benches.[9]

In the middle of the 1842–43 season Kimball began the process of altering the function of his so-called music saloon. His goal was to seduce the audience gradually, transforming the space into a true theater without diminishing the aura of respectability established by the somber decor and pseudo-scientific atmosphere of the museum itself. Slowly he began mounting more and more comic sketches and vocal interludes, and he briefly introduced operetta to his museum audience. In his third season, 1843–44, Kimball initiated his first dramatic presentation; on September 4, 1843, the museum presented George Colman Jr.'s play *The Blue Devils.*[10] It was an auspicious occasion, and for the next sixty years the Boston Museum continued to mount theatrical productions. They were almost certainly more lavish than those produced at many museums, but give a good sense of fare in the better lecture rooms.

89

The public's reception of Kimball's theater "museum style" was emphatically positive. By eliminating all offensive language, innuendo, and behavior—and by sustaining a family entertainment environment—Kimball succeeded in making even those with antitheater sentiments feel comfortable. Kimball wanted to expand the museum audience to include the largest possible cross-section of the populace. He convinced coach services to schedule a regular 10 P.M. pickup in front of his museum in order to attract patrons who did not live within walking distance.[11] He did not charge an extra admission to the theater, and although drinking was common in many theaters of this era, he refused to allow patrons to consume alcohol on the premises. In the 1848–49 season Kimball was forced to institute reserved seating, his open seating policy having finally proved too chaotic. To encourage family attendance thereafter, he devised "family slips" in which a block of up to seven seats could be reserved, at fifty cents each, and saved for an hour into the performance.[12]

In the fall of 1846 he moved the Boston Museum to yet another new building, on Tremont between School and Court Streets. According to the *Daily Evening Transcript,* the building's exterior was tasteful and elegant, and the interior well contrived and convenient.[13] The museum's main exhibition hall, known as the Great Hall, was highly decorative, with an arched ceiling sixty feet high and Corinthian columns. The room measured 103 feet in length and was 50 feet wide. The Great Hall was flanked by rooms displaying the museum's vast collection. At the end of the hall was a staircase twenty-five feet wide that branched into two staircases, leading visitors to two long galleries and ultimately to the theater, which seated 1,500 spectators.[14]

The new, elaborate theater was designed especially for the production of plays and spectacles. The walls were painted gray, the ceiling white, and the decorations along the proscenium and the stage boxes were white and gold painted on a background of light green. There were three chandeliers and seven candelabra. The stage was fifty feet deep by ninety feet wide, with a proscenium opening of thirty feet.[15] On either side of the stage were the manager's office and the greenroom. The dressing rooms were just below and, because they were not located in the basement, contained windows, a valued asset, since most nineteenth-century theatrical dressing rooms were dark and dingy. On the dressing room floor there were also a music room, a wardrobe, and a property room.[16] The theater was renovated in 1868, 1872, 1876, and again in 1880, when the Boston Museum was functioning solely as a theater. At that time the stage and orchestra were moved to a lower level to make room for a second gallery, which added about three hundred seats.[17] The new auditorium featured three tiers of seating above the orchestra, a parquet circle, and first and second balconies.

In the 1840s, in preparation for play production, the museum had assembled a stock company of fifteen to twenty professional actors. (Extra actors were hired on an as-needed basis for the large spectacle performances.)[18] The museum's stock company played in repertory, presenting a variety of plays during a single season.

According to Edward Mammen, in 1850 there were probably thirty-five museum stock companies. By 1860 the number had jumped to fifty.[19] But the quality of the productions mounted at the Boston Museum was superior to that of most museum stock companies, and many nineteenth-century star actors were attracted by the high caliber. Among them were E. L. Davenport (1845), Charlotte Cushman (1849), and Junius Brutus Booth.[20] Booth made his museum debut in August 1849 as Richard III. He returned the following year and played King Lear, Shylock, Richard III, and Hamlet.[21]

Booth's soon-to-be-famous son Edwin made his professional acting debut at the museum. On September 10, 1849, Edwin appeared as Tressel in his father's production of *Richard III*.[22] Edwin Booth, in fact, thought so highly of the Boston Museum's stock company that he brought it to New York for a four-week engagement many years later, in January 1884. There, the company performed various classics, among them *Othello, Hamlet, Richard III,* and *Macbeth.* Booth played the title role in all the plays, with the exception of *Othello,* in which he alternated the roles of Iago and Othello with Charles Barron, another actor in the company.[23]

A typical Boston Museum season during the 1850s also included several Elizabethan and eighteenth-century plays, among them Richard Sheridan's *The School for Scandal* and Oliver Goldsmith's *She Stoops to Conquer,* along with perhaps half a dozen plays by Shakespeare.[24] These classics were usually performed with a guest artist, a famous actor, in the lead role, since a typical museum crowd would not otherwise be drawn by such dramas. Although the element of refinement associated with the classics was enticing for the more literate spectator, it was the stars that brought in the crowds.

The stock company assembled by the managers of the Boston Museum was unusually talented, and a few of its members were under contract for many years. The comedian William Warren, whose first season with the museum was in 1847, acted in the company for over thirty years; his final performance was given on May 12, 1883.[25] The usual contract, however, was shorter.

George C. Howard and Caroline Fox, who ultimately achieved national fame for their portrayals of St. Clair and Topsy in the touring company of *Uncle Tom's Cabin,* were members of the museum company for two seasons, beginning in 1843.[26] Fox's older brother, the pantomimist George Lafayette Fox, also performed at the museum, as did other Fox siblings, their mother, and George H. Wyatt, their uncle. Howard and Caroline Fox performed in several plays together during the 1843–44 season, including a Christmas pantomime, *The Golden Age,* in which she played Sylva, Queen of the Fairies.[27] On October 31, 1844, Howard and Fox were married; she was fifteen years old and he was twenty-nine.[28] After the 1844–45 season, the Howard-Fox group left the museum and formed its own touring company, settling in Rhode Island from 1846 to 1850. (In 1851, Howard took over the management of Peale's Troy Museum in Troy, New York, where the Howard-Fox acting troupe became the resident stock company.)

• • •

The life of a member of the Boston Museum stock company was extremely hectic. From 1848 to 1875, the museum's rehearsal policy allowed one to three days for a revival, one week for a new play, and only three to five rehearsals for an afterpiece.[29] Actors rehearsed daily from 10 A.M. to 1 or 2 P.M.; they had the rest of the afternoon off, unless, of course, there was a matinee. During the early years, matinees were usually given on Saturdays and occasionally during the week, while evening performances, which began at 7:30, were presented every night except Saturday and Sunday. (For supposed religious reasons, the museum was closed on Saturday night; however, this practice stopped in 1871.) Actors arrived at the theater around 7 P.M. and did not leave until midnight.[30]

The repertory season itself was quite long: almost eleven months, from

91

September to mid-July.[31] Each night a different play was performed, and often there was doubling of roles in large-cast plays or when an actor fell ill. Although it was exhausting, the experience to be gained by a young actor as a member of the repertory company was unmatched. During his first four years at the Boston Museum, for example, William Warren performed 204 different roles.[32] During the company's six-week summer recess, the museum's theater offered variety acts by magicians, ventriloquists, and pantomimists.[33]

The wages an actor earned in the Boston Museum's repertory company were slightly lower than those of the legitimate theater, but there was the attraction of a certain job security. In the 1850s, lead players at the Boston Museum earned from thirty to sixty dollars a week, while members of the supporting cast earned from two to twenty dollars.[34] At Wallack's, a prominent New York theater erected in 1861, lead actors were paid thirty-five to eighty dollars a week, while others earned six to thirty dollars.[35] In any case, wages for actors cannot be compared to the hundreds of dollars a week many museum freaks earned.

During the early years of the Boston Museum, Kimball did not neglect the museum proper—its displays and exhibits—as a place of popular entertainment. His theater became increasingly important to him, however, and soon its survival took precedence over that of all the other attractions. By the 1850–51 season, the museum was mounting 126 plays. This dramatic explosion was tempered a bit in the ensuing decades, when the average number of plays produced a season fell to between forty and seventy.[36] But eventually the Boston Museum evolved into a full-fledged theater with a repertory company that mounted productions in blocks of weeks, usually with ten to twenty consecutive performances per play, as opposed to the earlier "nightly bill changes."[37]

In order to meet the needs of its expanded drama department, in 1843, the museum engaged a full production staff, including a stage manager (who functioned much as a modern-day director), a prompter (who functioned much as a modern-day stage manager), a musical director, a stage designer, a mechanic, a costumer, and a ballet mistress. William H. (Sedley) Smith was the museum's first stage manager, as well as a member of the acting company. He retired in 1860 and was succeeded briefly by E. F. Keach, a leading actor in the company. After Keach died in 1864, Kimball appointed an outsider, a nonactor named Richard Montgomery Field, to be both the manager and the producer of the company. Field ran the theater until the stock company disbanded in 1893.[38]

Discipline was a way of life for members of the museum's company; Kimball maintained an impressive list of rules and regulations for his actors. The heavy demands of repertory theater could result in sloppy performances, and, as a warning to the actors, Kimball set up a "forfeit system."[39] Exhibited on a wall in the greenroom was a code of conduct, a list accompanied by a corresponding inventory of fines for infractions, ranging anywhere from twenty-five cents to a week's wages or to discharge from the theater, depending on the severity of the offense.[40] Failure to know one's lines, for example, missing an exit, appearing onstage in inappropriate costume, or talking too loudly backstage were all offenses punishable by fines. Often the money accumulated from these fines was pooled in a fund to aid sick or destitute actors.[41] Although Kimball was sympathetic to their financial needs, he kept his company on a tight rein. In *Melodrama Unveiled: American Theatre and Culture, 1800–1850,* David Grimsted suggests that the forfeit system was used more as a "psychological threat" than anything else.[42]

93

Kimball also supported the common practice of benefit evenings, which enabled members of the company to make extra money. Most actors were allowed one benefit evening per season, although some company members, such as William H. Smith, were allocated two.[43] For benefit performances, an actor selected the play or part (or both) that he or she wanted to perform. Since benefit night was not part of the regular season, the performer was required to help solicit an audience for the event.[44] For his or her effort the actor was rewarded with a percentage of the box office receipts. (The benefit system had distinct advantages for managers: by offering benefit evenings they could keep actors' salaries to a minimum.) While earning sixty dollars a week as the company's foremost comedian, William Warren recorded that in 1864 he earned an additional thousand dollars from his benefits.[45] It was economically critical, therefore, for a stock company actor to maintain a good reputation and build up a local following. Naturally, the selection of the play was an important element in the success of a benefit performance. Actors prudently chose plays that had proved popular with audiences and were certain to bring in the crowds. By the late 1860s, however, the benefit policy had become unpopular, probably because of the difficulties involved in soliciting an audience and because the financial rewards were so uncertain that an actor could even lose money. By 1885 only three actors in the Boston Museum company were given benefit nights.[46]

Comedies, of course, could be seen at the Boston Museum. But the plays most often performed there, as at the majority of the dime museums, were melodramas, most of which could also be seen in the legitimate theaters of the period—plays such as Dion Boucicault's *The Octoroon* (1859) and Clifton W. Tayleure's *East Lynne* (1861). Museums had a special propensity for mounting plays that dealt with gambling, drinking, and avarice. Some of those familiar to the museum theatergoer bore such titles as S. F. Hill's *Six Degrees of a Crime, or Wine, Women, Gambling, Theft, and the Scaffold* (c. 1851; the one degree not mentioned in the title was murder) and *The Crock of Gold, or Toiler's Trails* (1845), by S. S. Steele, Esq. The plays examined problems that affected all classes, offering solutions from which both rich and poor could profit.[47] These ethical dramas, whose subject matter involved improving the world, were in line with contemporary Protestant dogma, which emphasized the value of deed and viewed prohibition as the means of ensuring an exemplary society. The temperance melodrama's particular message was that anyone who worked hard and stayed sober could expect to live comfortably and even become wealthy.[48] These dramas provided their audiences with a feeling of control by endorsing the traditional values and morals that were being threatened by a new and evolving industrial order. Temperance and other so-called uplifting themes especially attracted the puritanical spectator who would not normally attend the theater but who believed that watching moral plays, in an atmosphere as "educational" as that of a dime museum, was not sacrilegious. The moral lecture rooms of dime museums differed substantially from immoral playhouses where liquor and prostitution were part of the theatergoing experience.[49]

Intemperance was viewed as a major impediment to progress and modernization. According to John Frick reformers, "produced or endorsed an astonishing variety of activities—conventions, dances, meeting, picnics, balls, boating excursions, festivals, lectures and tent shows."[50] However, the most potent weapon in the temperance arsenal, Frick pointed out, was the drama. The dime museum lecture room, with its mixed-class audience and its air of respectability, was the perfect venue to disseminate the temperance message of abstinence and hope to the masses. More than a hundred temperance dramas were written in the nineteenth century, and many of them found a home in dime museums. Temperance plays often began with a scene of domestic tranquility; characters were often depicted in comfortable, if not affluent, surroundings. Once alcohol was introduced, a chain of events was set in motion that destroyed the family unit, and women and children were depicted as the innocent victims.[51] The final scenes of these dramas frequently illustrated redemption through a return to sobriety.

A perennial favorite of many museums was the temperance play *Ten Nights in a Bar-Room* (1858), adapted from an 1858 novel by T. S. Arthur. The protagonist of the play, Joe Morgan, begins as a prosperous miller. His excessive drinking, however, causes him to lose his business, his integrity, and his daughter. His partner, Simon Slade, gains control of the mill, then sells it to buy a tavern called the Sickle and Sheaf. One evening, Morgan's young daughter, Mary, follows him to the Sickle and Sheaf and tries to persuade him to give up drinking and come home. While pleading with him, she is mortally wounded by a flying bottle intended for her father.

On her deathbed, Mary makes her father promise to stop drinking. Overcome with grief, Morgan seeks solace from a bottle of whiskey he has stashed at home and enters a state of drunken delirium. But in the midst of his madness he remembers his pledge to Mary. The final act of the play takes place ten years after Mary's death and depicts a reformed and sober Morgan. Other moral dramas, such as T. P. Taylor's play *The Bottle* (1847), told stories with more tragic endings. As a result of Richard Thornbey's drinking, his family becomes destitute and one of his children dies of starvation. In the final acts of *The Bottle*, Thornbey kills his wife and is sent to a madhouse, where he eventually dies.

The plays performed on museum stages reflected the proprietors' ideas about audiences' standards of purity and piety. Often owners subjected plays to censorship, deleting any language they believed to be potentially offensive. Expressions such as "son-of-a-gun," "devil," "sucker," and even "liar" were considered highly objectionable. Dialogue changes were made routinely: "lusty" was changed to "fat," "nigger" to "Negro," "cuckold" to "fool," and "damn" to "curse" or "smother" (or it was cut out entirely).[52]

It was not uncommon for an actor in a museum company to be given the opportunity to have his or her play produced there. A few dime museum performers, including Charles H. Saunders (*The Gambler*, 1844) and William H. Smith (*The Drunkard, or the Fallen Saved*, 1844), wrote plays that became sentimental favorites with mid-nineteenth-century audiences. *The Drunkard* opened at the Boston Museum on February 25, 1844, and by May had played a record one hundred performances.[53] During the 1830s and 1840s, by comparison, few plays had runs of more than fifty nights; in the first half of the century only a dozen plays reached the fifty-plus mark.[54]

• • •

The most popular play of the time, of course, produced all over the country and in all kinds of performance spaces, was Harriet Beecher Stowe's *Uncle Tom's Cabin; or Life among the Lowly* (1852), adapted from her famous novel of 1852. Its production history is legendary, and to this day it is still one of the most successful plays ever produced on the American stage. Because there were no copyright protection laws in 1852, however, novelists could not control rights to their work, nor could they reap any financial gain from the success of stage adaptations.[55] Playwrights and in-house dramatists of the dime museums were free to rework novels and popular plays, omitting characters, killing some off, or inventing new ones in order to meet the needs of the museum's stock company. The consequences could be appalling for an author. Thus, even though Harriet Beecher Stowe had strong antitheater sentiments, she could not prevent her novel from being turned into a play by other authors.

There were many stage adaptations of *Uncle Tom's Cabin,* but the two most popular were those of George L. Aiken and H. J. Conway. (Coincidentally, both Conway and Aiken were in-house dramatists at Barnum's American Museum, Conway in the 1850s and Aiken in the 1860s.) The Aiken version was commissioned in 1852 by George C. Howard, manager of the Troy Museum Theatre Company. After reading the novel, he asked George L. Aiken, his wife's twenty-two-year-old cousin, to write the script; he believed that the role of Eva could be portrayed beautifully by his four-year-old daughter, Cordelia. (He gave Aiken forty dollars and a gold watch for his work.)[56] The role of Topsy, however, was difficult to cast. Aiken believed that no actress would put on blackface makeup, so he took some dramatic license and changed the character to a boy. Howard objected; he wanted to be as faithful to the novel as possible. Indeed, no actress had ever blackened up on stage before, and the museum company's soubrette refused to play the part. Eventually—going against tradition—Howard cast his wife, Caroline, as Topsy.[57] The final Aiken version of the novel, in six acts, eight tableaux, and thirty scenes, opened at the Troy Museum on November 15, 1852, and ran for one hundred performances.[58] In July 1853, Aiken's *Uncle Tom's Cabin* was produced in New York City at the National Theatre on Chatham Street and played for an unprecedented 325 performances.[59] Perhaps because of the length of the play, Howard imitated the format of the Boston Museum's 1844 production of *The Drunkard,* which omitted a curtain-raiser, an afterpiece, and other acts common in the theater of the period.[60] There may also have been "moral" considerations, resulting in an attempt to make the evening as little like conventional theater as possible.

On December 8, 1852, only several weeks after the Aiken version premiered in New York, the Boston Museum presented Conway's *Uncle Tom's Cabin*. The Conway version was different from the provocative but gloomy Aiken adaptation; it was a "watered-down pro-Southern version," which Robert Toll believes was popular because it was in touch with the taste of the general public in a time when the slavery issue was threatening to destroy the Union.[61] In the Conway version, the novel's antislavery message was toned down, Little Eva recovered, and Tom was saved from death by George Shelby.[62] Conway even added a bit of humor by creating the comic character of Penetrate Partysides, to capitalize on the talents and popularity of William Warren.[63] Even though many Northern dime museum proprietors were abolitionists, it was the Conway play that they most often presented. Proprietors hoped that the less controversial Conway script would attract a wider audience than the Aiken version.

While the Aiken adaptation still played to huge crowds at the National, Barnum, in a competitive move, mounted the Conway play at the American Museum in November 1853. In advertising his production, Barnum stated that the Conway version, as opposed to Aiken's, gave the spectator a "true picture of negro life in the South," and claimed that the Conway play was "the only just and sensible dramatic version of Mrs. Stowe's book."[64] He defended the Conway version, claiming that his adaptation did not "foolishly and unjustly elevate the negro above the white man in intellect and morals."[65]

In effect, it was a challenge, a sport, a way for Barnum to outsell the other productions of *Uncle Tom's Cabin*. A first-class showman, he was motivated chiefly by the desire for notoriety and money. Supposed quotes praising the play in the newspapers were intended as advertisements and not antiabolitionist sentiments belonging to Barnum himself. (Barnum, in fact, was a strong supporter of the Union.) He was not a critic; in spite of all his boosting of the Conway play, he mounted the Aiken version in 1866, with Mrs. Howard re-creating the role of Topsy. Barnum presented the same version again in 1868, this time employing the entire Howard family because the fame of the Howards was certain to bring crowds of spectators to his museum.[66]

If an issue or idea was topical, somehow the dime museum business capitalized on it. In particular, spectators loved to see the novels they read mounted as stage plays. Familiarity did not breed contempt; on the contrary, it created excitement. It was exhilarating to see one's favorite fictional characters come to life. And for those who were illiterate, plays allowed

**98** them to enjoy meeting such well-known characters as Lady Isabel of *East Lynne* and Little Eva of *Uncle Tom's Cabin*. Nathaniel Hawthorne's famous novel *The Scarlet Letter* was adapted for the stage by Aiken (1852), and Conway wrote his own version of Tom Taylor's *Our American Cousin,* titled *Our Irish Cousins* (1857). Victor Hugo's popular novel *Les Miserables* was performed in 1871 on the stage at Wood's Museum.[67] Dramatizations of Charles Dickens's novels, including *Oliver Twist* (c. 1846), *The Old Curiosity Shop* (c. 1846), and *Nicholas Nickelby* (c. 1846), also became fashionable after the author's 1842 visit to the United States.

• • •

During the first half of the century, dime museum theatrical evenings often included a drama followed by a farce, with musical interludes between the acts.[68] A theatrical evening at the Boston Museum or the American Museum could last five hours. The longer plays, usually five-act dramas, were preceded or followed by light comedies and musical interludes, pantomimes, and farces.[69] There were also variety turns. On September 3, 1866, for example, Fanny Turner, a female drummer, performed between the acts at Barnum's museum with her son "Allie Turner, the infant drummer."[70] Sometimes human oddities were known to appear between acts as well; sharing the stage with the Turners was General Grant Jr., a midget who danced.

Some evenings, especially during the Christmas season or when the stock company was on summer break, the Boston Museum presented a program of variety artists or mounted one of its familiar spectacles, such as the pantomimes of the Martinetti company or those of the illustrious George L. Fox and his company. Many of them were based on popular fairy tales such as *The Forty Thieves, and the Fairy of the Lake* (1848), *Little Red Ridinghood, or the Wolf at the Door* (1868), or *Cinderella* (1846).[71] Pantomime was a very popular summer fill-in, but the production demands of these displays were great. They usually required enormous casts, had scores that called for large orchestras, and included numerous scenes. For example, the Boston Museum's 1850 production of *The Enchanted Beauty, or A Dream of 100 Years,* (author and date unknown) contained scenes set, variously, in a castle, a French vineyard, a forest, and a farm.[72] But the popularity and financial success of pantomimes made up for the trouble and expense.

Most museums maintained a collection of generic backdrops, ranging from exterior rustic scenes to interior domestic ones that could be adapted to the requirements of almost any script. For the most part, as in many theaters, the sets were of the traditional "drop and wing" type. The rear of the stage was marked by a painted canvas drop or by two painted flats that met at the center. Along the side of the stage was a series of canvas wings that faced the audience. Actors made their entrances and exits between these flats. (The box set, with its three walls and ceiling, was a later innovation that appeared at the Boston Museum on November 24, 1862.)[73]

With the exception of some period clothing, most of the costumes were supplied by the actors themselves. This included everything from hosiery and shoes to wigs and other accessories. An extensive professional wardrobe was therefore crucial for a stock company actor. Edward Mammen, in his article on the Boston Museum stock company, noted that stage manager Smith once wrote a letter of recommendation for one of his young actors in which he praised not only her looks and talent but also her excellent wardrobe.[74]

•   •   •

Barnum's American Museum in New York established its stock company in 1849 under the management of the English-born Francis Courtney (F. C.) Wemyss, a longtime manager of Philadelphia's Chestnut Street Theatre Company. As a temperance advocate Barnum used his museum to disseminate the antiliquor message to a mass audience; his Lecture Room presented its fair share of domestic melodramas with themes about the perils of excessive drinking (see fig. 19). He also mounted many biblical dramas, however, such as Royall Tyler's *Joseph and His Brethren* (c. 1859) and Aiken's *Moses; or, Israel in Egypt* (1866), and staged several Shakespearean plays, such as *Romeo and Juliet* (1850) and *Macbeth* (1855). In addition to plays, the American Museum presented minstrel shows and variety entertainments.

At first, the museum's Lecture Room schedule provided only for evening performances and one matinee on Saturday. This schedule gradually expanded to include a Wednesday matinee and, in the hope of attracting more women and children, daily matinees. During the holidays, the mu-

100

FIGURE 19. Lecture Room, Barnum's American Museum, 1853. (Harvard Theatre Collection, Houghton Library.)

seum presented as many as twelve shows a day.[75] George C. D. Odell notes that by 1850, "Barnum's was no longer Barnum's; it was a theatre."[76]

Lecture room entertainments were an important aspect of the museum-going experience, and Barnum's increasingly expanded theater reflected this assumption. In November 1853, a critic for the *Illustrated News* complained that he had to make four attempts to get a seat for the American Museum's production of *Uncle Tom's Cabin*. Three times he arrived at the theater fifteen minutes before showtime, only to be confronted by a sign that read, "All seats in the lecture room are engaged or occupied." On his fourth attempt the critic had to wait outside the theater for an hour to get his seat.[77]

Barnum offered no intermissions or refreshments to his Lecture Room audience, which forced spectators to remain quietly in their seats throughout the program, creating a more subdued and refined atmosphere. Generally, his dramatic bills ran for a week, and on Wednesdays and Saturdays the matinee was the same as the evening bill. On all other days a farce was played in the afternoon time slot. During the summer season Fox's troupe was frequently in residence, presenting such pantomimes as *Jack and Gill*, *The Golden Age*, *The Frisky Cobbler*, and *The Red Gnome and Four Lovers*.[78]

• • •

Variety acts, which after midcentury were no longer associated with the legitimate theater in New York, continued to share the Lecture Room stage with moral dramas at Barnum's museum. In fact, in the post–Civil War era, the theaters in the larger dime museums rejuvenated variety by presenting it in clean, safe, family environments. It was essential for the survival of dime museums to have some element of live performance, and managers recognized that an established performance space could expand a museum's reputation, clientele, and revenues. Even New York's elite Eden Musée, which did not have a true theater and shied away from dramatic productions, presented such variety entertainers as vocalists, serpentine dancers, and illusionists in its famous Winter Garden.

101

Museums differed in their emphasis on the question of dramas versus variety shows. George Wood's museum in New York, for example, concentrated on plays and initiated a two-play-a-day policy. A program from April 13, 1874, shows Mr. and Mrs. E. L. Davenport performing in *Macbeth, Oliver Twist, St. Marc,* and a benefit performance of *A New Way to Pay Old Debts.*[79] By 1876 the museum was repossessed by John Banvard, who removed all its curiosities; in 1879 it was transformed into Daly's Theatre, one of the most reputable nineteenth-century legitimate houses in the city.[80] At New York's Gaiety Museum, where the tiny theater seated only three hundred spectators, the management tended to mount variety acts rather than plays.[81] Many of the more prominent dime museums, however, fell somewhere between these two approaches. Huber's Museum, for example, often provided a balanced menu of drama and variety. As mentioned earlier, Doris's Eighth Avenue Museum had three theaters and thus managed to cater to almost everyone's tastes. In its theater 1 it offered traditional melodramas and moral plays, in its theater 2, variety, and in its third theater, Punch and Judy shows.

The Grand Museum in New York operated two theaters, presenting variety in one space and stock company melodramas in the other. Bunnell's maintained only one theater but presented two different shows every day in alternating time slots. A bill for April 21, 1882, announced that the first show would offer "Ventriloquist Clever Carroll"; "Herr Singerhoff, the Successor to Ole Bull"; "the La Porte Sisters, Queens of Song"; "John Irish, Champion of the Bell Harmonica"; and "Charles Chestra, the Indian Rubber Man." The second show featured a piano overture by Herr Wiggins; songs by the Quaker City Quartet; a demonstration of the great

London Ethoscope; Japanese Tommy impersonating Adelina Patti; and Ion Ferrya, "the Man Flute." The performance concluded with a farce, *Grim Goblins*.[82] It was common during the 1880s and 1890s to find Irish or German performers (or performers pretending to be Irish or German) acting both in dime museum lecture rooms and on the vaudeville stage.

Austin and Stone's Museum, located at 4 Tremont Street in Boston, followed a schedule similar to Bunnell's, operating two theaters and providing two separate variety programs. Theater A presented five shows daily and Theater B four. According to a November 25, 1891, bill, each program contained six spots. The variety programs offered by dime museums did not differ much from one to another. The names of the performers might change, but the six-turn to eight-turn variety structure, which sometimes included a one-act playlet, remained constant. A bill from a dime museum theater in the 1880s resembled a typical small-time vaudeville bill, although it was somewhat shorter. It included several individual acts, such as vocalists, jugglers, and comedians, followed by a one-act play.

Standing Room Only signs grew commonplace as the theaters at dime museums, became not only an accepted part of the museum experience but a highly desirable one. Odell noticed that by the 1880s, the nature of museum advertising had begun to change; managers put less emphasis on their curio hall exhibits and more on the variety artists who were performing in their "theatoriums." It was the lecture room entertainments that had the real drawing power. In fact, when lecture rooms were dark, dime museum crowds were smaller.[83]

In the late 1880s, theater people began to form comedy teams that played to family audiences in dime museums.[84] These teams would float from museum to museum, spending from one to six weeks at a given location. They would perform individual sketches that could be integrated into a bill filled with works of the museum's stock company. The program often culminated in the joint production of a one-act play performed by the guest artists and the stock company.

Some of the more popular variety comedy teams were Mack and Bryant, the Reed Family, and Harry Thompson's Comedy Company, names found over and over in dime museum theater programs.[85] Richard Hyde and Louis Behman, who briefly managed the New Park Theatre, Museum and Menagerie in 1884, created a two-act comedy called *Muldoon's Picnic* (c. 1882), which was performed by many vaudeville companies and comedy teams and can also be found on numerous dime museum programs of the

1880s and 1890s. It was a "dung-boot comedy," says Douglas Gilbert, and it achieved nationwide notoriety.[86]

The smaller museums, those located in storefronts, mostly were not equipped for actual play production; their stages were small and their seating capacity limited. Instead, they tended to produce entertainments with a lower overhead than straight plays. For the most part they confined themselves to song and dance acts, comedians, and the like. When an actual play was mounted, it was usually cut to shreds so that it could be played in less than an hour, and there was rarely, if ever, any rehearsal time.[87] One observer wrote that when he visited a small museum in New York where *Uncle Tom's Cabin* was playing, he found the stage very meager, with a post in the center (no doubt a structural column). Little Eva was played by a "three hundred pound blond woman and Eliza crossed the ice in the kitchen," the only available backdrop.[88] The bloodhounds who followed her were described as a couple of sickly-looking pug dogs.

The seedier museums tended to hire down-and-out actors, and audiences were far from reticent when it came to showing their disapproval. The behavior of a spectator in these smaller dime museums tended to be on a par with that of a boisterous concert saloon patron. These unsophisticated museum theaters, however, provided training grounds for some notable young performers, including Al Jolson, Harry Houdini, and Weber and Fields.[89]

The lecture rooms of dime museums were among the first places in which variety (an ancestor of vaudeville) appeared, perhaps as early as the 1840s. Indeed, performance spaces in cheap museums had more in common with the concert saloons and variety halls of the day, which showcased a seedy kind of sketch and novelty entertainment. The lecture room entertainments of places like Huber's and Doris's Museums and the Boston Museum, on the other hand, were highly respectable. The variety performances of the larger dime museum theaters were family-oriented, devoid of "bad" language, and far from vulgar; they did not need cleaning up. Much of the entertainment presented in the lecture rooms of the better dime museums was "clean variety" as distinguished from the honky-tonk kind.

B. F. Keith, later a "clean" vaudeville mogul, had begun his career as a museum man. He worked at Bunnell's museum for a year, toured with Barnum's circus, and in January 1883 opened his own dime museum at 565–567 Washington Street in Boston. The museum had one exhibition,

FIGURE 20. Austin and Stone's Museum, c. 1891. (Billy Rose Theatre Collection, New York Public Library for the Performing Arts, Astor, Lenox and Tilden Foundations.)

"Baby Alice, the Midget Wonder."[90] For ten cents, a spectator could see this little girl (a premature infant) displayed on a stage six feet square in a fifteen-by-thirty-foot room. After a few weeks, he took on a partner, William Austin, and they renamed their establishment the New York Dime Museum. By February they had added several exotic displays, including "Dora, the Beautiful Tattooed Lady," "Warbler, the Mysterious Lady Warbler," and "Dahema, the Giant."[91] Shortly thereafter, however, Austin broke off his partnership with Keith and opened a competing museum with Frank Stone. Austin and Stone's museum was located at 4 Tremont Street; in September 1883 the duo claimed to be the owners of the largest museum in America (see fig. 20). Eight years later, in 1891, according to a boast on the museum's letterhead, nine million patrons had visited the establishment.[92]

Keith was not discouraged by Austin's defection, however, and by March 1883 he had found a new partner named Gardiner. During their brief union, the two managers expanded their museum to include a "theater room" on the second floor that could accommodate 123 seated spectators and 30 to 40 standees.[93] In 1884 Keith next paired up with George H. Batchelder, a circus man from Providence, Rhode Island. In the summer of 1885, with Batchelder's resources, they enlarged the theater again, raising the seating capacity to five hundred.[94] The museum was renamed Keith and Batchelder's Mammoth Museum, and was open from 10 A.M. to 10 P.M. Slowly, Keith began to switch the emphasis of the museum, and by the spring of 1885 the establishment was given a new name, the Gaiety Hall and Museum, which reflected the change.[95] The museum employed a conventional stock company of performers who rotated shows every two hours, but it was difficult to compete with Austin and Stone's two theaters and their in-house variety companies.

105

In addition, in an article published in 1898, Keith wrote that the old adage "Necessity is the mother of invention" never had a clearer application than in the "continuous performance idea of entertainment."[96] Keith developed the continuous variety or "vaudeville" bill to combat one of the dime museums' major difficulties with its lecture room productions— crowd control.[97] The hourly show structure created traffic control problems, since many patrons organized their museum visits around the lecture room schedule. The critic who attempted three times to see *Uncle Tom's Cabin* at Barnum's museum before getting a ticket, for example, finally saw the play only because he arrived an hour early and waited in the hall. Responding to such "problems within the economic and presentational structure of dime museum" lecture rooms, Keith eliminated the "waiting-in-the-hall" syndrome.[98] On July 6, 1885, with a twenty-seven-turn program, he introduced his continuous variety program to a Boston dime museum. Whether or not Keith was the first to implement this format at a dime museum, he did popularize it. After the Civil War, however, museum lecture rooms already had begun to operate on an all-day performance schedule. Bunnell's theater, for example, staged from six to eight shows daily and began a trend toward increasing the number of daily performances. In 1889, according to Odell's records, Worth was already regularly mounting continuous variety. But it would not be enough in the twentieth century.

# 6. Waxworks and Film

My childish fancy confused the living men and women swarming
along the street with the lifelike wax-figures in the showcases.
—William Henry Venable

Between 1840 and 1900 a mass market in imagery developed in the United
States. Owning paintings and etchings during the eighteenth century had
been a sign of status and affluence. By the mid-nineteenth century, however, because of advances in printing techniques, color lithographs decorated the walls of even the most humble parlors. The Western world was
becoming a densely visual environment, and the ubiquity of images contributed greatly to the dissemination of knowledge and the average person's perception of the world. Newspapers not only documented but illustrated current events, billboards provided alluring images of goods for sale,
and the art of photography was flourishing.[1] The quest for greater realism
permeated all aspects of late nineteenth-century culture. The aesthetics of
stage design changed rapidly, from flat, painted scenery to three-dimensional, solid realism. Imaginative technicians such as Steele MacKaye and
David Belasco brought the latest mechanical devices into the theater, including elevator stages, natural-looking overhead lighting, electrical lighting boards, and authentic props.[2] Dime museums provided provocative
images of the wonders of the universe, the human body, and faraway places,
as well as fragments of history and current events. The dime museum was
also one of the first institutions to show films, the quintessential optical
spectacle of the late nineteenth century.

"Images are more precise and richer" than the written word, John Berger
has written in *Ways of Seeing*.[3] Images, however, are not as exact as words
and often are deceiving. They perpetually challenge the viewer's sense of
authenticity: It looks real, but is it real? Can a work be genuine if it is a
reproduction? The wonderful profusion of images may have visually stimu-

lated Victorian Americans, but it also propelled them into a world of deceptions, hoaxes, and humbugging. Phineas T. Barnum thrived in this environment, as did the dime museum.

One of the most popular exhibits at any dime museum was the display of life-sized waxworks. The operational aesthetic of waxworks exhibits was "admiring the perfection of the fake."[4] Wax tableaux re-created and reinterpreted figures and moments in time for a specific audience that was amazed by the remarkable realism of the lifelike mannequins. The delight for the viewer was in being deceived. Standing before the "Assassination of Julius Caesar" tableau at New York City's Eden Musée, for example, spectators did not critique the fictionalized Roman Forum setting or question the theatrical logic of placing Caesar on a stretcher half covered with a sheet conveniently draped to expose his stab wounds (see fig. 21). And who was the unidentified man kneeling and weeping by Caesar's side, and who were the two women stretching out their arms toward him in grief? They were not mentioned in the description of the scene provided by the guidebook.[5] Eden Musée patrons were satisfied simply to know that all the essential figures—Cassius, Brutus, Marc Antony, and Caesar—were present and accounted for. The authenticity of a historical reproduction was not questioned as long as certain familiar elements and characters were included. This was an important part of the delight: the pleasure of seeing a three-dimensional re-creation of a famous moment was so rewarding and reassuring that it allowed the spectator not to be critical about the exhibit.

The Forum background in the Eden Musée's "Assassination of Julius Caesar" was created from the designer's own imagination. Wax artists often imitated well-known paintings, however, thus complicating the level of deception; interpretation begat interpretation, which was seen by the public as reality. Of the countless portraits painted of George Washington, which one was selected by artists as their model? Was "Washington" created to show how the man really looked, with the smallpox scars on his face and the mole under his ear, or was the goal to create a flawless paragon to represent the general who had liberated the United States?[6] Most exhibits simply re-created the famous painting by Emanuel Leutze of Washington crossing the Delaware. Artists in wax were no different from Barnum in attempting to give the public what it wanted, which was a pasteurized interpretation of the past. By standardizing or stereotyping historical moments and individuals, museum artists presented a diverse audience with a common vision of the past. Such shared images were both comforting and inspirational.

1. Cassius. 2. Brutus.     3. Marc Antony.    4. Julius Cæsar.

FIGURE 21. "The Assassination of Julius Caesar," Eden Musée catalog, 1905. (New-York Historical Society.)

The dime museum was a natural venue for itinerant waxworks. By the late eighteenth century waxworks had become a fashionable entertainment. Wax re-creations furthered the Enlightenment's cause of the dissemination of knowledge; historical tableaux were viewed as educational. Waxworks had first become popular in Europe, and foreign collections toured the East Coast of the United States as early as 1749. In August of that year the *New York Gazette* announced the arrival of a wax exhibition from Britain featuring images of the royal family of England, the Empress Queen of Hungary and Bohemia, and fourteen other famous figures. Daniel Bowen, one of the first Americans to manage a waxworks display, exhibited his figures from 1790 to 1810 at the Columbian Museum and American Coffee House in Boston, the American Museum of Wax Works in Philadelphia, and in New York at 74 Water Street, 75 Broad Street, and Edward Savage's Greenwich Street museum. His displays included George Washington "sitting under a canopy in his military dress," as well as the king and queen of England with the Prince of Wales.[7] In 1793 Gardiner Baker avidly advertised his waxworks collection.[8] As itinerant amusements, waxworks were booked into town halls and lecture rooms. Generally, showmen rented a space for only a day or so before moving on. "The Travelling Museum," an early nineteenth-century attraction, consisted of two horse-drawn caravans that could be joined to form one large exhibition room displaying twenty-seven wax figures. The mannequins included George Washington, General Lafayette, the revolutionary Jean Paul Marat, the Marquis de Sade, and Napoleon. Also in the exhibit was Hortensia Howard, a woman who had killed sixteen of her seventeen husbands by pouring melted lead in their ears as they slept.[9]

Creating quality wax displays was very expensive. The effigies themselves could cost as much as $250 each, a large sum at the time, and for elaborate costumes a museum might pay thousands.[10] Just as some dime museums devoted more time to theatrical productions than did others, museums varied in the quality and complexity of their waxworks departments. The larger dime museums had their own artistic staffs, whose members created a wide range of wax tableaux.[11] Smaller institutions either bought aging displays from larger ones or hired itinerant showmen to exhibit their waxworks.

For centuries craftsmen had been creating lifelike effigies in wax; however, these images were not often used for entertainment. The ancient Romans paraded wax figures at the funerals of influential men to represent the ancestors of the deceased, and afterward these effigies remained in the deceased's house.[12] Early Christians used wax for creating images of the saints and Jesus Christ. Until the middle of the eighteenth century it was a common custom in England to exhibit wax figures of departed noblemen and royalty at their funerals.[13] Seventeenth- and eighteenth-century death masks and wax bust-medallions immortalized heroes, martyrs, wealthy politicians, and aristocrats. Wax sculptures were used in medical schools to teach students anatomy. Abraham Chovet, a noted physician, frequently lectured from wax models; in 1774 he established an anatomical museum in Pennsylvania that displayed naked male and female effigies whose "external parts were removable" for better scrutiny.[14]

•   •   •

One of the greatest creators of life-sized figures in this era was a French citizen, Madame Tussaud. Born Anne Marie Grosholtz, she began training in the art of wax modeling at the age of six with a German sculptor, Dr. Philippe Curtius. Marie's mother worked as a housekeeper for Curtius, whom young Marie called "Uncle."[15] When Curtius moved to Paris in 1767, he took Marie and her mother with him. There he established a reputable waxworks museum known as the Salon de Cire located at 20 Boulevard du Temple. For many years Marie lived at Versailles, working as art tutor to Madame Elizabeth, the sister of Louis XVI. In 1789, several month before the storming of the Bastille on July 14, Marie left Versailles and returned to Paris. During the French Revolution, Marie was commanded by the revolutionary authorities to make death masks from the decapitated heads of the victims of the guillotine.[16] When Curtius died in 1794, he willed all his property, including the Salon de Cire, to Marie. A year later, in 1795, Marie married a civil engineer named Francois Tussaud. Postrevolutionary France did not have a stable economy, and, fearing for the future of her wax business, Madame Tussaud left Paris in October 1802 with her eldest son, Joseph, and settled in England. (She never returned to France or reunited with her husband.)

Before leaving for England, Madame Tussaud had entered into a partnership agreement with a phantasmagoria, a type of magic lantern performance, operated by Paul de Philipsthal. Philipsthal, who performed at the Lyceum in London, believed that his partner's wax displays would help attract patrons to the Lyceum. The partnership soon soured, however, chiefly because Madame Tussaud's wax museum was more successful than the magic lantern shows. After leaving the Lyceum, Madame Tussaud spent many years as an itinerant entrepreneur. In 1835, at the age of seventy-four, she settled permanently in London and opened a wax museum on Baker Street. When Barnum toured England with Charles Stratton in 1844, he was so impressed by her collection that he tried to buy it for his museum.[17]

Madame Tussaud died in 1850, leaving her collection to her two sons, Joseph and Francis. In 1884, her three grandsons, Joseph Randall, Francis Curtius, and Victor, moved four hundred wax statues and accessories to a new home in London's Marylebone Road. To this day it is Britain's most visited tourist attraction.[18]

•   •   •

Perhaps the most sophisticated and dramatic nineteenth-century wax presentation in America was created and produced by Joseph Dorfeuille and his twenty-four-year-old artistic protégé, Hiram Powers. In 1829 Dorfeuille hired Powers to repair wax figures damaged in shipment to the Western Museum of Cincinnati from New Orleans, where they had been manufactured. Powers, however, had a gift for working in wax and soon began to create original figures for Dorfeuille's museum.

The two men's greatest achievement was their theatrical depiction of Hell, known as "The Infernal Regions." Modeled after Dante's *Divine*

*Comedy* and Milton's *Paradise Lost,* "The Infernal Regions" presented a fascinating and frightening multimedia spectacle. (Actually, there were two hellish environments, one cold and one hot. In the cold Hell, men were shown freezing to death.)[19] At the entrance to the exhibit, patrons read the Dantesque sign, "Whoever Enters Here Leaves Hope Behind"; Minos, Lucifer, and Beelzebub greeted them at the door.[20] The figures were mechanical wax effigies that literally jumped out at passersby while emitting horrific cries. Visitors to "The Infernal Regions" were so intrigued by the realism of the figures that they were constantly touching them for confirmation that they were indeed wax. To minimize damage to his sculptures, Dorfeuille had to put up an iron grating charged with a mild electrical current.

111

In the center of "The Infernal Regions" sat the "King of Terrors" (see fig. 22). Costumed in red tights, with red horns and a forked tail, the king welcomed visitors with a wave of his pitchfork while ominous smoke swirled about him. Powers himself played the role of the devil, but he soon tired of the task and constructed an automated devil to take his place. Adept at theatrical engineering, he also devised sound effects of shrieks, groans, thunder, and the hissing of serpents. But no sooner had Powers abandoned one role than he created another, a more active character known as the "Evil One." Powers would roam about the chamber in costume, casually frightening unsuspecting patrons. Now the screams of real people intermingled with the exhibit's prepared sound effects, and the crowd became a vital part of the experience. At the end of the exhibition hall, ushering the shocked and shaken patrons out, stood a skeleton holding a sign that read,

> To this grim form, our cherished limbs have come,
> And thus lie mouldering in their earthly home;
> In turf bound hillock, or in sculptured shrine,
> The worms alike, their cold caresses twine;
> So far we all are equal, but once left,
> Our mortal weeds, of vital spark bereft,
> Asunder, farther than the poles were driven;
> Some sunk in deepest Hell, some raised to highest Heaven.[21]

Powers left the Western Museum of Cincinnati in 1834 after five years.[22] He went on to become a sculptor, first in Washington, D.C., and then in Florence. Rumors later circulated that there had been a rift between Powers

FIGURE 22. A wood engraving illustrating "The King of Terrors," c. 1830. (Cincinnati Historical Society.)

and Dorfeuille. In an interview, in fact, Powers admitted that he had left out of frustration, because Dorfeuille had broken his promise of a partnership. In addition, Powers claimed that Dorfeuille had shortchanged him on his salary.[23] After Powers left "The Infernal Regions" deteriorated; his successor, Linden Ryder, did not possess the skills needed to maintain such an elaborate presentation. Dorfeuille took the remains of the exhibition with him to New York, but his venture did not meet with much success. Ironically, all the infernal figures were destroyed in a fire.

"The Infernal Regions" had been an unprecedented nineteenth-century display of showmanship, its success completely dependent on Powers's mechanical skills and theatrical vision. The exhibition combined elements of stage design, lighting, sound, costuming, acting, and technology to create an utterly convincing and frightening atmosphere: Disney-like audio-animatronics in the technologically unsophisticated early nineteenth century. Automata themselves were not unprecedented; they had been quite popular in the eighteenth century, when mechanical toys and clocks with moving figures had amused millions. There were, for example, automaton chess players before the famous Ajeeb of the 1880s; among the most celebrated was Maelzel's Turk.[24] Automata were often used in magic shows, and Jean Eugène Robert-Houdin, the famous nineteenth-century magician, was well known for his animated figures. In 1844, in fact, he so impressed Barnum with his "smaller than life-size automated man" that could write with pencil and paper that Barnum bought the automaton and put it on display in London.[25]

The mechanics of automation, however, was rarely applied to such large figures as wax effigies. Mood at these exhibits was generally created by background paintings, costumes, and sometimes sound; rarely was an entire environment created. Even standard chambers of horrors, for example, were gruesome in terms of their subject matter, the nature of the items exhibited, and the depiction of human torture, but spectators never became real participants in the drama.

• • •

The popularity of chambers of horrors depended heavily on the attraction felt by nineteenth-century pleasure seekers to the genre of horror, which also produced such novels as Mary Shelley's *Frankenstein* (1818), Robert Louis Stevenson's *Strange Case of Dr. Jekyll and Mr. Hyde* (1887), and Bram Stoker's *Dracula* (1897). The typical dime museum chamber of horrors featured tools of torture and execution, as well as wax figures of such murderers, evildoers, and outlaws as Jesse James. The actor Otis Skinner remembered visiting the Boston Museum's chamber of horrors as a youth. The "dominant feature of these silent and awful dramas was blood—and lots of it," he wrote.[26] In his autobiography, Skinner also described two other powerful dime museum memories, "Three Scenes in a Drunkard's Life" and "The Pirates' Cabin." The first set of tableaux depicted the destruction of a family by alcohol. In the initial scene Skinner saw a comfortable family—mother, father, sister, and brother—merrily drinking champagne. The room was decorated with pretty wallpaper, and a cheerful cloth covered the dinner table. The second scene showed the family dressed in rags, drinking rum in their now-dilapidated home. The third, tragic tableau showed the final stage of the family's dissolution. The daughter wore cheap, tawdry clothes, suggesting that she was now a prostitute. The father, in a drunken rage, had killed his wife, who now lay dead on the floor, blood oozing from her forehead.[27] In "The Pirates' Cabin," Skinner recalled a "scene of carnage," with pirates "gloating" over bloody corpses.[28]

Why were these exhibits so popular? This is what Noël Carroll has called the paradox of the horror genre: the attraction of the repulsive?[29] Our exhilaration comes from our knowledge that the threat of the horror is not real. We can be thrilled by a fearsome spectacle or experience, knowing we will in no way be harmed. This is the principle of roller coasters and other rides designed to seem dangerous. Simply buying a ticket to such a ride attests to its safety and qualifies the experience, allowing fear or the illusion of fear to be pleasurable. Unexpected horror, random horror, horror not purchased, is never a pleasurable experience; almost by definition it causes actual terror. Purchased horror, commodified horror, fictional horror, is a compelling experience; it promotes both excitement and wonder. This is what the waxworks in a chamber of horrors offered.

Blood was hardly ever found in historical displays of war, but it was everywhere in a chamber of horrors, because the chamber was a place of dark fantasy and controlled unworldliness. As a result, the spectator could securely come face to face with images such as torture, execution, and blood that in the real world would cause great distress. Foreign barbarism was illustrated by tableaux depicting such spectacles as "The Hindoo Woman's Sacrifice" or methods of torture used by the Spanish during the Inquisition.[30] Effigies of local criminals often were displayed; in many ways dime museum waxworks served the same function as today's television docudramas: they immortalized the latest crime stories.[31]

A subgenre of fantasy is the happily-ever-after story. Fairy tales, which fall into the latter category, often were illustrated at dime museums; the Western Museum of Cincinnati, for example, had a tableau of Sleeping Beauty being awakened from her spell by true love's first kiss, as did Philadelphia's Ninth and Arch Museum.[32] With these three-dimensional fantasy visions, the dime museum truly entered the realm of hyperreality, in that fantasy was translated into reality. Thus, any authenticity offered by wax displays was by definition an illusion, a humbug.

At the dime museum waxworks, an intertextual interplay took place between the viewer and the wax tableaux. A spectator usually knew the rudiments of the event depicted before him, be it an electrocution or a scene from history. Knowing the story line, the spectator focused not on the narrative but on the details of the exhibit. For example, at the numerous displays of the surrender of General Lee's army at Appomattox Court House, viewers seemingly were not primarily concerned with who was in the room and what document they were signing; they focused perhaps on the wall of the room and its pictures, what each figure was wearing, whether the mannequins were wearing gloves, whether their hands looked real, whether there were fingernails on their fingers. What color was General Grant's hair? The spectators knew they were witnessing a re-creation, something fake; therefore, they concentrated on the mimicry of truth, on the seemingly realistic aspects of the scene—the costuming, makeup, lighting, and props. The operational aesthetic was the admiration of the perfection of the fake.

New York's Eden Musée maintained an impressive wax collection, one of the most thrilling in the United States during the nineteenth century. Its frightening Chamber of Horrors and its historical and contemporary tableaux were imitated by many museums. They were so popular that the museum "became one of the goals of the rustic visitor to the city."[33] The museum earned the reputation of having lifelike, artistic wax figures, its tableaux usually took as long as two weeks to complete. When the need arose, however, the staff could work miracles in twenty-four hours, as in the case of the death of a queen or a president.[34]

The museum's chief wax artist was Constant Thys. Thys did not cast the head of a figure, but he was responsible for all the detailing and essentially brought life to the effigy. The heads of these wax figures were created first by a sculptor. Then sketches and clay models were made, followed by a plaster cast, which was divided into seven sections. The sections were put together and filled with melted beeswax. It took only twenty minutes for most of the wax to harden, and the mold was turned upside down to allow the remaining wax to run out. The sculptor then was left with a mold not more than half an inch thick. A hot iron was used to make holes for the eyes. Once fake eyes were in place, hot wax was poured around the edges

115

to hold them in place. Holes also were drilled at the mouth for false teeth. Initially the mold was rough, and the artist used a spatula to smooth the surface.

**116**   Then came the detailing. Real hair, costing sixty cents an ounce, was sewn onto the head with a needle; it could take three days to complete a figure with long hair. Lashes, brows, and facial hair also were hand-sewn. For a male figure without a beard, facial hair still was meticulously applied to the cheeks and chin and then shaved to create a more natural look. The body was made out of wax and papier-mâché and then attached to the head. Coloring, painting wrinkles, and adding moles were done next. Then the figures were meticulously costumed. An iron rod ran through the sculptures from head to toe to keep them in place.[35] Each figure was inspected daily and repainted twice a year when the museum's staff also changed their seasonal garments. Two thousand individuals were immortalized in wax during the museum's first twenty-five years. "Queen Isabella Receiving Christopher Columbus," consisting of thirty figures, was said to have been the largest tableau in the world. The waxwork staff at New York's Eden Musée was also responsible for manufacturing the figures mounted at the Eden Musée in Chicago. In addition, the museum provided opportunities for the public to make its own wax moldings. Betrothed couples, for example, could go to the museum and have a mold made of their clasped hands.[36] After twenty-eight years at New York's Eden Musée, Thys died of a heart attack while working on the museum's Christmas display.[37] He was succeeded by two skilled craftsmen, Edward Hause and Frank Donnelly.

Not all dime museums had such elaborate wax displays, but as a general rule, any museum that called itself a "musée" regularly exhibited detailed waxworks. History, horror, famous artists and musicians, and fairy tales were not the only subjects of these wax displays. Museums mounted religious tableaux such as the Sacred Chamber of the Eden Musée and the Egyptian Musée of Philadelphia. The Eden Musée's display, as noted in chapter 3, had six tableaux, whereas the one in the Egyptian Musée had eight: "The Stable"; "The Savior Talking to the Learned Doctors"; "At the House of Martha and Mary"; "The Last Supper"; "The Savior Brought from Prison"; "The Crucifixion"; "Nicodemus and Joseph Bearing the Body of the Savior to the Sepulchre"; and "In the Tomb of the Savior after the Resurrection."[38] These exhibits helped many museums aspire to a high moral and didactic tone, although the stories they re-created were already so familiar to the average spectator that they were not exceptionally informative. To the non-English-speaking immigrant and the small child, however, wax re-creations were of some educational value. The wax museum business, in fact, still thrives in some tourist communities, although the film and television industries are now the leading producers of horror, fantasy, and religious drama.

117

•  •  •

The development of the cinema, wrote Stuart Ewen and Elizabeth Ewen "was one of the most powerful components of the new urban culture."[39] The movies provided cheap, accessible, and ever changing entertainment that entire families could enjoy. The emergence of the cinema as a new form of popular entertainment was greeted with amazement, and as early as 1897, short films could be seen on the daily programs of many large dime museums such as the Eden Musée in New York, Huber's Museum, Brandenburgh's Ninth and Arch Museum, and Austin and Stone's Museum. The flexibility and alterability of early projected motion pictures made them a perfect entertainment for the variety programs often offered in museum lecture rooms. From 1897 to 1899, in fact, the principal venue for most daily screenings was the dime museum. The popularity of cinema grew with such intensity that by 1899 vaudeville houses were also offering a daily menu of short films. By 1906, however, projected motion pictures no longer needed to be appended on other forms of popular entertainment; they had proved popular enough to merit their own performance space, the nickelodeon.

Waxworks displayed illusions of a static reality; the cinema presented filmic renderings of reality itself. There was a "close affinity between waxworks and motion pictures, both of which strove towards a realistic representation of nature and life," but a wax tableau of Admiral Dewey and his fleet could not compare in its realism to the film footage of the 1898 war with Spain.[40] Indeed, Charles Musser, the major scholar on cinema before the nickelodeon era, sees early motion pictures as emerging from other forms of optical wonders based on the phenomenon of "the persistence of vision," among them the zoetrope (William George Horner, 1833), the kinematascope (Cleman Seller, 1861), the kinetoscope (Edison, 1893), and especially the projected image spectacle of the magic lantern show (Christiaen Huygens, 1655).[41]

Beyond that, early films transported the spectator in ways that cosmoramas, panoramas, and the live stage could not: "the stage might represent reality but the motion picture could photograph it."[42] The first images produced by cinematography were easily comprehensible; familiar places, activities, and scenes from everyday life, such as a train pulling into a station or a house on fire, were among the first impressions captured on film. *Shooting the Chutes at Atlantic City, The Philadelphia City Hall,* and *The Delaware River,* for example, are the titles of a few of the films shown at the Ninth and Arch Museum in Philadelphia during the early 1890s.[43]

•   •   •

Visual spectacles had long been a staple of dime museums. Their cosmoramas offered glimpses of faraway places and historic monuments, and their shaddowgraphs particularly delighted children. Thus the magic lantern show was quickly absorbed by the dime museum business. According to X. Theodore Barber, who has chronicled the history of magic lantern exhibitions, Gardiner Baker's American Museum in New York presented magic lantern shows as early as 1776.[44] But the heyday of the magic lantern in the United States was the nineteenth century. Boston's Columbia Museum hired a lanternist in December 1806.[45] Edward Savage provided his New York audience with magic lantern shows during the 1807 season, and Charles Willson Peale's Philadelphia museum also engaged lanternists, heralding their slide shows as both scientific and educational.[46] By 1820, Rubens Peale, then manager of Peale's Philadelphia museum, presented lantern shows as often as four times a week. As proprietor of Peale's New York Museum, he devoted one evening a week to astronomical slide presentations.[47] According to Barber, Rubens Peale was a "lantern enthusiast" who eventually painted some of his own slides.

A typical magic lantern program featured a lecturer, often called "Professor" or "Doctor," who would project images from painted glass slides onto a wall or screen and provide descriptions of the pictures. (Early lantern slides were hand-painted, but by the late nineteenth century they were increasingly photographic.) The magic lantern itself was a box, with a vent on top, that housed an artificial illuminant. Inside the box was a concave mirror, placed behind the illuminant, and a lens, called a condenser, in front of the illuminant. The painted glass slide was inserted upside down in a carrier behind the lens tube. Magic lantern performances ranged in subject matter from science and travel to the demonic. Essentially, most lantern shows were collections of projected images that could be thematic, narrative, or merely a hodge-podge of unrelated scenes.

Because a lantern show could tell a story through a series of related pictures, contemporary literature often was illustrated on glass slides; *Uncle*

*Tom's Cabin,* for example, was illustrated in this way as early as 1856.[48] As literacy grew in the United States, people became eager to see their favorite narratives in visual interpretations. Poems, biblical stories, plays, and fairy tales were all hugely popular as subjects for lantern shows, the latter especially with children. The stories often showed the influence of the fast-growing temperance movement, which permeated all facets of popular entertainment, from melodramas to waxworks. Glass slide sets bore such titles as "The Drunkard's Progress: From the First Glass to the Grave," "The Drunkard's Reform," "The Evils of Drink," and "The Drunkard's Daughter." Popular stories and plays such as *The Bottle* and *Ten Nights in a Bar-Room* were made into lantern shows in 1847 and 1880, respectively.[49]

119

From 1803 to 1839, one of the most prevalent types of lantern show was the so-called phantasmagoria, or ghost show. So successful were these macabre presentations that their format eventually was codified: the show began with a tempest, complete with thunder and lightning; various phantoms would then appear from different directions. Slides were projected from behind a translucent screen, and several lanterns were used simultaneously to produce a composite image, a presentation requiring the use of several technically proficient lanternists. Often there would be an appearance by a celebrity ghost—George Washington, Thomas Jefferson, John Adams, or Mary Stuart. Characters from Shakespeare were popular, among them Macbeth and the Witches, Hamlet and the Ghost.[50]

A Belgian showman, Étienne-Gaspard Robertson, who is credited with making the phantasmagoria show into a multimedia event, devised a "fantascope" to create more vivid illusions. The fantascope used oil rather than a candle, which increased the brightness of the images, and it was mounted on a table with casters, which allowed lanternists greater flexibility in the manipulation of the pictures. The projected image of a phantom, for instance, would appear small from a distance but, as it approached the audience, would gradually increase to monstrous size before disappearing. Barber has observed that phantasmagoria were very well received at the American Museum in New York in the early 1800s while it was under the direction of Edward Savage.[51] Savage provided musical accompaniment and supposedly heightened the effect of the traditional thunderstorm by adding a streak of lightning.

The variety-format magic lantern show probably was the most prevalent type of lantern entertainment in the dime museums of the post-Barnum era. In the variety show, the lanternist generally projected indiscriminate images, with no clear through-line or theme. It was prudent for museums to begin their shows with scientific material because it reinforced the quasi-scientific tone of the enterprise. But scientific slides, for example, might be followed by illustrations from literature, painting, or architecture.

• • •

The mutascope, a precursor of the motion picture projection, was also frequently found in dime museums. The mutascope, invented in 1894 by Herman Castle, was a peephole device based on the same premise of the flick book or thumb book. A series of photographs were mounted on a reel and manually cranked by the viewer to give the illusion of motion.[52] While cosmorama stereoscopes and other so-called viewing devices were free, the mutascope cost a penny or a nickel to operate. It was the invention of the "vitascope," however, that "effectively launched projected motion pictures as a screen novelty in the United States."[53] A brand-new industry was established, and film manufacturing companies developed overnight: the American Mutascope Company, which later merged with the Biograph Company; the Vitagraph Company; the Edison Manufacturing Company; and the International Film Company, to name only a few. As with most new businesses, patent and licensing disputes were rife, as were fights over manufacturing, production, and distribution contracts. The history of the early cinema is filled with anecdotes of these battles and lawsuits.[54]

Americans first witnessed the commercial debut of a vitascope show on April 23, 1896, at Koster and Bial's Music Hall, a famous vaudeville house on Herald Square in New York.[55] By May of the following year there were several hundred vitascope machines throughout the country. The vitascope was invented by Francis Jenkins and Thomas Armat. They hired the team of Norman Roff and Frank C. Gammon as their American marketing agents, and the Edison Manufacturing Company was contracted to make the vitascopes and shoot the films for their projection. It was mutually decided, however, that Jenkins and Armat's vitascope should be marketed as the "Edison Vitascope" for greater acceptance and profitability. "The only thing Edison had contributed to the development of the Vitascope was the imprimatur of his name . . . a ruse which, no doubt, was largely responsible for the generous publicity."[56] The Edison Vitascope had heavy competition from European manufacturers; in fact, the Lumière Company's cinématographe dominated the American market until the spring of 1897, when the brothers Auguste and Louis Lumière were forced to leave the American market, most probably because of patent litigation with Edison.[57]

The Eden Musée in New York became one of the first entertainment institutions to make a major commitment to the exhibition of film. And commitment it was, for films were not rented but purchased; to maintain an exhibition schedule, houses had to acquire new footage at a fast pace. In addition, equipment had to be bought and technicians hired. The president of the Eden Musée, Richard Hollaman, selected the Lumière cinémato-graphe as the museum's motion picture projector. On December 18, 1897, the Eden Musée began to show films in its Winter Garden.[58]

Hollaman hired William Paley to make films exclusively for the museum because he recognized the necessity of perpetually updating and changing the daily film selection. This was a very shrewd decision, for the Eden Musée, as a film producer, could now control changes in its film exhibitions (important for an institution whose major drawing power was the variety of its programs) as well as changes in subject matter. The museum soon amassed a good library of film footage, copies of which it was able to sell to other exhibitors at a handsome profit. Musser has pointed out that from 1897 to 1899, "the Eden Musée was the only amusement center in New York to commit itself to motion pictures on a full-time basis. . . . This gave the Eden Musée a unique role in New York City and, because New York was the center of motion picture activity, in the United States as a whole."[59]

Films were not at first shown as they are today; footage was bought scene by scene and strung together on the same basis by the projection-ist. Exhibitors who could not afford a complete series of scenes could purchase a portion of the series at a time, and their projectionists func-tioned like modern-day film editors, rearranging the sequences of images and controlling the length, order, and narrative flow of each presentation.[60] As a result, exhibitors and their projectionists had a high degree of artistic control. In 1898, Hollaman hired Edwin Porter to work as his projectionist and to build projection machines and cameras exclusively for the mu-seum.[61]

As a direct result of the Eden Musée's exhibition of the popular *Passion Play of Oberammergau* in 1897, Edison brought patent suit against the museum. The suit was quietly settled in two days, and, as of February 1899, the musée became an Edison licensee. Paley went to work for the Edison Manufacturing Company and was immediately sent to Cuba to film the war that had begun in February 1898 when the U.S.S. *Maine* blew up in Havana harbor. By August the musée was screening a new war scene every day, and by the end of the month the museum's film library contained nearly two hundred such war scenes.[62] Daringly, the museum's cinema department attempted to create a film showing the entire Spanish-American War. Titled *Panorama of the War*, the film opened with a shot of the arrival of soldiers in Tampa, Florida, and included the Battle of San Juan Hill and the surrender of General Toral. Musser writes that "the use of editorial procedures was arguably most advanced at the Eden Musée," and that the museum's film of the war, employing twenty scenes, was an overwhelming success.[63] Paley was paid fifteen cents for every fifty feet of negative the museum bought, and made a thirty-cent royalty on every fifty feet the Edison Company sold. Eventually both Porter and Paley left the Eden Musée and went on to independent careers in the burgeoning film industry.[64]

The history of the early cinema is filled with stories of fierce competition. One of those battles concerned Edison and Siegmund Lubin. By 1896, Lubin, a German immigrant who had come to this country in 1876, built his first movie projector and produced his first film, *Horse Eating Hay*, in the backyard of his home at 1608 North Fifteenth Street in Philadelphia.[65] When his wife grew tired of the commotion associated with Lubin's filmmaking, he created a rooftop studio for himself at 912 Arch Street. He established a permanent working relationship with C. A. Brandenburgh's Ninth and Arch Museum; Musser believes that Lubin's rooftop studio was actually on top of the museum, although there is little absolute proof that the studio was not across the street.[66]

In the latter part of 1899 motion pictures became a permanent part of vaudeville programming.[67] By 1905, however, film had outgrown its home in vaudeville, and nickelodeons rapidly appeared in urban entertainment districts. This may not have immediately affected the crowds in the vaudeville houses, but it did have a direct impact on the crowds at the Eden Musée. In fact, the blossoming film industry was one of the reasons for the demise of the dime museum. Even though some of the more prosperous museums had managed to include film in their repertoire of entertainments, it was a short-lived venture. The new century, with its new technology and increased sophistication, witnessed the creation of new types of entertainment for a more liberated and heterogeneous society.

The advent of electricity had important consequences for the entertainment industry. The once darkened city streets were no longer ominous, and going out at night was swiftly incorporated into the average person's lifestyle. Electric streetcars, trolley lines, and the automobile also made nighttime excursions easier, and cities became twenty-four-hour playgrounds. Now, along with the legitimate theater and dime museums, there were vaudeville and burlesques houses and nickelodeons. In the summer, most cities now offered pleasure seekers amusement parks, presenting a variety of diversions for an admission of only twenty-five cents. As a result, the old dime museum was doomed to extinction.

# 7. The Dime Museum Reconfigured for a New Century

The amusement business situation of today is vastly different than it was in Barnum's museum days—but the human mind of today is still susceptible to the contagion of the germ of curiosity.

—Joe Tracy Emmerling

In the middle of the nineteenth century, entertainment promoters in several American cities had organized permanent displays of paintings, artifacts, waxworks, freak shows, and variety artists, thereby creating a new form of amusement center—the dime museum. With their combination of exhibits and live performances presented side by side in huge, ornate buildings, these urban places had become the embodiment of modernity. For those first learning about the wonders of the world, they were emporiums of weird and wonderful curiosities, comprehensible and unthreatening testimonials to society's progress in civilization, technology, and science. The dime museums were extremely democratic, and while the smaller, storefront versions may have attracted only a male working-class audience, the larger museums drew a heterogeneous, multiethnic, and interclass crowd. They also had cross-generational appeal. The dime museum cannot be labeled either a working-class or a middle-class amusement; it was open to anyone, male or female, rich or poor, who could afford the price of admission.

With the average number of hours in a work week declining and the number of legal holidays increasing, the advent of several other new types of respectable, family-oriented entertainment was inevitable. Many urban reformers had altered their views on recreation and now saw it as a form of social control over a fast-growing population. Large parks were created in the hope that the restorative powers of nature—meadows, streams, and trees—would bring tranquility and, ultimately, generate moderation and temperance. The park system was to be a powerful antidote to the forces of "degeneration and demoralization in the city."[1] By the end of the nineteenth century, recreation was accepted as the right of all people, whatever their social status. The ultimate demise of the dime museum business came about during the early years of the new century with the success of three relatively new urban amusements, vaudeville, film, and amusement parks. Ultimately, it was these forms, offering their own brands of exciting, cheap, and ever-changing entertainment, that lured away most of the old dime museum's audience.

If the large dime museums fostered patriotism, affirmed the common person's worth, restored his dignity, and perpetuated the dream of a prosperous life, the movies did it better and more cheaply. The cinema was the culmination of those democratizing tendencies in the field of entertainment that had been at work throughout the century.[2] The cinema was compelling, controlled, and accessible, and it catered to women, children, and immigrants. The nickelodeon may have revolutionized American mass entertainment, but it was not until the end of the first decade of the twentieth century, when large urban theaters and vaudeville houses converted into movie houses, that film became thoroughly respectable. Movie houses appeared in residential neighborhoods and in commercial areas: they moved into traditional amusement centers, absorbing the audiences of the dime museums.

One could find anything on the screen: movies about local murders, such as *The Unwritten Law* (1907), based on the sensational murder of Stanford White by Harry K. Thaw; about crime, such as *The Gentleman Burglar* (1908); and about history, such as *Nero and the Burning of Rome* (1908) and *The Midnight Ride of Paul Revere* (1907). There were romances like *The Lover's Guide* (1908) and *Buying a Title* (1908) and comedies like *A Sculptor's Welsh Rarebit Dream* (1908) and *The Painter's Revenge* (1908), as well as "actualities."[3] Early films were pleasurable, informative, and often, as in *Life of an American Fireman* (1903), *How They Do Things on the Bowery* (1902), and *Rube and Mandy at Coney Island* (1908), the central figure was an average man. While critics feared that films were an evil influence, calling them silly and a waste of time, "if not actually pernicious," audiences loved them.[4] The motion picture industry as a chronicler of contemporary events and urban life became the technological successor to waxworks, "distant vision" exhibits, and melodrama.[5] To this day film is the most enduring and powerful of commercialized leisure activities, perpetually informing, arousing, terrorizing, thrilling, moving, and inspiring its audiences. While the advent of the movies as an independent industry hastened the demise of the dime museum as an institution, it was not the sole culprit. Progress was partly to blame; the machine itself was becoming both the source and the means of entertainment. Nowhere was this more apparent than at an outdoor amusement park.

126

•  •  •

The extension of transportation lines, including subways, trolleys, and ferries, made day trips easier for city families, and the outdoor amusement parks represented a new form of commercial entertainment for an increasingly industrial society. Coney Island, on the stretch of beach from Sheepshead Bay to Gravesend Bay in Brooklyn, New York, was one of America's first permanent amusement parks. Once known as a scandalous and unsavory place, Coney Island was transformed between 1897 and 1904 into a technologically sophisticated center of mass entertainment that attracted patrons from all socioeconomic levels.[6]

Amusement park audiences represented social and cultural melting pots. As the second generation of rural migrants and European immigrants came of age, they began to break away from the principles and practices of their own cultures. These younger people wanted fun, adventure, and the chance for social interaction. An excursion to Coney Island provided the ideal opportunity to fraternize and flirt. Tunnel rides like the "Canals of Venice" offered the perfect pretext for innocent kissing, and Coney Island also boasted one of the largest dance floors in the world, accommodating three thousand couples.[7]

Captain Paul Boyton, the famous nineteenth-century American who swam the English Channel, opened Coney Island's first family-oriented, enclosed, outdoor amusement park in July 1895. Boyton was a showman who presented water spectacles complete with seals and sea lions. Before 1895, he had been an itinerant performer traveling with his aquatic circus, and his name can be found on many programs from dime museums of the 1880s. He established Sea Lion Park as a permanent home for his aquatic performances. The dime museum environment, with its multiplicity of attractions all under one roof, may have influenced Boyton's imaginative decision to enclose Sea Lion Park with a fence, separating it from everyday reality. It was a friendly place where families could spend hours of pleasure without spending much money above the twenty-five-cent admission fee. Soon, other showmen followed Boyton, and eventually Coney Island had three parks: Steeplechase (1897–1965), Luna (1903–46, on the Sea Lion Park property), and Dreamland (1904–11).

These parks traded on many of the methods of dime museum management, such as using a single-price admission, barring alcohol, buying lots of publicity, and forbidding vulgar language. As the dime museums had done, the amusement parks competed with one another for patrons and were forced to keep creating new attractions. Managers often simply changed the names of rides from season to season. Just to pique visitors' curiosity, Luna Park's great naval spectacle, "War of the Worlds," changed its name twice in two years. Luna Park also created "Fire and Flames," a spectacle in which a four-story building was set on fire; the audience watched as firemen conquered the flames and saved "victims" from the conflagration. Dreamland sought to outdo this reenactment by burning down a six-story building. In a spirit of competition, Luna Park electrocuted an elephant named Topsy, and Dreamland created a midget community.

Coney Island, with its beachfront resorts, three amusement parks, independent entertainments, and sideshow attractions, was the culmination of one nineteenth-century form of recreation cultivated for the masses. It was a clean, safe environment where patrons could not only marvel at wonders but experience them firsthand. Machines, which had before been used solely as a means to an end, were here utilized as engines of entertainment themselves. Here, technology was tamed but not miniaturized, as in the museums, or merely displayed to exemplify scientific progress, as at the world's fairs. Instead, it was transformed into "objects of amusements."[8] Technology was not feared or revered; it was simply experienced. Machines were not threatening or productive; they promised nothing more than "the pleasure of the event itself."[9] Mechanical rides like "Shoot-the-Chutes," the "Barrel of Fun," "Helter Skelter," or the "Human Roulette Wheel" tossed and tumbled laughing, gasping pleasure seekers. It was entertaining to experience the ride, but it was equally amusing to watch strangers bounce and twirl. Electricity was used as decoration, and scenography created mood and atmosphere. By 1907, 1.3 million lights decorated Luna Park's towers and buildings; in fact, Luna Park was known as the Electric Eden. Coney Island became the embodiment of the fantasy of a smoothly running mechanical world. Technological advances had made the United States a superpower, and in the naval spectacle "War of the Worlds," audiences watched as the American fleet defeated Germany, Britain, Spain, and France. While such amusements showed how well technology could be controlled, nature demonstrably could not be. Freaks of nature as well as freaks of culture still held a fascination for the early twentieth-century pleasure seekers, and many dime museum anomalies found work at Coney Island.

Lilliputia, a midget city in the heart of Dreamland, was not a sideshow but a permanent municipality of three hundred midgets, organized by Samuel W. Gumpertz. A longtime showman, Gumpertz was an acrobat, an actor, a member of Buffalo Bill's Wild West Show, and a theater producer. He was hired by William Reynolds, Dreamland's developer, in 1903 to manage the little people's town.[10] It had been constructed at half scale, and everything, from the bathrooms and bedroom furniture to the fire department, was in precise proportion. The town also had its own government and operated like any municipality. Spectators entered Lilliputia and, like Gulliver, could walk among the midgets, who might be shopping, cleaning, or doing any other ordinary task. It was here that Mrs. Tom Thumb and her second husband, Count Primo Magri, eventually lived.

On May 27, 1911, a fire destroyed Dreamland. Reynolds and the board of directors did not rebuild the park; it was financially too risky, and Reynolds was already developing the Chrysler Building in Manhattan. But after the disaster, Gumpertz, a true showman, put up a tent outside the ruins and reopened a "congress of freaks," an attraction, like circus side-shows, loosely based on the dime museum idea.[11] While the embers of the fire were still smoldering, Gumpertz turned Dreamland into a popular sideshow attraction, displaying a collection of "living wonders" from all over the world. Gumpertz was a big promoter of non-Western freaks and imported more than three thousand attractions for Dreamland.[12] It was his efforts that turned Coney Island into the "world's capital of the eccentric and the bizarre," and he became known as the godfather of the freak.[13]

Coney Island by 1905 was the amusement capital of the United States. Many exhibits that had proved successful at both the Chicago World's Columbian Exposition of 1893 and the Pan-American Exposition of 1901 were brought to the Brooklyn shore, many of them with roots in the dime museum. In 1901 Dr. Martin Arthur Couney exhibited premature babies in incubators in a pavilion at the Buffalo Pan-American Exposition. The tiny infants had been born at least three weeks before the end of the normal forty weeks of gestation. Two years later, Couney was persuaded to come to Coney Island. The doctor was aware that he was running a sideshow, but he did his best to emphasize the scientific aspects of his venture. He never accepted money for his services from the families of his patients, and his exhibitions always began with a lecture describing in detail many of the machines found in his miniature hospital. But the Incubator Pavilion was not much different, after all, from Meade's Midget Hall in the previous century. The displays at Meade's may have been cruder and less scientific than those of the Incubator Pavilion, but the wonder of seeing tiny beings living against the odds was in both cases very compelling.

129

Coney Island became the unofficial capital of the new mass culture. The amusement park represented a cheap alternative recreation that competed with the dime museums for patrons as well as performers. The festive outdoor atmosphere, flamboyant architecture, exotic landscaping, mechanical amusements, and public socializing provided pleasure seekers with constant stimulation and activity in an environment that was the antithesis of the grim city. As Kathy Peiss aptly stated, Coney Island was the "apotheosis of summer entertainment." [14]

• • •

By the beginning of the new century the dime museum was in a state of decline. Museums competed for customers with the circus, the legitimate theater, art galleries, and amusement parks. Certain forms of entertainment, such as variety and film, that had been featured in dime museums now "competed on their own against the establishments that had nurtured them." [15] The idea of a museum as an entertainment center with just a hint of the educational gradually disappeared, and museums reclaimed their former objective of edifying their patrons. At the beginning of the nineteenth century there was a coming together of natural history and art museums with freak shows, waxworks, theater, and variety performance. The beginning of the twentieth century witnessed their fragmentation. Significant pieces of art and authentic objects of natural history were displayed in prestigious public museums; human oddities found work at circuses and amusement parks; waxworks could be found at the parks or in wax museums; and talented variety performers made names for themselves in vaudeville, theater, and film. Though it may not be obvious today, all the individual amusements that were once assembled in the dime museums still form part of the American cultural fabric. Although the dime museum as an institution was obsolete by World War I, the need for cheap, accessible, escapist entertainment endured. While twentieth-century popular culture ultimately came to be defined by the electronic mass media, voyeurism, patriotism, and sensationalism remained dominant themes. [16]

One of the most famous and popular twentieth-century descendants of the old dime museum is the "Ripley's Believe It or Not!" odditorium. In 1918, Robert Ripley was working at the *New York Globe* as a sports illustrator. One day when sports news was sparse, Ripley, using his imagination and knowledge of sports trivia, created nine cartoons and called the section "Believe It or Not!" The response was extremely positive, and "Believe It or Not!" became a daily feature.

By 1929 Ripley's cartoons had been published in book form, and he was one of the top sports cartoonists in the country, as well as one of the most sought-after and highest-paid lecturers. By 1930 he had his own radio show and a contract with Warner Brothers to make twenty-six movie shorts. In 1933 he created a "Believe It or Not Odditorium" for the Chicago World's Fair, featuring exhibits of shrunken human heads, medieval torture machines, and Oriental curiosities. After the fair, Ripley toured with a company of twenty-five living oddities and some three hundred inanimate objects.[17] At one point his collection contained over four thousand items. Some of his more famous freaks were Grace McDaniels, the "Mule Faced Woman," Roy Bard, the "Ossified Man," Leo Congee, the "Human Pin Cushion," and Paul Whitaker, a black man from Georgia who could pop his right eye out a full inch beyond the socket. Paul Desmule, the "Armless Man," used his toes to hurl knives with ten-inch blades at a human target.[18] He also demonstrated how he prepared breakfast for himself, shaved, washed his face, and combed his hair. In 1934, Desmule married his human target, Miss Mae Dixon, in a Barnumesque public wedding ceremony at Horticultural Hall in Boston where Ripley's museum was on display.

In 1939 Ripley purchased two Fiji Mermaids who were strikingly similar to the one Barnum had exhibited in 1843. Ripley, aware of Barnum's legacy, captioned this exhibit the "World's Greatest Fake!"[19] Norbert Pearlroth, a researcher for Ripley for fifty years, attributes his success to the "primary human urge to flee from the daily grind into the realm of the incredible." "Curiosity," said Pearlroth, "is a fundamental trait."[20] In 1940 there were three Odditoriums running simultaneously in America: at the Golden Gate International Exposition in San Francisco; at the New York World's Fair; and on Broadway in New York City. In addition, Ripley had a number of traveling companies touring the world. Robert Ripley died in 1949, and the trustees of his estate, believing that without him the enterprise would collapse, sold it when the market value was high. The business has changed hands several times over the decades and is now owned by Ripley Entertainment, which as of 1996 operates fifteen permanent "Believe It or Not!" museums throughout the United States.[21] There are also museums in Australia, England, Denmark, Thailand, Indonesia, Korea, the Philippines, and Mexico. Each Ripley museum is unique in its architecture and collection of oddities and also in their presentation.

Perhaps as a direct result of Ripley's success and the onset of the Great Depression, a new generation of proprietary museums developed in the 1930s. Dime museums opened across the country, in Detroit (W. G. Wade's Hollywood Freak Museum), Houston (Marine Firestone Museum), St. Louis (Erber's Show of Living Wonders), and Baltimore (John T. McCaslin's Baltimore Museum), to name a few. *Billboard Magazine*, a show business trade paper, devoted a column to chronicling museum activity from 1930 to 1940. The majority of these museums had penny arcades, displayed miscellaneous objects and freaks and showcased variety artists. They were usually small; John T. McCaslin's Baltimore Museum, for example, was just one room. Along the left side of the long, narrow room were the freaks, along the right side the inanimate objects and wax displays, and at the far end was a small stage.[22] Most of these proprietary museums closed by World War II; there were a few exceptions, however, such as Huber's Museum, on West Forty-second Street, which did not close until around 1965. Huber's was famous for Professor Heckler's Traveling Flea Circus, a show where trained fleas could be seen pulling wagons, swinging weights, and dancing.[23]

• • •

The wax museum is perhaps the most prevalent modern proprietary museum. It can be found wherever tourists congregate—in Los Angeles, Niagara Falls, and Las Vegas, among other tourist meccas. In the 1970s there was an International Association of Wax Museums based in Chicago. The organization claimed fifty members from twenty-three states and six foreign countries.[24] (It has since disbanded.) "Much of the character of the old, frankly proletarian museum has been lost," wrote Brooks McNamara in 1974, "but at least a touch of the old brass and fraudulent gentility remains, transformed into a middle-class idiom."[25]

When New York's Eden Musée closed in 1916, Gumpertz purchased the collection and opened a new Eden Musée next door to his Coney Island freak show. When visitors entered the gates of Gumpertz's new pavilion, they saw the same wax policeman who for decades had guarded the door of the Eden Musée in the city. Gumpertz displayed all the Eden Musée's historical scenes and throughout the years added many of his own tableaux.

131

He struggled, as had dime museum impresarios before him, to earn respect for his establishment. "Everything in the Eden Musée," said Gumpertz in defense of his wax displays, "is taken from the pages of history . . . we show actual punishments which are meted out by various countries to their criminals, and in showing these scenes we are doing good. All these scenes, I insist, are moral lessons."[26] Forever fascinated by crime scenes, he created a series of tableaux called "The Squealer," illustrating what happened to an informer in the underworld. Local murders also captivated Gumpertz; one of his more popular exhibits was a depiction of the Snyder-Gray murder.

Ruth Snyder and her lover, Judd Gray, had been convicted of murdering Snyder's husband, Albert, in 1927. Gumpertz's three-tableaux display showed the lovers conferring at a restaurant, the crime scene, and Snyder's electrocution at Sing Sing. Gray also died there, but his execution was not depicted in the tableau, probably because the newspapers had portrayed him as the victim of a wicked temptress. The Snyder case, according to Ann Jones, was a media event, but it was a morality play "meant almost exclusively for the edification of women." Ruth Snyder was cast as the source of evil, "as Eve in league with Satan," and Judd Gray was depicted as "a decent, red-blooded, upstanding American citizen" caught like a fly in her web.[27] Up-to-date depictions of homicides were in vogue, and the wax museums that still existed operated like tabloid newspapers, mounting many electrocution scenes minutes after a criminal's death. For good measure, throughout the years Gumpertz also added wax replicas of contemporary celebrities, including Charlie Chaplin, Douglas Fairbanks, and Mary Pickford.[28]

The atmosphere of the modern wax museums may differ from that of their nineteenth-century prototypes, but the contents remain very similar, with re-creations of celebrities and historical figures and events. For example, Wax U.S.A. in Lake George, New York, includes a wax figure of John F. Kennedy sitting in a real Lincoln Continental, which the museum claims he had actually owned.[29] The Musée Conti in New Orleans is a wax museum devoted to local history; patrons are treated to thirty-one tableaux depicting the history of the city from 1699 to the present. Included is a reproduction of Napoleon, seated in a bathtub, telling his brothers he will sell Louisiana to the Americans.[30] The Stars Hall of Fame in Orlando, Florida, is dedicated to reenacting "great moments" in television, film, and music; it features a re-creation of a snow scene from *Doctor Zhivago* starring a waxy Julie Christie, Omar Sharif, and Rod Steiger.[31]

Two wax museums devoted to the African American experience have opened in the past decade: the Great Blacks in Wax Museum in Baltimore, owned by Elmer Martin and Joanne Martin, and the Harlem Museum in New York, operated by Raven Chanticleer.[32] Both contain replicas of Martin Luther King Jr. and Malcolm X, and their goal is to encourage a collective cultural connection and to foster pride in being African American. The Baltimore collection exhibits one hundred "role models," spanning more than three thousand years of black history, from the Egyptian Pharaoh Akhenaton to Supreme Court justice Thurgood Marshall.[33]

•   •   •

The "Guinness World of Records" museums are late twentieth-century versions of the "Ripley's Believe It or Not!" odditorium and relatives of the dime museum. The Guinness organization maintains museums in New York City, Las Vegas, Gatlinburg, Tennessee, San Francisco, Hollywood, and Niagara Falls, Ontario. As spectators walk through the halls of the museum they become absorbed in what the souvenir guidebook calls a world "of the strongest, the longest, the shortest, the loudest, the brightest, and the greatest."[34]

The New York City museum is located on the concourse level of the Empire State Building. The space is divided into a number of sections displaying records from the fields of entertainment, sports, agriculture, and nature, among others. In the so-called Human World, for example, there is a life-sized replica of Robert Pershing Wadlow, "the tallest officially recorded man in history," who was 8 feet 11.1 inches tall at his death at the age of twenty-two in 1940. Also included in the exhibition are depictions of Pauline Muster, a Dutch midget who measured 24 inches when she died at the age of nineteen in 1895, and Robert Earl Hughes, who is said to have been the heaviest person in the world, weighing 1,069 pounds at his death at the age of twenty-two in 1958.[35] According to the museum's archive, Anna Swan (1846–1888) and Martin Van Buren Bates (1845–1919), freaks from the old dime museum era, still hold the record for being the tallest married couple. At the Guinness museum, antique trial and test machines coexist with modern technology in the form of video displays that "chronicle man's adventure in space" or bring to life "living legends from the world of sports."[36] In the American Fact File section, there is a large glass cabinet called the Guinness Boutique. Displayed are some of the world's most expensive items, such as the most costly pair of sports shoes, mink-lined ruby-tipped golf shoes costing $23,000, and the most expensive bottle of wine ever sold, a 1787 Chateau Lafite claret signed by Thomas Jefferson and sold at auction in 1985 for $157,500.

134                              •   •   •

More than anything else, the institution of the dime museum helped introduce and standardize the concept of the freak show. "Once human exhibits became attached to organizations," wrote Robert Bogdan, "distinct patterns of constructing and presenting freaks could be institutionalized, conventions that endure to this day." [37] The freak show was—and is—about spectacle: it is a place where human deviance is enhanced, dressed, coiffed, and propped up for the entertainment of a paying audience. The freak show is about relationships, *us* versus *them*, the normal versus the freaks. It is about culture, which determines what is freakish and what is not. In one sense, the definition changes over time.

Charles Stratton ("Tom Thumb") died on July 15, 1883, at the age of forty-five. During his lifetime he had earned an enormous fortune, but because of poor investments and a lavish lifestyle, he left only a small estate, valued at about $16,000, in addition to some minor real estate holdings. The most valuable asset he left to his wife, Lavinia Warren, was his name.[38] Lavinia had grown accustomed to a life of luxury, complete with yachts, fine jewelry, and handmade dresses. After Stratton's death Lavinia returned to show business; "Mrs. Tom Thumb" was still a bankable star.

On April 6, 1885, at the Church of the Holy Trinity on Madison Avenue, she married Count Primo Magri, another midget, eight years her junior. Magri was skilled at fencing, boxing, and music and played the piano and the piccolo.[39] The couple depended mainly on the fame of Lavinia's dead husband, however, and often exhibited themselves as "Mrs. General Tom Thumb and Her Husband" (see fig. 23). In December 1888, they appeared in a play called *Two Strings to Your Bow* at the Grand Museum's lecture room in New York. According to George C. D. Odell, the title highlighted Lavinia's two marriages.[40]

In fact, however, Lavinia and the count did try to escape from the "General's" image by forming their own troupe, called the Lilliputian Opera Company. The two also toured in vaudeville shows and made several films. But by the turn of the century, the days of the glorified freak show were over, and the couple found it difficult to earn a living like the one Lavinia and her first husband had made fifty years earlier. There was no longer an abundance of dime museums with organized freak show exhibi-

135

FIGURE 23. Mrs. General Tom
Thumb and Count Magri,
broadside, Grand Museum, c.
1889. (New-York Historical Society.)

tions, as there had been in the 1880s and 1890s. Even when freaks could find work in a dime museum, the salaries they earned were no longer inflated.

In a desperate move to gain financial security, the couple lived for several years at Gumpertz's Lilliputia. The name of General Tom Thumb proved rewarding once again for Lavinia and Gumpertz, and millions of people came to Lilliputia to see the famous couple. Unfortunately, however, Lavinia was never able to reclaim the social or financial status she had while married to Charles Stratton. She died on November 25, 1919, at the age of seventy-eight.

With the demise of the dime museums during the early part of the century, freak performers became largely itinerants. Anomalies who wanted to exhibit themselves for money could still find work at world's fairs, amusement parks, carnivals, and the circus. Over a forty-year period, from 1893 to 1933, the United States hosted six world's fairs: Chicago, 1893; Buffalo, 1901; St. Louis, 1904; San Francisco, 1915; Philadelphia, 1926; and Chicago, 1933.[41] At these fairs, where technological progress was being showcased, human anomalies remained as testaments to man's inability to conquer nature completely. Freaks were usually relegated to the fair's midway, an annexed area that housed such lowbrow—and immensely popular—attractions as human anomalies, foreign villages, and menageries. World's fairs never lasted more than about two years and generally ran only from May to October; thus a freak was guaranteed perhaps six months of work at a time. As the decades passed, however, it became more and more difficult for freaks to find legitimate jobs.[42] The circus sideshow guaranteed a performer more stable work, but the sideshow traveled, and it was difficult for freaks to become part of a rooted community. The luxury of living in a city and exhibiting at dime museums from September to July was a thing of the past; the permanent, standing freak show was part of a bygone era.

Lilliputia and Gumpertz's Dreamland Circus Sideshow were two of the few twentieth-century freak shows not associated with a traveling carnival or circus. Gumpertz operated his Dreamland Circus Sideshow for well over thirty years; he followed in the footsteps of Phineas T. Barnum, E. M. Worth, and George H. Huber to become a czar of the twentieth-century freak show world. His sideshow attracted many freaks who were tempted by the life in the seaside resort. It provided them the opportunity, then rare, to live and work in a stable and thriving community. Everybody at Coney Island knew "Jolly Irene, the Fat Lady," who weighed 689 pounds, "Lady Olga, the Bearded Lady," and "Captain Fred Walters, the Blue Man."

Nate Eagle was another twentieth-century czar of freakdom who fol
lowed the path of Gumpertz. He entered the world of show business as a
carnival barker but in his later years, during the 1950s, managed the
circus sideshow for Ringling Brothers. Eagle first achieved notoriety for his
creation of a Midget City for Chicago's Century of Progress Exposition of
1933–34. Eagle's Midget City, which had forty-five buildings, was so
successful that he grossed nearly $2 million for the fair. The city maintained
a resident company of eight to ten midgets, all of whom spent the winter
months in Sarasota, Florida, near Eagle himself. After the success of his
Chicago venture, Eagle was asked to create a miniature world for the 1935
San Diego Exposition. Not only did he create a midget city but he also
organized a scandalous nudist colony exhibit called Zoro Gardens. Naked
men and women from twelve different countries could be seen at Zoro
Gardens "gossiping, dozing on artificial rocks, and fishing in homemade
ponds."[43] Ironically, Eagle would not allow the men to walk unclothed,
believing this immoral: they had to wear loincloths.

137

The display was a phenomenal attraction, and male visitors were known
to bring their lunches to the exhibit and casually watch naked women
talking and playing while they ate their meals. Although the expo—and
Eagle—made money from this exhibit, the California authorities were
annoyed. But, always the clever showman, he wore them down with his
arguments for the viability of Zoro Gardens. In the end, the two sides
reached a compromise. A major complaint was that there was too much
loitering at the exhibit. So Eagle encircled the garden with a long wooden
walkway and hustled the customers around it at a fast pace.

The freak shows of the nineteenth-century dime museums had elevated
the status of human anomalies to that of celebrities; many became famous
and dined with presidents and foreign dignitaries. In the twentieth century,
the exploitation of freaks for profit began to be frowned upon. In part
because of the ensuing world wars and their devastating effects on the
bodies of survivors, there arose a gradual awareness of society's responsibil-
ity toward people with disabilities. Prostheses were devised for those who
lacked limbs, modern medicine demystified many of nature's mutations,
and hormone therapy was administered to people with growth problems.

• • •

Traditional outdoor amusements began to lose their appeal as movies,
radio, and television began to occupy a greater portion of America's leisure
time. For the most part, world's fairs have been replaced by permanent

theme parks, and with these shifts many American performance traditions have been lost. But Dick Zigun, a young man from Barnum's hometown of Bridgeport, Connecticut, for the past fifteen years has devoted his energy to preserving popular entertainment forms. Zigun, a playwright and graduate of the Yale Drama School, founded Coney Island, USA, a museum and theater company dedicated to reviving the parades, sideshows, and other performance elements typical of Coney Island at the turn of the century.[44] Together with Valerie Haller, whom he hired as design director in 1988, Zigun presents a continuous sideshow, or "Ten-in-One," for the 1990s. Zigun either produces his own entertainments, Sideshows by the Seashore, or provides a venue for other sideshows, such as Bradshaw's Circus of World Curiosities, which was at Coney Island in 1989.

At these performances there are no born freaks; "nobody would be exhibited because of a deformity," Zigun has said. His freaks are "performance-oriented, rather than gawker-oriented."[45] The cast includes "Miss Electra, the Electric Girl," the "Human Block Head," and the "Illustrated Man." It is this sensibility, as it were, that prevents the Coney Island, USA, freak show from affecting its audiences on a truly visceral level. Without the real human anomalies, with only a cast of self-made freaks, it is little more than a magic show. It does not shock or revolt us. On the other hand, Fred Siegel, who worked at Coney Island, USA, has argued in the *Drama Review* that it is a "viscerally titillating place where performers violate their bodies with spikes, swords, and fire and walk off the platform unharmed."[46] The pleasure, Siegel concluded, comes from matching wits with a sideshow performer, which many spectators see as a game.[47] Perhaps the pleasure is derived from figuring out whether the performers are deceitful in the acts. Does Todd Robbins really eat a light bulb, or is his performance the fake we imagine it to be?

One reason this kind of freak show cannot inspire a true sense of wonderment, however, is that self-made freaks fail to amaze the modern spectator. In our late twentieth-century culture the self-made freaks on the platform are not very different from the people we see at the downtown mall or on the subway. We have developed a very vocal subculture that believes the body is a personal canvas to be reconfigured as the owner sees fit. Body jewelry and the piercing of cheeks, nose, navel, and nipple, which have never been associated with Western notions of beauty, have become very popular in the 1990s.

Tom Singman, a California lawyer, recently visited the Gauntlet, a piercing parlor that has stores in Los Angeles and New York, to get his thirteen-

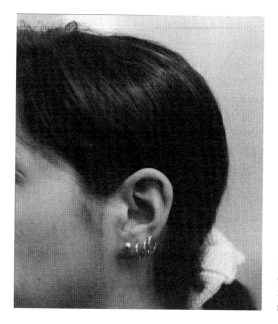

**139**

FIGURE 24. A contemporary
example of mainstream body
modification: the earlobe of a
second-grade teacher.

year-old daughter a "belly-button pierce." "There I was," he recalled,
"gobbling down pierce-care hints, as if this were the most normal thing in
the world. Then it hit me: this *was* normal. Not 1950's normal, but maybe
1990's normal."[48] Body piercing as an organized phenomenon is entering
its seventeenth year, according to Stace Maples, a guest editorial writer for
*Piercing Fans International Quarterly.*[49] While the piercing of genitalia still
seems outrageously freakish to most of us, ear, nose, navel, and nipple
piercing is now mainstream, and the Gauntlet advertises in the Manhattan
yellow pages (see fig. 24).

Tattooing, now frowned upon because of the health risks, is a booming
industry. Tattoos are seen not as the mark of the criminal or the macho
insignia of soldiers and sailors, but as living art. Celebrities like Cher,
Whoopi Goldberg, and Prince all sport tattoos. *Body Art,* a magazine
published in England, is devoted solely to tattooing, body jewelry, body
painting, and body modification.[50] *Glamour* magazine, in its fashion-con-
scious "Dos & Don'ts" section, recently allotted space to tattoos.[51] According to the magazine, they are more than acceptable; they are hip (see
figs. 25 and 26).

During the 1960s and 1970s, Americans witnessed a cultural and aes-

140

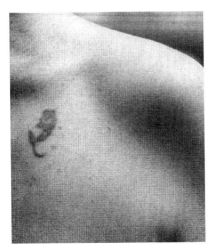 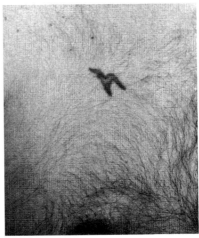

FIGURE 25. *(left)* Tattoo belonging to the executive director of a law firm. FIGURE 26. *(right)* Tattoo belonging to a partner of a law firm.

thetic revolution in which many artists created projects that challenged the perception of the human body and its function. Many performance artists transformed their bodies, turning themselves into freaks in order to shatter cultural taboos about bodily functions and human sexuality. Vito Acconci, originally a poet, "abandoned the space of the written page for a place in which the body was assigned the task of going beyond the poetic function."[52] In *Conversation* (1970 and 1971), he experienced the possibility of transforming his male body into a female one by burning the hairs on his chest, pulling his nipples, hiding his penis between his legs, and attempting to walk, dance, and sit with his penis between his thighs. Performance artists break down barriers between life and art and use their bodies as a canvas for expression, a visualization of their artistic message. Karen Finley claims control over her body by pouring food over it; she pours a can of yams down her back and buttocks. Her art is shocking, revolting to some, and yet powerful in its message; "the result is both fascinating and horrifying to behold, because audiences can't help but recognize their most mortifying obsessions in the fast-flowing bile."[53]

Certain nineteenth-century freaks suggested ambiguous types of sexuality and aroused the erotic fantasies of a repressed audience. Modern body artists, using their own tissue as the medium of expression, challenge twentieth-century social concepts of sex and individuality. While the nineteenth-century spectator feared the consequences of the Industrial Revolution, the twentieth-century audience is anxious about the loss of autonomy and control brought on by an overindustrialized, computer-oriented society.

In 1983 and 1984, performance artists Linda Montano and Tehching Hsieh attached themselves to each other with an eight-foot rope tied at the waist. Their project, titled *Rope,* called for them to remain joined for an entire year. In essence, their contrived lifestyle of enforced intimacy mirrored the interdependency of natural Siamese twins. Montano and Hsieh, as individual artists, explored how a state of perpetual attachment would affect them as people and as artists. (One stipulation of their project was that they could not touch each other for the year, but audiences were unaware of this condition.) Seeing a man and a woman joined together evokes taboo topics and erotic images. While witnessing any part of *Rope,* spectators might ask such questions as, How do they go to the bathroom, shower, or even sleep? Is each celibate for a year? With the Montano-Hsieh piece, the questions might probe deep into their relationship. Just as Chang and Eng, the original Siamese twins, had conflicting personalities, Montano and Hsieh disagreed about the intent of their project and "eventually discovered themselves in a contextual tug of war, literally pulling each other in opposite directions."[54] His approach was more formal, while she wanted to explore the personal and spiritual implications of their bondage.

Through body piercing to body art, many Americans are symbolically illustrating that they are in control of their lives as well as negating the importance of the body in mass culture. Thus, in a world where body modification is accepted and body piercing and tattooing commonplace, the performer who hammers nails into his tongue or drives spikes up his nose is no longer outrageously freakish. Many self-help organizations, such as Robbins Research International, end their seminars with physically challenging activities like walking barefoot on hot coals. Completing a fire-walk supposedly helps demonstrate the power of the mind. Without the so-called gawking that was an intrinsic part of the nineteenth-century freak show, Zigun's shows become interpretive spectacles, with twentieth-century sensibilities imposed on a once-popular tradition. Coney Island, USA's "Ten-in-One" is a sideshow but not a freak show. The problem for a modern promoter, therefore, is how to reconfigure the nineteenth-century freak show for a late twentieth-century audience. What kinds of exhibitions would be grotesque, fascinating, politically correct, and a sure draw?

The most obvious modern form of the freak show is the television talk show, an environment in which dysfunctional human beings parade themselves in front of an audience. If, as Odell claimed, the old-time freak show made spectators feel at ease with their lot in life, so too does the daytime talk show, which prompts viewers to tell themselves, "I'm so glad that's not me." As the dime museum freak show transforms itself into the television talk show, attention shifts from physical to psychological freakishness. Although today's talk shows promote themselves as "discussion programs" and do indeed occasionally address a politically important issue, their basic appeal is pure voyeurism. People in bizarre situations more or less out of their control, either psychologically or physically, hold themselves up to public scrutiny.

These shows are both alluring and revolting, but also indisputably successful. Taboo subjects, ranging from homosexuality among teenagers to sexual relations between unmarried relatives, are aired daily from 9 A.M. to 5 P.M. In 1995 a glance at a *TV Guide* revealed seventeen talk shows, not including the prime-time magazine and tabloid shows, which incorporate similar devices. With a press of a button audiences could tune into Oprah Winfrey, Phil Donahue, Sally Jessy Raphaël, Geraldo Rivera, Montel Williams, Jerry Springer, Gordon Elliott, Maury Povich, Jenny Jones, Richard Bey, or Ricki Lake.

Talk shows recycle many of the conventions of the earlier freak shows. For example, television hosts closely resemble the lecturers of the dime museum freak shows, as they guide their audience from exhibit to exhibit, explaining the pathetic plight of each person in turn. As with the freaks shows of the dime museum, the sensational aspects of television talk shows are played down and the educational ones heightened so that the spectacles are legitimized. Sometimes actual midgets or other deformed or disabled persons appear on talk shows, but mostly these appearances are promoted as enlightening and informative. Like the "doctors" who provided medical testimonials at a dime museum freak show, psychologists and other behavioral "experts" often appear, supposedly to help the audience understand a particular problem and to validate the show's subject. Just as traditional freak shows had codified elements, the same freakish stories are used over and over again. The "performance" may change with each show, but the stories remain the same.

The crudeness of talk show entertainment, or "confrontainment," which can be viewed every hour during daytime programming, promises to change the face of television. James B. Twitchell believes that talk shows, or television's sideshows, as he labels them, have begun to dominate programming, as they are the favorites of a younger, less sophisticated audience. He believes that the "end of the twentieth century promises to reverse what the nineteenth century had separated as high culture and low culture. Where the elite threatened to exile the vulgar, now the vulgar threatens to suffocate the elite."[55] A would-be Barnum cannot profitably exploit our continuing fascination with human freaks; the only show people who make big money exhibiting human anomalies these days are those who produce television shows.

# Epilogue

Although it might be easier to remember Phineas Taylor Barnum as a circus man, we should not neglect the tremendous contribution he made to the entertainment industry with his dime museum concept. In a city where there was no zoo or aquarium or even a museum of natural history, Barnum's American Museum presented New York families, regardless of income or nationality, a safe place to enjoy a multitude of entertainments. His genius was his "knack of knowing what the public wanted."[1] Much of the museum's success resulted from its ability to attract women and children. Barnum's matinees were devised specifically for the female patron, and many afterpieces, such as *Cinderella* and Punch and Judy shows, were tailored for children. Liquor was banned from the museum's theater and the theater's illicit third tier was redesigned by Barnum into a "family circle."[2] Strolling musicians, live animals, and mechanical figures fascinated even the youngest of spectators. Barnum loved to see children laugh. He once said that "there was no picture so beautiful as ten thousand smiling, bright-eyed, happy children, and no music so sweet as their clear-ringing laughter."[3]

The reason for the success of Barnum's American Museum was three-fold: first, he created a clean and safe environment for whole families; second, he got patrons to return again and again by changing his exhibits constantly; and last, he promoted his museum as an educational experience. Barnum's three strategies are still winning ones today, and the successful entertainment establishments are those that follow the formula laid out by him over 150 years ago. Although the dime museum does not exist today, Barnum has indeed left a legacy. In tracing the performance genealogy of many entertainment forms, including the circus, movies, wax museums, and theme parks, one can find a connection to the dime museum industry.

Walt Disney is to the amusement world of the twentieth century what Barnum was to that of the nineteenth. While Barnum popularized and reinterpreted the museum concept, Disney took the standard outdoor amusement park and transformed it into something altogether new called a theme park. He believed in the importance of the family, and family entertainment was the backbone of his whole business.[4] Like Barnum, Disney provided his audiences with "popular and inoffensive entertainment"; he knew his audience and provided them with the types of amusements they desired.[5] Disneyland, in Anaheim, California, was dedicated on

July 17, 1955, and its enormous success changed American attitudes toward amusement parks in general and revived a seemingly moribund industry.[6] Disneyland was the prototype; all other theme parks are imitations.

Disneyland, a distant relative of the American Museum, was the first family-oriented outdoor amusement center designed for the post–World War II baby boom generation. It was extraordinarily clean and safe, in contrast to the decaying amusement parks that still existed in the mid-fifties. It had a single entrance, to facilitate crowd control, and there was also a single admission price. There were a variety of live performances, from organized shows to parades, marching bands, and wandering players dressed as Disney cartoon characters that children could embrace. Disney constantly changed and expanded his offerings; the park was something he could keep building, "keep plussing and adding to." When Disneyland opened in 1955, Fantasyland had just six attractions. In 1983, after extensive renovations, it had sixteen attractions.[7]

Disneyland attracted patrons from all incomes, and while hardly cheap, the single-price admission ticket serves the same purpose as the ten- or twenty-five-cent admission policy at the dime museum: making the entertainment economically democratic in its own way. When all spectators pay the same admission price for the same entertainments, points out Bruce A. McConachie, it erases one of "the traditional markers of class distinction."[8] This illusion of economic equality, however, quickly vanishes outside the amusement environment.

Although theme parks in general play up their educational aspects, they are primarily interested in providing entertainment. Thus, just as with the dime museums, the history or the ideas taught are skewed to make the exhibits that much more entertaining. If the historical truth is too controversial, a more nostalgic, homogenized version will be substituted. The Disney Imagineers defend this process: "We carefully program out all the negative unwanted elements and program in the positive elements."[9] At the "American Adventure," a twenty-eight-minute presentation of America narrated by Mark Twain and Ben Franklin, nothing is mentioned about Vietnam. There are no Holocaust, threat of nuclear war, ghettoes, homeless, or poor. There are no McCarthy hearings, civil rights demonstrations, Kent State, or Watergate. A viewer sees only positive images and people who are icons, as opposed to representatives of history. Disney realism, concludes Michael Wallace, is "utopian in nature"; it does not reproduce the past but improves it.[10] The reason for this is that theme parks are basically about fantasy and escape, and the two goals of escape and educa-

145

tion are fundamentally at odds. Education is not simply a matter of disseminating information; true instruction is stimulating, thought-provoking, and a powerful agent for understanding the present.

There is no denying that history is manipulated when it is transformed into entertainment. "Issues of illusion and deceit, . . . of beauty as process or disguise," wrote Neil Harris, "are dilemmas of antiquity and should not be localized as agonizingly modern."[11] Slavery and the status of African Americans, for example, were such controversial topics in the nineteenth century that dime museums rarely acknowledged blacks in their waxworks displays. Pre–Civil War minstrel shows and African freaks marketed as missing links and savages appeased white audiences' curiosity about blacks, but these exhibits merely reaffirmed the then common belief, even among Northerners, that blacks were inferior. Post–Civil War tableaux were certainly pro-Union, but the inhumanity of slavery was never depicted. Historical displays were created to promote nationalism; most war tableaux were designed to honor the heroic efforts of General Grant and the Union soldiers and to celebrate the victory of the North. Slavery was illustrated only in an occasional emancipation scene. Dime museum managers consciously avoided the politically charged discourse of race, and although Booker T. Washington was represented in the 1905 "People Talked About" exhibit at the Eden Musée, for the most part, American black culture was ignored.

At Colonial Williamsburg in Virginia, a living history museum that tries to re-create the historic village, the original creators totally neglected the fact that, in the eighteenth century, this Southern town was over 50 percent black.[12] The curators wanted to avoid the volatile issue of race. These historical silences, like the silence about Vietnam in the "American Adventure," simply reflect the traditional cowardice of mass-market entertainers. "For many people," states Cary Carson, Williamsburg vice president for research, "history is the core of patriotism, a kind of sacred text, a refuge where they can turn to reaffirm their faith."[13] People will not readily pay to see an unpatriotic version of history, however truthful it may be.

Historical accuracy is not a concept one associates readily with dime museums. Managers paid meticulous attention to authentic detailing of costumes and hairstyles—thus allowing these institutions to claim a certain genuineness for their exhibits—but the nineteenth-century showmen usually lied to the public about the larger issues. Audiences had few choices, however, when it came to popular entertainment, so the humbugging, deceit, and stereotyping were not much criticized. If a freak, for example, was heralded as the "heaviest man alive," most people believed at that moment he was. Phony exhibits are not as easily tolerated by late twentieth-century audiences, so managers must expend tremendous effort on packaging: the grander the spectacle, the more likely the public will be to flock to see it. Wonder is no longer felt for the person or the event displayed or for history retold, but for the display and the retelling themselves. The irony is that in this misdirection of interest and manipulation of history for the sake of "production values," the truth, the very source of the historical text, is lost, ignored, or betrayed.[14]

**147**

The relationship between mass culture and popular historical consciousness thus involves not only the translation of history into fiction but the textual interplay, complex and contradictory, among sponsor, producer, and assumed audience. When historical events are reenacted or reconstructed as entertainment spectacles, the chasm between fact and fiction becomes pronounced. Robert Rydell believes that even what is labeled "progress" becomes translated into utopian statements about the future.[15] For-profit entertainment institutions, from as far back as Charles Willson Peale's Philadelphia museum, have a greater obligation to fill the pockets of their investors than to enlighten the public about history. Although Peale hoped to make his museum a national institution and obtain government sponsorship, this dream was never realized. Instead, his museum depended on ticket sales and in the end succumbed to the public's desire for other forms of entertainment.

In spite of all the humbugging, the primary reason for the success of theme parks like Disneyland is that they are marketed as family entertainment. They mimic the dime museum philosophy of offering something for everyone. With the huge baby boom generation now becoming parents, family recreation has grown increasingly important. Even the gambling city of Las Vegas has turned "family" with its new MGM Grand Hotel and theme park. The travel and entertainment industry must find amusements all family members can enjoy. In many dual-income families and single-parent households, parents and children have less "quality" time, and the family outing or vacation has taken on new meaning and importance.

Today family entertainment enterprises are not only marketed as vacation resorts but are used as urban renewal projects. The Disney Company is planning to revive New York City's Forty-second Street area with a hotel and amusement complex, and the Tussaud organization has promised to create a "335,000 square-foot complex housing robotic and interactive wax exhibits" at a nearby location—a sort of dime museum for the next century.[16] These attractions, wrote Paul Goldberger, are aimed at luring "members of the middle class who once gave American cities their destiny, but for the last generation have stayed away in droves."[17] Ironically, almost 170 years ago, in 1830, the New York Institute evicted Scudder's American Museum because it was attracting too many people to the neighborhood.[18]

# Appendix A. Chronology

1727 American Philosophical Society established (cabinet prototype).
1759 British Museum opens.
1774 Charleston Museum opens.
    Dr. Abraham Chovet opens Anatomical Museum in Philadelphia.
    Continental Congress bans plays and other public entertainments.
1778 Federal law prohibits theater in any form.
1782 Du Simitière opens his collection to the public.
1786 Charles Willson Peale opens American Museum in Philadelphia.
1791 Tammany Museum in New York opens.
1798 Old Trowbridge Museum in Albany opens.
1800 Washington, D.C., becomes new capital of United States.
1810 Scudder's American Museum in New York opens.
1820 Western Museum of Cincinnati opens.
1825 Peale's New York Museum opens.
    Showboat brings entertainment to towns along Erie Canal.
1835 Madame Tussaud's opens at the Bazaar in London.
1841 Boston Museum opens.
1842 Barnum's American Museum in New York opens on New Year's day.
    Barnum makes a deal to promote Charles Stratton.
1843 Virginia Minstrels form first Caucasian group to work in blackface.
1846 Smithsonian Institution opens.
1848 New York Museum of Anatomy opens.
1849 Astor Place Riot, New York.
1852 Harriet Beecher Stowe's *Uncle Tom's Cabin* is published.
    George Aiken's adaptation of *Uncle Tom's Cabin* debuts in Troy, New York.
1853 Conway's version of *Uncle Tom's Cabin* has premiere in New York City.
    New York Crystal Palace opens.
1859 Charles Darwin's *Origin of Species* is published.
1864 Colonel Joseph H. Wood opens Chicago Museum.
1866 *The Black Crook* opens at Niblo Garden.
1868 George Wood opens museum in New York.
1869 Colonel Joseph H. Wood opens museum at Ninth and Arch Street in Philadelphia.
    American Museum of Natural History opens.

1870 Metropolitan Museum of Art opens.
Barnum signs circus contract with William C. Coup.

1871 Great Chicago Fire.

1876 Philadelphia Centennial.
George Bunnell reduces admission charge to his museum from twenty-five cents to ten cents.
Boston Museum of Fine Arts opens.

1877 Edison demonstrates the phonograph.

1879 Wood's New York museum becomes Daly's Theater.

1883 B. F. Keith opens dime museum in Boston.

1884 Eden Musée opens in New York.

1885 Charles A. Brandenburgh opens Ninth and Arch Museum in Philadelphia.

1888 Worth's Museum opens in New York.

1889 Gunther moves Libby Prison from Virginia to Chicago.
John B. Doris opens Harlem Museum.

1890 William Kemmler is first man to be electrocuted, in Auburn, New York.
Huber takes over management of Worth and Huber's Palace Museum.

1891 Chicago's Eden Musée opens.

1892 Concert hall and dime museum licenses expire.

1893 Chicago World's Columbian Exposition.
Continuous vaudeville bill at Worth's Museum, September 2.

1894 Holland brothers open first kinetoscope parlor on Broadway with ten machines.

1895 Sea Lion Park opens at Coney Island.

1896 Vitascope makes its debut at Koster and Bial's Music Hall.

1897 New York Eden Musée shows first film.
Steeplechase opens at Coney Island.

1901 Buffalo Pan-American Exposition.

1903 Luna Park opens at Coney Island.
Edwin S. Porter makes *The Great Train Robbery.*

1904 Dreamland opens at Coney Island.
St. Louis Exposition.

1933 Chicago's Century of Progress Exposition.

1939 New York World's Fair.

1955 Disneyland opens in California.

# Appendix B. Dime Museums

The following is a list of nineteenth-century dime museums that I have come across during my research. Not all the dime museums listed below were included in the text. I hope that this list will continue to grow as scholars become more familiar with the subject. A word of caution for researchers: Not all institutions called museums were actually dime museums. For example, New York's Franklin Museum was solely a theater.

**BOSTON**

Austin and Stone's Museum
B. F. Keith's Museum
Boston Eden Musée
Boston Museum and Gallery of Fine Arts (referred to as the Boston
    Museum)
Gaiety Museum
Grand Museum
Keith and Batchelder's Mammoth Museum (changed to the Gaiety Hall
    and Museum)
New York Dime Museum

**CHICAGO**

Arthur Putney's Museum
Chicago Eden Musée
Clark Street Museum
Colonel Wood's Museum
Congress Museum
Epstein's Museum
Globe Museum
Libby Prison Museum
London Dime Museum
Olympic Museum
West Side Museum
Whit John's Museum
Wonderland Compound

NEW YORK

Alexander's Museum

Apollo Museum

Barnum's American Museum

Barnum's New American Museum (Barnum and Van Amburgh Museum)

Banvard's Museum

Berlin Academy of Waxworks

Broadway Museum and Menagerie

Bunnell's New American Museum (Bunnell's Museum)

Bunnell's Old London Museum

Chatham Square Museum

Doris's Eighth Avenue Museum

Doris's Harlem Museum

Dr. Kahn's Museum of Anatomy

Eden Musée

Egyptian Museum

European Museum

Gaiety Museum

George Wood's Museum and Metropolitan Theatre (changed to Wood's Museum and Menagerie but referred to as Wood's Museum)

Globe Dime Museum

Gothic Museum

Grand Dime Museum

Huber's Mammoth Eighth Avenue Museum

Huber's Palace Museum (later known as Huber's Museum)

Hyde and Behman's New Park Theatre Museum and Menagerie

International Museum

Kimball's Star Museum

Mammoth Museum

Meade's Midget Hall

Morris and Hickman's East Side Museum

Mt. Morris Museum

New Natural Museum

New York Museum

New York Museum of Anatomy

Standard Museum

Worth and Huber's Palace Museum

Worth's Model Museum and Family Theatre

Worth's Museum

## PHILADELPHIA
Brandenburgh's Ninth and Arch Museum
Chestnut Street Dime Museum
City Museum
Colonel Joseph H. Wood's Museum
Eighth Street Museum
Egyptian Musée
Great European Museum
Hagar and Campbell's New Dime Museum
Peck's Great Dime Museum
South Street Museum
Temple Theatre and Egyptian Musée

## OTHER CITIES
Anderson's Musée, Wilkes-Barre, Pennsylvania
Beach Street Museum (city unknown)
Bristol's Museum, Worcester, Massachusetts
Charles Hunt's Museum, Baltimore
Drew's Museum, Cleveland
Drew's Museum, Providence
Geary's Wonderland, Ft. Wayne, Indiana
Grand Museum, Allegheny, Pennsylvania
Harry Davis Eden Musée, Pittsburgh
Harry Davis Museum, Altoona, Pennsylvania
Herzog's Museum, Baltimore
Litt Museum, Milwaukee
McGinley's, St. Louis
Miracle Museum, Pittsburgh
Musée, Youngstown, Ohio
Newark Dime Museum, Newark
Pacific Museum of Anatomy and Natural Science, San Francisco
Peck and Fursman's Museum (city unknown)
Pleasant Street Museum, Providence
Punnell's Museum (city unknown)
Trowbridge Museum, Albany, New York
Troy Museum, Troy, New York
Vine Street, Cincinnati
Westminster, Providence

Wonderland, Buffalo
Wonderland, Detroit
Wonderland, Erie, Pennsylvania
Wonderland, Rochester, New York

**154**

# Notes

NOTES TO THE PREFACE

1. See Patricia Click, *The Spirit of the Times: Amusements in Nineteenth Century Baltimore, Norfolk, and Richmond* (Charlottesville: University Press of Virginia, 1989).

NOTES TO CHAPTER 1

1. See J. Orosz, "Curators and Culture: An Interpretive History of the Museum Movement in America, 1773–1870" (Ph.D. diss., Case Western Reserve, 1986); and Charles Coleman Sellers, *Mr. Peale's Museum: Charles Willson Peale and the First Popular Museum of Natural Science and Art* (New York: Norton, 1979).

2. See Richard D. Altick, *The Shows of London: A Panoramic History of Exhibitions, 1600–1862* (Cambridge: Harvard University Press, 1978), for a discussion on cabinets of wonders.

3. The Linnaean system was named after Carolus Linnaeus (1707–78), a Swedish biologist.

4. See George C. D. Odell, *Annals of the New York Stage,* vols. 2–4 (New York: Columbia University Press, 1927–49).

5. See Orosz, "Curators and Culture"; Sellers, *Mr. Peale's Museum;* and Neil Harris, "Cultural Institutions and American Modernization," *Journal of Library History* 16, no. 1 (winter 1981).

6. Gunther Barth, City People (New York: Oxford University Press, 1980), 21; Lawrence W. Levine, *Highbrow/Lowbrow: The Emergence of Cultural Hierarchy in America* (Cambridge: Harvard University Press, 1988), 176.

7. Robert C. Toll, *Blacking Up* (New York: Oxford University Press, 1974), 4.

8. Madelon Powers, "Decay from Within: The Inevitable Doom of the American Saloon," in *Drinking,* ed. Susanna Barnes and Robin Room (Berkeley: University of California Press, 1991), 113.

9. Roy Rosenwieg, *Eight Hours for What We Will* (New York: Cambridge University Press, 1983), 103.

10. Ruth Bordin, *Women and Temperance* (Philadelphia: Temple University Press, 1981), 5.

11. John Frick, " 'He Drank from the Poisoned Cup': Theatre, Culture and Temperance in Antebellum America," *Journal of American Drama and Theatre* 4, no. 2 (spring 1992): 32.

12. John Kasson, *Amusing the Million: Coney Island at the Turn of the Century* (New York: Hill and Wang, 1978), 4; Stuart Ewen and Elizabeth Ewen, *Channels*

*of Desire: Mass Images and the Shaping of American Consciousness* (New York: McGraw-Hill, 1982), 15, 30.

13. Toll, *Blacking Up,* 10.

14. Claudia D. Johnson, "That Guilty Third Tier: Prostitution in Nineteenth Century American Theatres," in *Victorian America,* ed. Daniel Walker Howe (Philadelphia: University of Pennsylvania Press, 1976), 113.

15. Levine, *Highbrow/Lowbrow,* 31; Paul DiMaggio, "Cultural Entrepreneurship in Nineteenth Century Boston," in *Rethinking Popular Culture,* ed. Chandra Mukerji and Michael Schudson (Berkeley: University of California Press, 1991), 374–75.

16. Brooks McNamara, " 'A Congress of Wonders': The Rise and Fall of the Dime Museum," *Emerson Society Quarterly* 20 (3rd Quarter 1974): 219.

17. Don Wilmeth, *Variety Entertainment and Outdoor Amusements* (Westport, Conn.: Greenwood, 1982), 95.

18. Kasson, *Amusing the Million,* 4.

19. Ibid., 101.

20. Ibid., 6.

21. Susan Porter Benson, Stephen Brier, and Roy Rosenzweig, eds., *Presenting the Past: Essays on History and the Public* (Philadelphia: Temple University Press, 1986), xvii, xix.

22. Moses Kimball's Boston Museum was an exception. Kimball was very civic-minded and mounted a display titled "The Horror of Slavery."

23. Barth, *City People,* 65.

24. T. Allston Brown, *A History of the New York Stage* (New York: Benjamin Bloom, 1964), 592.

25. See A. H. Saxon, *Selected Letters of P. T. Barnum* (New York: Columbia University Press, 1983), for the correspondence between Kimball and Barnum.

26. Ibid., 12; the "General" is General Tom Thumb.

27. P. T. Barnum was known as the "prince of humbugs" for his out-and-out lies and exaggerations about his museum exhibits.

28. Star Museum advertisement, 1889; Austin and Stone's letterhead, n.d.; New York Museum of Anatomy advertisement, n.d., New York Public Library for the Performing Arts.

29. Toll, *Blacking Up,* 21.

30. Paul G. Sifton, "Pierre Eugène Du Simitière (1737–1784): Collector in Revolutionary America" (Ph.D. diss., University of Pennsylvania, 1960), 35; Orosz, "Curators and Culture," 64.

31. The Charleston Museum (1774–78), instituted under the auspices of the town library, was destroyed by a fire. Although it is considered the first attempt at establishing an American museum of natural history, for my purposes I consider it a prerevolutionary museum.

32. Sifton, "Pierre Eugène Du Simitière," 10.

33. Ibid., 23, 454, 464.

34. Ibid., 37.

35. Sellers, *Mr. Peale's Museum,* 12.

36. Orosz, "Curators and Culture," 51, 52; Sifton, "Pierre Eugène Du Simitière," 445.

37. Dillon Ripley, *The Sacred Grove* (Washington, D.C.: Smithsonian Institution Press, 1969), 35.

38. Kenneth Hudson, *A Social History of Museums* (Atlantic Highlands, N.J.: Humanities Press, 1975), 38–39.

39. Ibid., 10.

40. Orosz, "Curators and Culture," 66; Sifton, "Pierre Eugène Du Simitière," 450.

41. Hudson, *Social History of Museums,* 35; these items were collected between 1790 and 1792.

42. Orosz, "Curators and Cultures," 150.

43. Sellers, *Mr. Peale's Museum,* 28.

44. Due to poor eyesight, Rubens Peale did not become a painter, as did many of his siblings; he became a museum man instead.

45. Sellers, *Mr. Peale's Museum,* 215.

46. Catha Grace Rambusch, "Museums and Other Collections in New York City, 1790–1870" (M.A. thesis, New York University, 1965), 37; Odell, *Annals of the New York Stage,* 3:294.

47. Odell, *Annals of the New York Stage,* 3:475, 367.

48. In 1839, the board of trustees of Peale's New York Museum applied for incorporation under a new name, the New York Museum of Natural History and Science.

49. Saxon, *Selected Letters of P. T. Barnum,* 14–15.

50. Robert M. McClung and Gale S. McClung, "Tammany's Remarkable Gardiner Baker," *New-York Historical Society Quarterly* 42 (April 1958): 146.

51. Program, American Museum, 1 June 1791, New-York Historical Society.

52. McClung and McClung, "Tammany's Remarkable Gardiner Baker," 148.

53. Broadside, 25 November 1793, New-York Historical Society.

54. McClung and McClung, "Tammany's Remarkable Gardiner Baker," 152.

55. Ibid., 143.

56. *New York Herald,* 29 September 1794; McClung and McClung, "Tammany's Remarkable Gardiner Baker," 155.

57. McClung and McClung, "Tammany's Remarkable Gardiner Baker," 152.

58. Ibid., 156.

59. Ibid., 156. Peale wrote that he believed the collection was given to Baker as payment of back wages.

60. Loyd Haberly, "The American Museum from Baker to Barnum," *New-York Historical Society Quarterly* 43, no. 3 (July 1959): 275, 276.

61. McClung and McClung, "Tammany's Remarkable Gardiner Baker," 168.

62. Haberly, "American Museum from Baker to Barnum," 278.

63. Ibid.

64. Ibid., 279.

**158** 65. Odell, *Annals of the New York Stage,* 2:566.

66. John Scudder, *A Companion to the American Museum* (New York: G. F. Hopkins, 1823), New-York Historical Society.

67. Haberly, "American Museum from Baker to Barnum," 283–84.

68. Rambusch, "Museums and Other Collections," 42.

69. Even though John Scudder, Jr. did not finish medical school, he was known as Dr. Scudder.

70. Haberly, "American Museum from Baker to Barnum," 286.

71. Louis Leonard Tucker, " 'Ohio Show-Shop': The Western Museum of Cincinnati 1820–1867," in *A Cabinet of Curiosities: Five Episodes in the Evolution of American Museums,* ed. Whitfield J. Bell Jr. (Charlottesville: University Press of Virginia, 1967), 73.

72. Ibid., 72, 75.

73. Elizabeth R. Kellogg, "Joseph Dorfeuille and the Western Museum," *Journal of the Cincinnati Society of Natural History* 22 (April 1945): 22. It was not uncommon for universities to support museums. In the East, Harvard had already established the University Museum (1784) and Yale the Peabody Museum (1802).

74. Tucker, " 'Ohio Show-Shop,' " 84.

75. Ibid., 89. According to Odell, laughing gas was offered at a lecture given at the Chatham Museum in New York in 1830.

76. Tucker, " 'Ohio Show-Shop,' " 85.

77. Haberly, "American Museum from Baker to Barnum," 287.

NOTES TO CHAPTER 2

1. Neil Harris, *Humbug: The Art of P. T. Barnum* (Chicago: University of Chicago Press, 1973), 57. Harris uses the word "aesthetic"; he believes that Barnum's techniques involved a "philosophy of taste."

2. Catalog, American Museum, n.d., Special Collections Department, Adelphi University.

3. Phineas T. Barnum, *Struggles and Triumphs; or, The Life of P. T. Barnum, Written by Himself* (1869), 107.

4. Edward K. Spann, *The New Metropolis* (New York: Columbia University Press, 1891), 23.

5. David Nasaw, *Going Out* (New York: Basic Books, 1993), 4.

6. Brooks McNamara, " 'A Congress of Wonders': The Rise and Fall of the Dime Museum," *Emerson Society Quarterly* 20 (3rd Quarter 1974): 218.

7. George C. D. Odell, *Annals of the New York Stage* (New York: Columbia University Press, 1927–49), 5:58.

8. Irving Wallace, *The Fabulous Showman* (New York: Knopf, 1959), 77.

9. A. H. Saxon, *P. T. Barnum: The Legend and the Man* (New York: Columbia University Press, 1989), 108.

10. Barnum, *Struggles and Triumphs,* 96.

11. Ibid., 97.

12. Barnum's obituary, *New York Herald,* 7 April 1891; Neil Harris, in his biography, claimed that it was fifteen months before Barnum paid back his loan. Yet Barnum, in *Struggles and Triumphs,* claimed that it took him only twelve months (12). As we know, Barnum tended to exaggerate, and I trust Harris's meticulous research skills.

13. Odell, *Annals of the New York Stage,* 6:74.

14. William W. Appleton, "The Marvelous Museum of P. T. Barnum," *Revue d'Histoire du Théâtre* 15 ( January–March 1963): 61.

15. Robert C. Toll, *On with the Show* (New York: Oxford University Press, 1976), 34.

16. Saxon, *P. T. Barnum,* 74; James B. Twitchell, *Carnival Culture* (New York: Columbia University Press, 1992), 61, 63.

17. An accounting of tickets sold for various Barnum enterprises as compiled by Barnum, 1879. Unidentified clipping, n.d., New York Public Library for the Performing Arts.

18. Even Moses Kimball had trepidations about displaying such a fraudulent exhibit.

19. Saxon, *P. T. Barnum,* 121; Joseph Bryan, *P. T. Barnum: The World's Greatest Showman* (New York: Random House, 1956), 64. Bryan gives the following statistics: $3,341 was earned during the first four weeks the mermaid was exhibited, compared with $1,272 in revenue the four weeks before the mermaid's arrival.

20. A. H. Saxon, *Selective Letters of P. T. Barnum* (New York: Columbia University Press, 1983), 39.

21. Ibid., 111.

22. Harris, *Humbug: The Art of P. T. Barnum,* 77.

23. Saxon, *P. T. Barnum,* 120–21.

24. Phineas T. Barnum, *The Humbugs of the World* (New York: Carleton, 1866), 259.

25. Ibid., 270.

26. Harris, *Humbug: The Art of P. T. Barnum,* 77.

27. Barnum, *Humbugs of the World,* 12.

28. Robert Bogdan, *Freak Show: Presenting Human Oddities for Amusement and Profit* (Chicago: University of Chicago Press, 1988). Johnson, also known as "Zip," had one of the longest successful careers of any sideshow attraction, from

1860 to his death in 1926. The name "Zip," according Bogdan, came from "Zip Coon," a figure in early minstrel music shows. See James W. Cook Jr., "Of Men, Missing Links, and Nondescripts: The Strange Career of P. T. Barnum's 'What is It?' Exhibition," in *Freakery: Cultural Spectacles of the Extraordinary Body,* ed. Rosemarie Garland Thomson (New York: New York University Press, 1996), 139–57.

29. Unidentified clipping, n.d., New York Public Library for the Performing Arts.

30. All descriptions were obtained from illustrated guidebooks to Barnum's American Museum stored in the New York Public Library for the Performing Arts, the Special Collections Department at Adelphi University Library, and the New-York Historical Society. The date of the Adelphi book is not known, but it was probably printed in the 1860s. The book at the New York Public Library also had no date, but I am fairly certain it is a duplicate of the one at the New-York Historical Society, which was published in 1850. There is a small book at the New-York Historical Society, titled *Sights and Wonders in New York,* that contains a description of the American Museum in 1849. Before Barnum's $50,000 worth of renovations, spectators were forced to go immediately upstairs on entering.

31. Because of the rapidly changing nature of many of the exhibits, it is difficult to give a comprehensive look at the American Museum. The dates of most of the guidebooks can only be guessed. After Barnum's major renovations were completed, the museum contained six rooms for viewing his collection: one on the ground floor, three on the second floor, and one each on the third, fourth, and fifth floors. In the 1860s, Barnum moved his wax displays into the Cosmorama room and placed the Cosmorama Department on the fifth floor.

32. Catalog, American Museum, n.d., Special Collections Department, Adelphi University.

33. Barnum's "American Museum Illustrated," n.d., New York Public Library for the Performing Arts.

34. Saxon, *Selected Letters of P. T. Barnum,* 43.

35. Barnum's obituary, *New York Herald,* 7 April 1891; Barnum's "American Museum Illustrated," 1850, New-York Historical Society.

36. The American Museum's first production of *Uncle Tom's Cabin* was presented on November 7, 1853. Subsequent productions were mounted in 1855, 1858, 1865, 1866, and 1868.

37. Freaks were often cast as midgets and giants in plays performed in the lecture room. A more detailed discussion of these performances occurs in chapter 4.

38. "The Grand Aquaria at Barnum's!" n.d., New York Public Library for the Performing Arts.

39. Christine Stansell, *City of Women* (New York: Alfred A. Knopf, 1986), 83–86.

40. Nasaw, *Going Out,* 26.

41. Kathy Peiss, *Cheap Amusements* (Philadelphia: Temple University Press, 1986), 163.

42. Gunther Barth, *City People* (New York: Oxford University Press, 1980), 129.

43. Spann, *New Metropolis,* 94–103.

44. Wallace, *The Fabulous Showman,* 154.

45. Barnum, *Struggles and Triumphs,* 241.

46. Saxon, *P. T. Barnum,* 196; see 199–205 for a discussion of Barnum's finances. Apparently, Barnum overleveraged himself before the clock scandal; Saxon postulates that he sold his museum in anticipation of his financial troubles.

47. *New York Herald,* 19 September 1883.

48. Barnum, *Struggles and Triumphs,* 350.

49. Barnum's "American Museum Illustrated," 1850, New-York Historical Society.

50. Broadside, Barnum's New Museum, 2 September 1865, New-York Historical Society.

51. Saxon, *P. T. Barnum,* 109.

52. T. Allston Brown, *A History of the New York Stage* (New York: Benjamin Bloom, 1964), 2:523, 526, 541.

53. "Prospectus of Barnum's Museum Company," n.d., clipping file, New York Public Library of the Performing Arts.

54. Barnum, *Struggles and Triumphs,* 115.

NOTES TO CHAPTER 3

1. *Cincinnati Billboard,* 28 December 1928, 98–99; George Middleton, *Circus Memoirs* (Los Angeles: George Rice, 1913), 68.

2. Program, Ninth and Arch Museum, 3 April 1889, Free Library of Philadelphia.

3. *Cincinnati Billboard,* 28 December 1928, 98–99.

4. Joseph Jackson, ed., *The Encyclopedia of Philadelphia* (Philadelphia: National Historical Association, 1931).

5. Program, European Museum, n.d., Free Library of Philadelphia.

6. Ibid.

7. Perry R. Duis and Glen E. Holt, "Chicago As It Was: Cheap Thrills and Dime Museums," *Chicago* 26, no. 10 (October 1977): 106. Colonel Joseph H. Wood is the same man who operated the Philadelphia Wood's Museum twenty years later. The New York Wood's Museum was operated by George Wood.

8. "Journal and Program of the Letter Carriers' Association of Chicago," 1889, clipping file, Chicago Historical Society.

9. John Barron, "It's Like This," n.p., n.d., Chicago Historical Society.

10. Ibid.

11. See George C. D. Odell, *Annals of the New York Stage,* vol. 5 (New York: Columbia University Press, 1927–49).

12. Program, Hope Chapel, 1860, New York Public Library for the Performing Arts.

13. "A Visit to the Eden Musée," published in connection with the Dewey celebration, 28–30 September 1899, Museum of the City of New York; "The Eden Musée's Twenty-fifth Anniversary," *Saturday Evening Mail,* 22 February 1908.

14. "A Visit to the Eden Musée."

15. See Odell, *Annals of the New York Stage,* vols. 12–14.

16. Ibid., 13:338; "The Eden Musée Is Thirty Years Old," *New York Times,* 5 April 1914.

17. "A Visit to the Eden Musée."

18. Henry Collins Brown, *Valentine's Manual of Old New York* (New York: Valentine's Manual, 1926), 12:194.

19. A number of guidebooks or monthly catalogs to the Eden Musée are available at the New-York Historical Society as well as the Theatre Collection at the New York Public Library. Specifically, I was able to view guidebooks from the years 1884, 1885, 1886, 1887, 1890, 1897, 1898, 1899, 1905, 1906, 1907, and 1909.

20. Guidebook, Eden Musée and Chamber of Horrors, Boston, n.d., private collection of Brooks McNamara, 3.

21. Odell, *Annals of the New York Stage,* 12:539; guidebook, Eden Musée, 1885, New-York Historical Society, New York Public Library for the Performing Arts.

22. "A Visit to the Eden Musée."

23. Ibid.

24. Luc Sante writes in *Low Life* (New York: Farrar, Straus and Giroux, 1991) that Ajeeb was a pseudo-automaton and that a dwarf inhabited his body. This is the first account I have read that postulates this theory pertaining to Ajeeb. However, the obituary of Peter J. Hill from the *Sun* on January 24, 1929, claimed that Hill was concealed inside Ajeeb. Ajeeb first appeared at the Eden Musée in the 1884–85 season.

25. Odell, *Annals of the New York Stage,* 13:123. By 1889 all the guidebooks illustrate that the Sacred Chamber was replaced by the Historical Chamber.

26. Guidebook, Eden Musée, 1898, New-York Historical Society; Odell, *Annals of the New York Stage,* 13:337.

27. "A Visit to the Eden Musée."

28. Ibid.

29. "Kemmler's Death by Torture," *New York Herald,* 7 August 1890.

30. Guidebooks, Eden Musée, 1898, 1899, 1905, 1909, New-York Historical Society, New York Public Library for the Performing Arts; "A Visit to the Eden Musée."

31. "A Visit to the Eden Musée."

32. Edward K. Spann, *The New Metropolis* (New York: Columbia University Press, 1981), 91.

33. Ibid., 92.

34. Susan D. Moeller, "The Cultural Construction of Urban Poverty: Images of Poverty in New York City, 1890–1917," *Journal of American Culture* 18, no. 4 (winter 1995): 3, 7.

35. Guidebook, Eden Musée, November 1887, New-York Historical Society.

36. Guidebook, Boston Eden Musée, n.d., private collection of Brooks McNamara.

37. Barnum's "American Museum Illustrated," n.d., New York Public Library for the Performing Arts.

38. Claire McGlinchee, *The First Decade of the Boston Museum* (Boston: Bruce Humphries, 1940), 21.

39. "A Visit to the Eden Musée"; guidebook, Eden Musée, 1885, New-York Historical Society, New York Public Library for the Performing Arts.

40. "Eden Musée Is Thirty Years Old."

41. Charles Musser, "The Eden Musée in 1898: The Exhibitor as Creator," *Film and History* 11, no. 4 (December 1981): 77.

42. "Eden Musée Is Thirty Years Old."

43. Unidentified clipping, n.d., Museum of the City of New York.

44. *Cincinnati Billboard,* 8 December 1928, 98–99.

45. Alvin F. Harlow, *Old Bowery Days* (New York: D. Appleton, 1931), 378–79.

46. John Frick, *New York's First Theatrical Center: The Rialto at Union Square* (Ann Arbor, Mich.: UMI Research Press, 1985), 93.

47. Ibid.

48. Odell, *Annals of the New York Stage,* 10:704; see Frick, *New York's First Theatrical Center,* 109, for different location at 109 Bowery.

49. Odell, *Annals of the New York Stage,* 11:364.

50. Guidebook, Eden Musée, November 1887. He must have been semiretired, because I ran across a program dated January 15, 1900, for G. B. Bunnell's Grand Opera House located at 206–10 Meadow Street in New Haven, Connecticut.

51. *New York Recorder,* 17 July 1910.

52. Frick, *New York's First Theatrical Center,* 98.

53. Odell, *Annals of the New York Stage,* 14:127. See my discussion on variety, vaudeville, and the dime museums in chapter 5.

54. Frick, *New York's First Theatrical Center,* 102; Odell, *Annals of the New York Stage,* 14:673.

55. Odell, *Annals of the New York Stage,* 15:155, 158.

56. "Huber's Museum in the Discard," *New York Telegraph,* 17 July 1910.

57. Odell, *Annals of the New York Stage,* 15:149.

58. Ibid., 15:150.

59. Ibid.; this story reminds one of Kafka's *Hunger Artist,* whose central character is on "exhibition" as he attempts to go without food for a record length of time. Of course the irony is that in order to achieve the goal, "the ultimate fast," one has to die, as did both the fictitious hunger artist and Mr. Stratton.

60. Odell, *Annals of the New York Stage,* 15:167

61. Ibid., 15:169; T. Allston Brown, *A History of the New York Stage* (New York: Benjamin Blomm, 1964), 2: 591.

62. Odell, *Annals of the New York Stage,* 14:409.

63. Ibid., 14:130. On July 28, 1895, the *Clipper* announced that George Huber had purchased Doris's Eighth Avenue Museum and would open it on August 19 as Huber's Mammoth Eighth Avenue Museum.

64. Ibid., 14:671.

65. Brown, *Valentine's Manual of Old New York,* 264.

66. Odell, *Annals of the New York Stage,* 13:532.

67. Harlow, *Old Bowery Days,* 479.

68. Ibid.

69. Jordan and Beck claimed to be members of the Royal College of Surgeons in London. Guidebook, New York Museum of Anatomy, 1863, New-York Historical Society.

70. A similar embryology exhibit, titled "Prenatal Development," can be seen today at Chicago's Museum of Science and Industry. This exhibit originated at the 1933–34 Chicago World's Fair.

71. Guidebook, New York Museum of Anatomy, 1863, New-York Historical Society.

72. Ibid.

73. Ibid.

74. Brooks McNamara, " 'A Congress of Wonders': The Rise and Fall of the Dime Museum," *Emerson Society Quarterly* 20 (3rd Quarter 1974): 223. Cure-alls were very popular during the mid-nineteenth century. Museum guidebooks were filled with advertisements for such products as "Brandreth's Vegetable Pills" for stomach disorders and "M'Alister's All-Healing Ointment," which supposedly cured tumors, ulcers, sores, piles, burns, and corns.

NOTES TO CHAPTER 4

1. Robert Bogdan, *Freak Show: Presenting Human Oddities for Amusement and Profit* (Chicago: University of Chicago Press, 1988), 9.

2. Gahan Wilson, "Freaks," 25 April 1966, 26, clipping file, New York Public Library for the Performing Arts.

3. Richard Altick, *The Shows of London: A Panoramic History of Exhibitions, 1600–1862* (Cambridge, Mass.: Harvard University Press, 1978), 37.

4. Shakespeare, *The Tempest,* ed. Frank Kermode (London: Methuen, 1954), **165** 2. 2.27–34.

5. Altick, *Shows of London,* 44.

6. Wilson, "Freaks," 26.

7. Felix Isman, *Weber and Fields* (New York: Boni and Liveright, 1924), 50.

8. "Huber's Museum in the Discard," *New York Telegraph,* 17 July 1910.

9. Barry Gray, *Cincinnati Billboard,* 8 December 1928.

10. Weldon B. Durham, ed., *American Theatre Companies* (Westport, Conn.: Greenwood, 1986), 69.

11. George Middleton, *Circus Memoirs* (Los Angeles: George Rice, 1913), 73.

12. Robert C. Toll, *On with the Show* (New York: Oxford University Press, 1976), 279; Walter Bodin and Burnet Hershey, *It's a Small World* (New York: Coward-McCann, 1934), 240; William G. Fitzgerald, "Side-Show III," *Strand Magazine,* June 1897, 3: 521; Wilson, "Freaks," 28.

13. Isman, *Weber and Fields,* 42.

14. Ibid., 44.

15. Bogdan, *Freak Show,* 121, 124.

16. "Barnum and Brady, Pictures from the collection of Frederick Hill Meserve," clipping file, New York Public Library for the Performing Arts; George C. D. Odell, *Annals of the New York Stage* (New York: Columbia University Press, 1927–49), 7:503.

17. See Odell, *Annals of the New York Stage,* vols. 12–16.

18. According to a listing from Odell, when the sisters performed at Doris's museum in 1892, they were billed as twins. I am not certain whether they were twins or whether this was just a bit of old-fashioned humbuggery.

19. Bogdan, *Freak Show,* 247.

20. Although as Wild Men the Davis brothers did not speak, they did speak English offstage.

21. *Sketch of the Life, Personal Appearance, Character and Manners of Charles S. Stratton, the Man in Miniature Known as General Tom Thumb* (New York: Van Norden and Amerman, 1847), 16, New-York Historical Society, New York Public Library for the Performing Arts.

22. *Sketch of the Life of Miss Millie-Christine; or, Christine-Millie,* New York Public Library for the Performing Arts.

23. Alvin Goldfarb, "Gigantic and Minuscule Actors on the Nineteenth-Century American Stage," *Journal of Popular Culture* 10, no. 2 (fall 1976): 270–71.

24. Ibid., 271–73.

25. Rollin Lynde Hartt, *The People at Play* (New York: Arno Press, 1975), 94.

26. B. A. Botkin, *New York City Folklore* (New York: Random House, 1956), 409.

27. Ibid.

28. Odell, *Annals of the New York Stage,* 15:455.

29. Stuart Ewen and Elizabeth Ewen, *Channels of Desire: Mass Images and the Shaping of American Consciousness* (New York: McGraw-Hill, 1982), 13.

30. Bogdan, *Freak Show,* 110, 219; Middleton, *Circus Memoirs,* 70.

31. *Life of the Living Aztec Children* (1860) was forty-eight pages long.

32. Most of the photographs available to scholars are from surviving copies of cartes de visites.

33. Bogdan, *Freak Show,* 13, 104.

34. Frederick Drimmer, *Very Special People: The Struggles, Loves and Triumphs of Human Oddities* (New York: Amjon, 1973), 103; "The Fat Man and His Friends," *American Heritage* 17, no. 4 (June 1966): 36.

35. Similarly, the Hollywood studios used to fabricate love affairs between their stars in order to promote movies.

36. Odell claims that Worth was upset by Coffey's wife soliciting, but his anger might have been an act to cover some action devised by Coffey and Worth together; controversy, as we know from Barnum, breeds profit. John Frick, in his account of the story, claims that Worth was about to sue Coffey for breach of contract.

37. Bogdan, *Freak Show,* 131.

38. P. T. Barnum, *Struggles and Triumphs* (1869), 308.

39. Hector Rosenfeld, "Barnum's First Freaks," *New York Times Magazine,* 22 May 1904.

40. Bogdan, *Freak Show,* 157.

41. Ibid., 297.

42. William G. Fitzgerald, "Side-Show III," gives the following statistics: he weighed 853 pounds and she weighed 553, for a total of 1,406 pounds.

43. Leslie Fiedler, *Freaks: Myths and Images of the Secret Self* (New York: Simon and Schuster, 1978), 214–18.

44. Ibid., 207.

45. See Odell, *Annals of the New York Stage,* vols. 12–15.

46. "The Great Baby Show," *New York Times,* 26 November 1877; "The National Baby Show," *New York Times,* 27 November 1877; "The Babies' Second Day," *New York Times,* 28 November 1877.

47. Don Wilmeth, *American and English Popular Entertainments* (Detroit: Book Tower, 1980), 241.

48. Drimmer, *Very Special People,* 15.

NOTES TO CHAPTER 5

1. Robert C. Allen, "B. F. Keith and the Origins of American Vaudeville," *Theatre Survey* 21, no. 2 (November 1980): 112.

2. Henry Dickinson Stone, *Theatrical Reminiscences* (New York: Benjamin Bloom, 1873), 237.

3. Ibid., 233.

4. Ibid.

5. Claire McGlinchee, *The First Decade of the Boston Museum* (Boston: Bruce Humphries, 1940), 56.

6. Howard Malcom Ticknor, "The Passing of the Boston Museum," *New England Magazine* 27, no. 4 (June 1903): 381–82; McGlinchee, *First Decade of the Boston Museum*, 28.

7. Ticknor, "Passing of the Boston Museum," 383; McGlinchee, *First Decade of the Boston Museum*, 48.

8. McGlinchee, *First Decade of the Boston Museum*, 48.

9. The number of spectators that the museum's theater could accommodate varies from source to source. Most scholars cite 1,200. McGlinchee, *First Decade of the Boston Museum*, 30, 48 (900 or 1,200 spectators); Laurence Senelick, *The Age and Stage of George L. Fox, 1825–1877* (Hanover, NH.: University Press of New England, 1988), 22 (1,200 spectators); Harry Birdhoff, *The World's Greatest Hit: "Uncle Tom's Cabin"* (New York: S. F. Vanni, 1947), 29 (1,200 spectators).

10. McGlinchee, *First Decade of the Boston Museum*, 61.

11. Ibid., 52

12. Ibid., 55

13. Ibid., 49.

14. Ticknor, "Passing of the Boston Museum," 385; McGlinchee, *First Decade of the Boston Museum*, 49–50.

15. McGlinchee, *First Decade of the Boston Museum*, 50.

16. Ibid., 50–51; Weldon B. Durham, ed., *American Theater Companies* (Westport, Conn.: Greenwood, 1986), 68–73.

17. Durham, *American Theater Companies*, 68–69; *Daily Evening Transcript*, 4 November 1846, suggests 1,500 seats, whereas McGlinchee in *The First Decade of the Boston Museum* concludes that there were 600 seats.

18. McGlinchee, *First Decade of the Boston Museum*, 59.

19. Edward W. Mammen, "The Old Stock Company: The Boston Museum and Other Nineteenth Century Theaters," *Bulletin of the Boston Public Library* 19, nos. 1–4 (January–April 1944): 1–5.

20. See McGlinchee, *First Decade of the Boston Museum;* Ticknor, "Passing of the Boston Museum"; Durham, *American Theater Companies.*

21. Mammen, "Old Stock Company," 6–7.

22. McGlinchee, *First Decade of the Boston Museum*, 97–98; Mammen, "Old Stock Company," 59; Ticknor, "Passing of the Boston Museum," 394.

23. George C. D. Odell, *Annals of the New York Stage* (New York: Columbia University Press, 1927–49), 12:338.

24. Mammen, "Old Stock Company," 10; McGlinchee, *First Decade of the Boston Museum*, 108.

25. McGlinchee, *First Decade of the Boston Museum*, 77–87.

26. Ibid., 23.

27. Senelick, *Age and Stage of George L. Fox*, 26.

28. McGlinchee, *First Decade of the Boston Museum*, 73; Jean Linzee, a descendant of the Howard family, wrote in an unpublished manuscript that the Howards were married on October 31, 1844, and that George Howard had joined the Boston Museum company in October 1843.

29. Durham, *American Theater Companies*, 70.

30. Mammen, "Old Stock Company," 29; Durham, *American Theater Companies*, 69.

31. Ticknor, "Passing of the Boston Museum," 390.

32. McGlinchee, *First Decade of the Boston Museum*, 60.

33. Ticknor, "Passing of the Boston Museum," 390.

34. Mammen, "Old Stock Company," 50–51.

35. Durham, *American Theater Companies*, 69; Mammen, "Old Stock Company," 50.

36. Durham, *American Theater Companies*, 70.

37. Mammen, "Old Stock Company," 9–10.

38. Ticknor, "Passing of the Boston Museum," 394.

39. David Grimsted, *Melodrama Unveiled: American Theatre and Culture, 1800–1850* (Chicago: University of Chicago Press, 1968), 97.

40. Mammen, "Old Stock Company," 15.

41. Durham, *American Theater Companies*, 70.

42. Grimsted, *Melodrama Unveiled*, 97.

43. McGlinchee, *First Decade of the Boston Museum*, 49–50.

44. According to an 1849–50 guide book in the New York Public Library for the Performing Arts, benefit performances were excluded from the museum's season pass.

45. Durham, *American Theater Companies*, 70; Grimsted, *Melodrama Unveiled*, 62.

46. Mammen, "Old Stock Company," 51, 62.

47. Judith N. McArthur, "Demon Rum on the Boards: Temperance Melodrama and the Tradition of Antebellum Reform," *Journal of the Early Republic* 9 (winter 1989): 527.

48. Senelick, *Age and Stage of George L. Fox*, 33; McArthur, "Demon Rum," 528.

49. Bruce A. McConachie, "Museum Theatre and the Problem of Respectabil-

ity for Mid-Century Urban Americans," in *The American Stage*, ed. Ron Engle and Tice L. Miller (New York: Cambridge University Press, 1993), 74.

50. John Frick, " 'He Drank From the Poisoned Cup': Theatre, Culture, and Temperance in Antebellum America," *Journal of American Drama and Theatre* 5, no. 2 (spring 1992): 23–24.

51. McArthur, "Demon Rum," 522, 529–38.

52. Mammen, "Old Stock Company," 5.

53. McGlinchee, *First Decade of the Boston Museum*, 24.

54. Grimsted, *Melodrama Unveiled*, 87.

55. Birdhoff, *World's Greatest Hit*, 260–61.

56. Daniel C. Gerould, ed., *American Melodrama* (New York: Performing Arts Journal, 1983), 15.

57. Thomas F. Gossett, *"Uncle Tom's Cabin" and American Culture* (Dallas: Southern Methodist University Press, 1985), 43; Senelick, *Age and Stage of George L. Fox*, 59.

58. Senelick, *Age and Stage of George L. Fox*, 18. Senelick equates these hundred performances with a seven-year run in a New York City theater.

59. Robert C. Toll, *On with the Show* (New York: Oxford University Press, 1976), 153.

60. Senelick, *Age and Stage of George L. Fox*, 27–28. According to Senelick, *Uncle Tom's Cabin* has mistakenly been assumed to have pioneered this innovation.

61. Robert C. Toll, *Blacking Up* (New York: Oxford University Press, 1974), 92.

62. Program for *Uncle Tom's Cabin*, Boston Museum, c. 1880, New York Public Library for the Performing Arts.

63. Odell, *Annals of the New York Stage*, 6:316–17.

64. Birdhoff, *World's Greatest Hit*, 88.

65. Gossett, *"Uncle Tom's Cabin" and American Culture*, 274; Toll, *On with the Show*, 153.

66. Program, New American Museum, 1866, New-York Historical Society; T. Allston Brown, *A History of the New York Stage* (New York: Benjamin Bloom, 1964), 2:5, 8.

67. Brown, *History of the New York Stage*, 3:532.

68. Mammen, "Old Stock Company," 9.

69. Ibid., 10.

70. Brown, *History of the New York Stage*, 2:6.

71. McGlinchee, *First Decade of the Boston Museum*, 134, 140, 145.

72. Grimsted, *Melodrama Unveiled*, 104; McGlinchee, *First Decade of the Boston Museum*, 140.

73. Mammen, "Old Stock Company," 52–55.

74. Ibid., 56, 100.

75. Brown, *History of the New York Stage*, 2:5.

76. Odell, *Annals of the New York Stage*, 6:73.

77. *Illustrated News*, 26 November 1853.

**170**    78. Odell, *Annals of the New York Stage*, 6:249.

79. Program, Wood's Museum, 13 April 1874, New York Public Library for the Performing Arts.

80. Odell, *Annals of the New York Stage*, 10:216. Ada Rehan was a member of the stock company of Wood's Museum before it became Daly's Theatre. She later became the "darling" of Daly's company.

81. Odell, *Annals of the New York Stage*, 5:172.

82. John Frick, *New York's First Theatrical Center: The Rialto at Union Square* (Ann Arbor, Mich.: UMI Research Press, 1985), 94–96.

83. Odell, *Annals of the New York Stage*, 15:172.

84. See Shirley Staples, *Male-Female Comedy Teams in American Vaudeville* (Ann Arbor, Mich.: UMI Research Press, 1984).

85. See Odell, *Annals of the New York Stage*, vol. 15.

86. Douglas Gilbert, *American Vaudeville: Its Life and Times* (1940), 13–14. Hyde and Behman also operated a variety theater in Brooklyn for over fifteen years, beginning in 1877.

87. Brooks McNamara, " 'A Congress of Wonders': The Rise and Fall of the Dime Museum," *Emerson Society Quarterly* 20 (3rd Quarter 1974): 228.

88. Unidentified clipping, n.d., New York Public Library for the Performing Arts.

89. Odell, *Annals of the New York Stage*, 15:734; Felix Isman, *Weber and Fields* (New York: Boni and Liveright, 1924), 27, 45; Armond Fields and L. Marc Fields, *From the Bowery to Broadway: Lew Fields and the Roots of Popular Entertainment* (New York: Oxford University Press, 1993); Allen, "B. F. Keith," 155.

90. Albert F. McLean Jr., "Genesis of Vaudeville: Two Letters from B. F. Keith," *Theatre Survey* 1 (1960): 90.

91. Allen, "B. F. Keith," 106.

92. Program, Austin and Stone's Dime Museum, 28 November 1891, New York Public Library for the Performing Arts.

93. Allen, "B. F. Keith," 106; McLean, "Genesis of Vaudeville," 90–91.

94. McLean, "Genesis of Vaudeville," 91.

95. Allen spells it "Gayety," but according to a 17 May 1885 program, it is spelled "Gaiety"; Albert F. McLean in his article on B. F. Keith spells it "Gaiety" as well.

96. B. F. Keith, "The Vogue of Vaudeville," in *American Vaudeville*, ed. Charles W. Stein (New York: DaCapo Press, 1984), 15.

97. Allen, "B. F. Keith," 112–14.

98. Ibid., 113.

NOTES TO CHAPTER 6

1. Stuart Ewen and Elizabeth Ewen, *Channels of Desire: Mass Images and the Shaping of American Consciousness* (New York: McGraw-Hill, 1982), 171, 176, 258.

2. A. Nicholas Vardac, *From Stage to Screen* (Cambridge: Harvard University Press, 1949), 108–55; Howard Taubman, *The Making of the American Theatre* (New York: Coward-McCann, 1965), 112.

3. John Berger, *Ways of Seeing* (London: British Broadcasting Corporation and Penguin Books, 1972), 10.

4. Umberto Eco, "Travels in Hyperreality," in *Travels in Hyperreality* (New York: Harcourt Brace Jovanovich, 1986), 44.

5. Guidebook, Eden Musée 1899, New-York Historical Society.

6. Alice Elizabeth Chase, *Famous Paintings* (New York: Platt and Munk, 1962), 76; George C. D. Odell, *Annals of the New York Stage* (New York: Columbia University Press, 1927–49), 13:337.

7. A. J. Wall, "Wax Portraiture," *New-York Historical Society Quarterly* 9, no. 1 (April 1925): 16–17.

8. "Museum and Wax-Works," broadside, 25 November 1793, New-York Historical Society.

9. "Travelling Museum," bill, n.d., New-York Historical Society. The date of the flyer falls between 1825 and 1829 since the museum was said to contain a "Portrait Painting of John Quincy Adams, President of the United States."

10. "The Eden Musée's Twenty-fifth Anniversary," *Saturday Evening Mail*, 2 February 1908.

11. "A Visit to the Eden Musée," published in connection with the Dewey Celebration, 28–30 September 1899, Museum of the City of New York.

12. "Concerning Waxworks," *Showman*, 13 December 1901, 218.

13. Pauline Chapman, *Madame Tussaud in England* (London: Quiller Press, 1992), 10.

14. Charles Coleman Sellers, *Patience Wright: American Artist and Spy in George III's London* (Middleton, Conn.: Wesleyan University Press, 1976), 35.

15. Sources vary as to whether or not Curtius really was Marie's uncle.

16. Chapman, *Madame Tussaud in England*, 4.

17. *Madame Tussaud's Illustrated Guide*, 1986, 39, author's collection.

18. *Madame Tussaud's Illustrated Guide*, 1897, 30–31, New York Public Library for the Performing Arts.

19. Louis Leonard Tucker, " 'Ohio Show-Shop': The Western Museum of Cincinnati, 1820–1867," in *A Cabinet of Curiosities: Five Episodes in the Evolution of American Museums*, ed. Whitfield J. Bell Jr. (Charlottesville: University Press of Virginia, 1967), 91.

20. Ibid., 92.

21. Ibid., 91.

22. Powers was hired in 1829 and left in 1834.

23. Tucker, " 'Ohio Show-Shop,' " 96.

24. Ernest Wittenberg, "Échec!" *American Heritage* 11, no. 2 (February
**172** 1960): 84; on April 22, 1827, Maelzel had displayed another of his automatons, the "American Chess Player," at John Scudder's American Museum in New York.

25. Milbourne Christopher, *The Illustrated History of Magic* (New York: Thomas Y. Crowell, 1973), 138.

26. Otis Skinner, *Footlights and Spotlights* (Indianapolis: Bobbs-Merrill, 1924), 14.

27. Ibid., 14, 15.

28. Ibid., 15.

29. Noël Carroll, *The Philosophy of Horror* (New York: Routledge, 1990), 160. I do not agree with every point Carroll makes, but he is one of the few scholars to attempt to analyze the genre of horror. The book discusses only film and fiction, not waxworks.

30. "A Visit to the Eden Musée."

31. During the past decade, television programming has been filled with reenactments of murders and other crimes. The two movies about the Menendez murders, for example, retell the story of how two young men from Beverly Hills killed their parents, allegedly for money. Three television movies were made about Amy Fisher, a young Long Island woman who shot her alleged lover's wife in the face. For months the media devoted hours of news coverage to these stories, and yet the public willingly watched reconstructed events everyone knew about.

32. Tucker, " 'Ohio Show-Shop,' " 86; Program, Ninth and Arch Museum, n.d., Philadelphia Free Library.

33. Henry Collins Brown, ed., *Valentine's Manual of Old New York* (New York: Valentine's Manual, 1927), 194.

34. "A Visit to the Eden Musée."

35. "Life-Like but Only Wax," *New York Saturday News,* 7 January 1891; "Tweaked Caesar's Nose, Pinched Columbus's Ear," n.d., Museum of the City of New York.

36. "Life-like but Only Wax."

37. "Dies at the Feet of Santa He Had Modelled in Wax," unidentified obituary for Constant Thys, n.d., New York Public Library for the Performing Arts.

38. Guidebook, Egyptian Musée, n.d., New York Public Library for the Performing Arts.

39. Ewen and Ewen, *Channels of Desire,* 82.

40. Charles Musser, *Before the Nickelodeon* (Berkeley: University of California Press, 1991), 117.

41. See Charles Musser, *The Emergence of the Cinema: The American Screen to 1907* (New York: Scribner's, 1990); A. R. Fulton, "The Machine," in *The Ameri-*

*can Film Industry,* ed. Tino Balio (Madison: University of Wisconsin Press, 1966), 21–24; Richard Balzer, *Optical Amusements: Magic Lanterns and Other Transforming Images,* exhibition catalog, Museum of Our National Heritage, Lexington, Mass., February 15–October 15, 1987, 67. "Scope" comes from the Greek word for viewer.

**173**

42. Vardac, *From Stage to Screen,* 250.

43. Musser, *Emergence of Cinema,* 234.

44. X. Theodore Barber, "Evenings of Wonders: A History of the Magic Lantern Show in America" (Ph.D. diss., New York University, 1993), 13.

45. Musser, *Emergence of Cinema,* 27.

46. Barber, *Evenings of Wonders,* 30–31.

47. Ibid., 39–40.

48. Ibid., 491.

49. Ibid., 438–41.

50. Ibid., 26–28; Odell, *Annals of the New York Stage,* 2:302.

51. Balzer, *Optical Amusements,* 3; Barber, *Evenings of Wonders,* 29.

52. Balzer, *Optical Amusements,* 64, 76.

53. Musser, *Emergence of Cinema,* 109.

54. See Musser, *Emergence of Cinema;* Charles Musser, "The American Vitagraph, 1897–1901: Survival and Success in a Competitive Industry," in *Film before Griffith,* ed. John L. Fell (Berkeley: University of California Press, 1983).

55. Robert C. Allen, "Contra the Chaser Theory," in *Film before Griffith,* ed. Fell, 105.

56. Robert C. Allen, "Vitascope/Cinématographe: Initial Patterns of American Film Industrial Practice," in *Film before Griffith,* ed. Fell, 148.

57. Ibid., 152. When Edison applied for his American patent on August 24, 1891, he decided not to spend the extra $150 for a foreign application. In July 1901, however, a judge gave Edison a virtual monopoly on film production.

58. Musser, *Before the Nickelodeon,* 117.

59. Ibid., 118, 142.

60. Ibid., 124.

61. Charles Musser, "The Early Cinema of Edwin Porter," *Cinema Journal* 19, no. 1 (winter 1979): 4, 5.

62. Musser, *Before the Nickelodeon,* 135.

63. Ibid., 135, 137; Musser, *Emergence of Cinema,* 258–59.

64. Musser, *Before the Nickelodeon,* 142–43.

65. Linda Kowall, "Siegmund Lubin: The Forgotten Filmmaker," *Pennsylvania Heritage* 12, no. 1 (winter 1986): 18.

66. Letter from Geraldine Duclow, head Librarian at the Theatre Collection, Philadelphia Free Library; Musser, *Emergence of the Cinema,* 236, 285; Anthony Slide, *Early American Cinema* (Metuchen, N.J.: Scarecrow Press, 1994), 19.

67. Musser, *Before the Nickelodeon,* 142.

NOTES TO CHAPTER 7

1. Paul Boyer, *Urban Masses and Moral Order 1820–1920* (Cambridge: Harvard University Press, 1978), 238–39; Neil Harris, *Humbug: The Art of P. T. Barnum* (Chicago: University of Chicago Press, 1973), 185; Roy Rosenzweig, *Eight Hours for What We Will* (New York: Cambridge University Press, 1983), 179.

2. Foster Rhea Dulles, *A History of Recreation: America Learns to Play* (New York: D. Appleton-Century Company, 1940), 293.

3. Charles Musser, *Before the Nickelodeon* (Berkeley: University of California Press, 1991), 428–32

4. Dulles, *History of Recreation,* 290.

5. Stuart Ewen and Elizabeth Ewen, *Channels of Desire: Mass Images and the Shaping of American Consciousness* (New York: McGraw-Hill, 1982), 212.

6. John Kasson, *Amusing the Million: Coney Island at the Turn of the Century* (New York: Hill and Wang, 1978), 3, 8; Andrea Stulman Dennett and Nina Warnke, "Disaster Spectacles at the Turn of the Century," *Film History* 4 (1990): 101; Kathy Peiss, *Cheap Amusements* (Philadelphia: Temple University Press, 1986), 129.

7. Richard Snow, *Coney Island: A Postcard Journey to the City of Fire* (New York: Brightwaters Press, 1984), 63; Peiss, *Cheap Amusements,* 132–36.

8. Kasson, *Amusing the Million,* 73.

9. Ibid.

10. Snow, *Coney Island,* 100. From 1893 to 1898 Gumpertz was promoting a variety of amusements in St. Louis. He helped Harry Houdini, who was a struggling dime museum entertainer. Alva Johnston, "Profiles: Boss of the Big Top," *New Yorker,* 13 May 1933.

11. Alva Johnston, "Profiles: Boss of the Circus," *New Yorker,* 6 April 1933.

12 Robert Bogdan, *Freak Show: Presenting Human Oddities for Amusement and Profit* (Chicago: University of Chicago Press, 1988), 56.

13. Edo McCullough, *Good Old Coney Island* (New York: Scribner's, 1957), 258, 265.

14. Peiss, *Cheap Amusements,* 125.

15. Bogdan, *Freak Show,* 38.

16. Robert Snyder, *The Voice of the City* (New York: Oxford University Press, 1989), xv.

17. "Ripley Gleans Curious Facts on Every Hand," *New York Times,* 27 December 1934.

18. "Ripley's Show Boasts 25 Wonders," *New York Times,* 26 December 1934; "5,000 Enjoy Ripley's Odditorium at Opening of Show Here," *Washington Times,* 5 January 1934.

19. Guidebook, Ripley's Believe It or Not! 44.

20. William Allen, "Believe It or Not! Even Though Robert Ripley Died in 1949, His Feature Still Appears in 328 Newspapers in 38 Countries!!!" *Saturday Review,* February 1973, 49.

21. Ibid., 51.

22. *Billboard,* 12 March 1932, 44.

**175**

23. "Max Schaffer, 83, Who Operated Hubert's Museum Arcade, Dies," *New York Times,* 15 February 1974; O. O. McIntyre, "New York Day by Day," n.d., New York Public Library for the Performing Arts.

24. Stanley Carr, "Notes: Wax Museums Are Not on the Wane," *New York Times,* 17 August 1975.

25. Brooks McNamara, " 'A Congress of Wonders': The Rise and Fall of the Dime Museum," *Emerson Society Quarterly* 20 (3rd quarter 1974): 230.

26. Oliver Pilat and Jo Ranson, *Sodom by the Sea* (Garden City, N.Y.: Doubleday, Doran and Company, 1941), 206.

27. Ann Jones, *Women Who Kill* (New York: Holt, Rinehart and Winston, 1980), 260–61.

28. McCullough, *Good Old Coney Island,* 266.

29. Carr, "Notes."

30. Guidebook, Musée Conti, n.d., New York Public Library for the Performing Arts.

31. Randy Mink, "Movie Stars Cast in Wax Entertain Florida Tourists," *New York Post,* 5 August 1980.

32. "Wax Figures in Black Cut Chains of Stereotypes," *New York Times,* 28 December 1988; Mel Tapley, "Visit Raven Chanticleer's Wax Museum," *New York Amsterdam News,* 4 December 1993.

33. "Wax Figures in Black."

34. Souvenir guidebook, Guinness World of Records, author's collection.

35. Lucia Zarate was only twenty inches tall, even smaller than Pauline Muster.

36. Souvenir guidebook, Guinness World of Records, author's collection.

37. Bogdan, *Freak Show,* 11.

38. Frederick Drimmer, *Very Special People: The Struggles, Loves and Triumphs of Human Oddities* (New York: Amjon, 1973), 233; Bogdan, *Freak Show,* 158.

39. A. H. Saxon, ed., *The Autobiography of Mrs. Tom Thumb* (Hamden, Conn.: Archon Books, 1979), 170–72.

40. George C. D. Odell, *Annals of the New York Stage* (New York: Columbia University Press, 1927–49), 14:133.

41. R. Reid Badger, *The Great American Fair* (Chicago: Nelson Hall, 1979), 131.

42. Pilat and Ranson, *Sodom by the Sea,* 179.

43. Robert Lewis Taylor, "Profiles: Talker-II," *New Yorker,* 26 April 1958.

44. Janice Paran, "Home Is Where Their Art Is," *American Theater,* October 1992, 34.

45. Douglas Martin, "The Rebirth of a Sideshow at Coney Island," *New York Times*, 4 September 1992.

46. Fred Siegel, "Theater of Guts: An Exploration of the Sideshow Aesthetic," *Drama Review* 35, no. 4 (winter 1991): 108.

**176**   47. Ibid.

48. Tom Singman, "Navel Maneuvers," *New York Times Magazine*, 22 January 1995, 20.

49. Stace Maples, "Viewpoint," *Piercing Fans International Quarterly*, no. 42 (1995): 3.

50. Advertisement, *Piercing Fans International Quarterly*, no. 42, 34.

51. "Dos & Don'ts," *Glamour*, January 1995, 112.

52. François Pluchart, "Risk as the Practice of Thought," in *The Art of Performance*, ed. Gregory Battick and Robert Nickas (New York: Dutton, 1984), 127.

53. C. Carr, "Unspeakable Practices Unnatural Acts: The Taboo Art of Karen Finley," *Village Voice*, 24 June 1986.

54. Linda Frye Burnham, "*High Performance*, Performance Art, and Me," *Drama Review* 30, no. 1 (Spring 1986): 15.

55. James B. Twitchell, *Carnival Culture* (New York: Columbia University Press, 1992), 224, 225, 243.

## NOTES TO THE EPILOGUE

1. Robert Bogdan, *Freak Show: Presenting Human Oddities for Amusement and Profit* (Chicago: University of Chicago Press, 1988), 9.

2. See Bruce A. McConachie, "Museum Theatre and the Problem of Respectability for Mid-Century Urban Americans," in *The American Stage*, ed. Ron Engle and Tice L. Miller (New York: Cambridge University Press, 1993).

3. Neil Harris, *Humbug: The Art of P. T. Barnum* (Chicago: University of Chicago Press, 1973), 286.

4. *Disneyland: The First Thirty Years* (Los Angeles: Walt Disney Productions, 1985), 115.

5. James H. Bierman, "Disney's *America Sings*," *Drama Review* 20, no. 2 (June 1976): 67.

6. Randy Bright, *Disneyland: The Inside Story* (New York: Harry Abrams, 1987), xiv.

7. *Disneyland: The First Thirty Years*, 84, 104.

8. McConachie, "Museum Theatre and the Problem of Respectability," 76.

9. Michael Wallace, "The Politics of Public History," in *Past Meets Present*, ed. Jo Blatti (Washington, D.C.: Smithsonian Institution Press, 1987), 44.

10. Michael Wallace, "Mickey Mouse History: Portraying the Past at Disney World," *Radical History Review* 32 (1985): 37.

11. Harris, *Humbug: The Art of P. T. Barnum*, 292.

12. Kate F. Stover, "Is It *Real* History Yet? An Update on Living History Museums," *Journal of American Culture* 12, no. 2 (summer 1989): 15. The situation at Williamsburg has been partially rectified: an assistant director for African American programs has been hired to help interpret the colonial black experience.

177

13. Fergus M. Bordewich, "Williamsburg: Revising Colonial America," *Atlantic Monthly* 262, no. 6 (December 1988): 31.

14. Richard Schechner, "Restoration of Behavior," in *Between Theatre and Anthropology* (Philadelphia: University of Pennsylvania Press, 1985), 35. The debate between museum professionals and academic historians on the best way to present history is lengthy and continuing.

15. Robert Rydell, *All the World's A Fair* (Chicago: University of Chicago Press, 1984), 4.

16. Brett Pulley, "Tussaud's and Movie Chain Join Disney in 42d Street Project," *New York Times*, 16 July 1995.

17. Paul Goldberger, "The New Times Square: Magic That Surprised the Magicians," *New York Times*, 15 October 1996.

18. Loyd Haberly, "The American Museum from Baker to Barnum," *New-York Historical Society Quarterly* 43, no. 3 (July 1959): 284.

# Selected Bibliography

Adams, T. R. "The Museum and Popular Culture." New York: American Association for Adult Education, 1939.

Alden, W. L. *Among the Freaks.* New York: Logmans, Green, and Company, 1896.

Allen, Robert C. "B. F. Keith and the Origins of American Vaudeville." *Theatre Survey* 21, no. 2 (November 1980): 105–15.

———. "Contra the Chaser Theory." In *Film before Griffith,* edited by John L. Fell, 105–15. Berkeley: University of California Press, 1983.

———. "Vitascope/Cinématographe: Initial Patterns of American Film Industrial Practice." In *Film before Griffith,* edited by John L. Fell, 144–52. Berkeley: University of California Press, 1983.

Allen, William. "Believe It or Not! Even Though Robert Ripley Died in 1949, His Feature Still Appears in 328 Newspapers in 38 Countries!!!" *Saturday Review,* February 1973.

Altick, Richard D. *The Shows of London: A Panoramic History of Exhibitions, 1600–1862.* Cambridge: Harvard University Press, 1978.

Appleton, William W. "The Marvelous Museum of P. T. Barnum." *Revue d'Histoire du Theatre* 15 (January–March 1963): 57–62.

Ardman, Harvey. "Phineas T. Barnum's Charming Beast." *Natural History* 82 (February 1973): 47–57.

"The Babies' Second Day." *New York Times,* 28 November 1877.

Badger, R. Reid. *The Great American Fair.* Chicago: Nelson Hall, 1979.

Ballantine, Bill. *Wild Tigers and Tame Fleas.* New York: Rinehart, 1958.

Balzer, Richard. *Optical Amusements: Magic Lanterns and Other Transforming Images.* Exhibition catalogue, Museum of Our National Heritage, Lexington, Mass., February 15, 1987.

Bank, Rosemarie. "Hustlers in the House: The Bowery Theatre as a Mode of Historical Information." In *The American Stage,* edited by Ron Engle and Tice L. Miller, 47–59. Cambridge: Cambridge University Press, 1993.

Barber, Lynn. *The Heyday of Natural History, 1820–1870.* New York: Doubleday, 1980.

Barber, X. Theodore. "Evenings of Wonders: A History of the Magic Lantern Show in America." Ph.D. diss., New York University, 1993.

Barnum, Phineas T. *The Humbugs of the World.* New York: Carleton, 1866. Reprint, Detroit: Singing Tree Press, 1970.

———. *Struggles and Triumphs; or, The Life of P. T. Barnum, Written by Himself.* 1869. Reprint, New York: Arno Press, 1970.

Barron, John. "It's Like This." N.p., n.d. Chicago Historical Society.

Barth, Gunther. *City People*. New York: Oxford University Press, 1980.

Benson, Susan Porter, Stephen Brier, and Roy Rosenzweig, eds. *Presenting the Past: Essays on History and the Public*. Philadelphia: Temple University Press, 1986.

**180**  Berger, John. *Ways of Seeing*. London: British Broadcasting Corporation and Penguin Books, 1972.

Bierman, James H. "Disney's *America Sings*." *Drama Review* 20, no. 2 (June 1976): 63–72.

Birdhoff, Harry. *The World's Greatest Hit: "Uncle Tom's Cabin"*. New York: S. F. Vanni, 1947.

Bode, Carl. *The Anatomy of American Popular Culture, 1840–1861*. Los Angeles: University of California Press, 1959.

Bodin, Walter, and Burnet Hershey. *It's a Small World*. New York: Coward-McCann, 1934.

Bogdan, Robert. *Freak Show: Presenting Human Oddities for Amusement and Profit*. Chicago: University of Chicago Press, 1988.

Booth, Michael R. "The Drunkard's Progress: Nineteenth Century Temperance Drama." *Dalhousie Review* 44, no. 2 (1964–1965): 205–12.

Bordewich, Fergus M. "Williamsburg: Revising Colonial America." *Atlantic Monthly* 262, no. 6 (December 1988): 26–32.

Bordin, Ruth. *Women and Temperance*. Philadelphia: Temple University Press, 1981.

Botkin, B. A. *New York City Folklore*. New York: Random House, 1956.

Boyer, Paul. *Urban Masses and Moral Order, 1820–1920*. Cambridge: Harvard University Press, 1978.

Bright, Randy. *Disneyland: The Inside Story*. New York: Harry Abrams, 1987.

Brown, Henry Collins, ed. *Valentine's Manual of Old New York*. 16 vols. New York: Valentine's Manual, 1927.

Brown, T. Allston. *A History of the New York Stage*. 3 vols. New York: Benjamin Bloom, 1964.

Bryan, Joseph. *P. T. Barnum: The World's Greatest Showman*. New York: Random House, 1956.

Buckland, F. T. *Curiosities of Natural History*. 4 vols. London: Richard Bentley, 1890.

Burke, Michael. "The Tallest Lady in the World." *Yankee*, November 1988.

Burnham, Linda Frye. "*High Performance*, Performance Art, and Me." *Drama Review* 30, no. 1 (spring 1986): 15–51.

Carmichael, Bill. *Incredible Collectors, Weird Antiques, and Old Hobbies*. Englewood Cliffs, N.J.: Prentice-Hall, 1971.

Carr, C. "Unspeakable Practices Unnatural Acts: The Taboo Art of Karen Finley." *Village Voice*, 24 June 1986.

Carrington, Hereward. *Side-Show and Animal Tricks.* Kansas City, Mo.: Sphinx, 1913.

Carroll, Noël. *The Philosophy of Horror.* New York: Routledge, 1990.

Chapman, Pauline. *Madame Tussaud in England.* London: Quiller Press, 1992.

Chase, Alice Elizabeth. *Famous Paintings.* New York: Platt and Munk, 1962. **181**

Christopher, Milbourne. *The Illustrated History of Magic.* New York: Thomas Y. Crowell, 1973.

Clair, Colin. *Human Curiosities.* New York: Abelard-Schuman, 1968.

Clapp, William W. *A Record of the Boston Stage.* New York: Benjamin Bloom, 1968.

Click, Patricia. *The Spirit of the Times: Amusements in Nineteenth Century Baltimore, Norfolk, and Richmond.* Charlottesville: University Press of Virginia, 1989.

Cole, Catherine. "Sex and Death on Display." *Drama Review* 37, no. 1 (1993): 43–60.

Coleman, Lawrence Vail. *The Museum in America.* 3 vols. Washington, D.C.: American Association of Museums, 1939.

"Concerning Waxworks." *The Showman,* 13 December 1901.

Cook, James W., Jr. "Of Men, Missing Links, and Nondescripts: The Strange Career of P. T. Barnum's 'What Is It?' Exhibition." In *Freakery: Cultural Spectacles of the Extraordinary Body,* edited by Rosemarie Garland Thomson, 139–57. New York: New York University Press, 1996.

Cook, Olive. *Movement in Two Dimensions: A Study of the Animated and Projected Pictures Which Preceded the Invention of Cinematography.* London: Hutchinson, 1963.

Cooperthwaite, Derek R. "Ripley's Believe It or Not! A Guide to the Collection of Oddities and Curiosities." N.p.: Ripley International, 1978.

Cullen, Jim. *The Civil War in Popular Culture.* Washington, D.C.: Smithsonian Institution Press, 1995.

Darrah, William C. *Cartes de Visites in Nineteenth Century Photography.* Philadelphia: Darrah, 1981.

Dennett, Andrea Stulman, and Nina Warnke. "Disaster Spectacles at the Turn of the Century." *Film History* 4 (1990): 101–11.

DiMaggio, Paul. "Cultural Entrepreneurship in Nineteenth Century Boston." In *Rethinking Popular Culture,* edited by Chandra Mukerji and Michael Schudson, 374–97. Berkeley: University of California Press, 1991.

DiMeglio, John E. *Vaudeville U.S.A.* Bowling Green, Oh.: Bowling Green University Press, 1973.

*Disneyland: The First Thirty Years.* Los Angeles: Walt Disney Productions, 1985.

Dizikes, John. "P. T. Barnum: Games and Hoaxing." *Yale Review* 67 (1978): 338–56.

Drimmer, Frederick. *Very Special People: The Struggles, Loves and Triumphs of Human Oddities*. New York: Amjon, 1973.

Duis, Perry R., and Glen E. Holt. "Chicago as It Was: Cheap Thrills and Dime Museums." *Chicago* 26, no. 10 (October 1977).

**182**    Dulles, Foster Rhea. *A History of Recreation: America Learns to Play*. New York: D. Appleton-Century Company, 1940.

Durham, Weldon B., ed. *American Theater Companies*. Westport, Conn.: Greenwood, 1986.

Eco, Umberto. "Travels in Hyperreality." In *Travels in Hyperreality*. New York: Harcourt Brace Jovanovich, 1986.

"The Eden Musée's Twenty-fifth Anniversary." *Saturday Evening Mail*, 22 February 1908.

Edwards, Richard H. *Popular Amusements*. New York: Associated Press, 1915.

Emmerling, Joe Tracy. "The Chain Museum in the Offering." *Billboard*, 28 March 1931.

Erenberg, Lewis. *Steppin' Out*. Westport, Conn.: Greenwood, 1981.

Ewen, Stuart, and Elizabeth Ewen. *Channels of Desire: Mass Images and the Shaping of American Consciousness*. New York: McGraw-Hill, 1982.

"The Fat Man and His Friends." *American Heritage* 17, no. 4 (June 1966): 34–39.

Fell, John L., ed. *Film before Griffith*. Berkeley: University of California Press, 1983.

Ferris, Helen. *Here Comes P. T. Barnum: P. T. Barnum's Own Story*. New York: Harcourt, Brace, 1932.

Fiedler, Leslie. *Freaks: Myths and Images of the Secret Self*. New York: Simon and Schuster, 1978.

Fields, Armond, and L. Marc Fields. *From the Bowery to Broadway: Lew Fields and the Roots of American Popular Entertainment*. New York: Oxford University Press, 1993.

Fitzgerald, William G. "Side-Show I." *Strand Magazine*, March 1897.

———. "Side-Show II." *Strand Magazine*, April 1897.

———. "Side-Show III." *Strand Magazine*, May 1897.

———. "Side-Show III." *Strand Magazine*, June 1897.

———. "Side-Show IV." *Strand Magazine*, July 1897.

———. "Side-Show V." *Strand Magazine*, August 1897.

Frick, John. *New York's First Theatrical Center: The Rialto at Union Square*. Ann Arbor, Mich: UMI Research Press, 1985.

———. "Victims of the Bottle from Printed Page to Gilded Stage: T. P. Taylor's Dramatization of George Cruikshank's Serial Illustration *The Bottle*." In *Performing Arts Resources*, edited by Barbara Naomi Cohen-Stratyner. New York: Theatre Library Association, 1991.

———. " 'He Drank from the Poisoned Cup': Theatre, Culture, and Temperance in Antebellum America." *Journal of American Drama and Theatre* 4, no. 2 (spring 1992): 21–41.

Fulton, A. R. "The Machine." In *The American Film Industry,* edited by Tino Balio. Madison: University of Wisconsin Press, 1966.

Gerould, Daniel C., ed. *American Melodrama.* New York: Performing Arts, 1983.

Gilbert, Douglas. *American Vaudeville: Its Life and Times.* 1940. Reprint, New York: Dover Press, 1968.

Goldberger, Paul. "The New Times Square: Magic That Surprised the Magicians." *New York Times,* 15 October 1996.

Goldfarb, Alvin. "Gigantic and Minuscule Actors on the Nineteenth-Century American Stage." *Journal of Popular Culture* 10, no. 2 (fall 1976): 267–79.

Gorham, Maurice. *Showmen and Suckers: An Excursion on the Crazy Fringe of the Entertainment Worlds.* London: Percival Marshall, 1951.

Gossett, Thomas F. *"Uncle Tom's Cabin" and American Culture.* Dallas: Southern Methodist University Press, 1985.

"The Great Baby Show." *New York Times,* 26 November 1877.

Green, Mabel. "Wax Museum Lacks Horrors." *New York Sun,* 25 April 1940.

Grey, Alex, and Allyson Grey. "Linda Montano and Tehching Hsieh's One Year Art/Life Performance." *High Performance* 7, no. 3 (1984): 24–30.

Grimsted, David. *Melodrama Unveiled: American Theatre and Culture, 1800–1850.* Chicago: University of Chicago Press, 1968.

Gurney, Gene. *America in Wax.* New York: Crown, 1977.

Haberly, Loyd. "The American Museum from Baker to Barnum." *New York Historical Society Quarterly* 43, no. 3 (July 1959): 272–87.

Haines, George W. *Plays, Players and Playgoers! Being Reminiscences of P. T. Barnum and His Museums.* New York: Bruce, Haines, 1874.

Halttunen, Karen. *Confidence Men and Painted Women.* New Haven: Yale University Press, 1982.

Haraway, Donna. "Teddy Bear Patriarchy: Taxidermy in the Garden of Eden, New York City, 1908–1936." *Social Text* 11 (winter 1984): 20–64.

Harlow, Alvin F. *Old Bowery Days.* New York: D. Appleton, 1931.

Harris, Neil. *Humbug: The Art of P. T. Barnum.* Chicago: University of Chicago Press, 1973.

———. "Cultural Institutions and American Modernization." *Journal of Library History* 16, no. 1 (winter 1981): 28–47.

Harrison, Barbara Grizzuti. "Flesh, Food and Fashion." *Mirabella,* January 1995.

Hart, Scott. "How Circus Freaks Are Made." May 1946. Freaks clipping file, New York Public Library for the Performing Arts.

Hartt, Rollin Lynde. *The People at Play.* Boston: Houghton Mifflin, 1909. Reprint, New York: Arno Press, 1975.

183

Havig, Alan. "The Commercial Amusement Audience in Twentieth Century American Cities." *Journal of American Culture* 5, no. 1 (1982): 1–19.

Henderson, Mary C. *The City and the Theatre.* Clifton, N.J.: James T. White, 1973.

Hewitt, Edward Ringwood, and Mary Ashley Hewitt. *The Bowery.* New York: Putnam, 1897.

Hingston, Edward. *The Genial Showman: Being Reminiscent of the Life of Artemus Ward.* New York: Harper and Brothers, 1870.

Howells, W. D. *Literature and Life.* Port Washington, N.Y.: Harper and Brothers, 1902. Reprint, New York: Kennikat, 1968.

"Huber's Museum in the Discard." *New York Telegraph,* 17 July 1910.

Hudson, Kenneth. *A Social History of Museums.* Atlantic Highlands, N.J.: Humanities Press, 1975.

Hutton, Lawrence. *Curiosities of the American Stage.* New York: Harper and Brothers, 1891.

Ireland, Joseph N. *Records of the New York Stage, 1750–1860.* New York: Benjamin Bloom, 1866. Reissued 1966.

Isman, Felix. *Weber and Fields.* New York: Boni and Liveright, 1924.

Isman, Felix, and Wesley W. Stout. "Weber and Fields." *Saturday Evening Post,* 31 May 1924.

Jackson, Joseph, ed. *The Encyclopedia of Philadelphia.* Philadelphia: National Historical Association, 1931.

Johnson, Claudia D. "That Guilty Third Tier: Prostitution in Nineteenth Century American Theatres." In *Victorian America,* edited by Daniel Walker Howe, 111–20. Philadelphia: University of Pennsylvania Press, 1976.

Johnston, Alva. "Profiles: Boss of the Circus." *New Yorker,* 6 April 1933.

———. "Profiles: Boss of the Big Top." *New Yorker,* 13 May 1933.

Jones, Ann. *Women Who Kill.* New York: Holt, Rinehart and Winston, 1980.

"Journal and Program of the Letter Carrier's Association of Chicago." 1889.

Kasson, John. *Amusing the Million: Coney Island at the Turn of the Century.* New York: Hill and Wang, 1978.

Katz, Herbert, and Marjorie Katz. *Museums, U.S.A.* Garden City, N.Y.: Doubleday, 1965.

Keith, B. F. "The Vogue of Vaudeville." In *American Vaudeville,* edited by Charles W. Stein, 15–20. New York: DaCapo Press, 1984.

Kellogg, Elizabeth R. "Joseph Dorfeuille and the Western Museum." *Journal of the Cincinnati Society of Natural History* 22 (April 1945): 3–29.

Kemlo, Karen. *Ripley's Believe It or Not! A Guide.* N.p. Ripley's Entertainment, January 1996.

"Kemmler's Death by Torture." *New York Herald,* 7 August 1890.

Koepp, Stephen. "Do You Believe in Magic." *Time,* 25 April 1988.

Kowall, Linda. "Siegmund Lubin: The Forgotten Filmmaker." *Pennsylvania Heritage* 12, no. 1 (winter 1986): 18–27.

Lambert, William. "Show Life in America." East Point, Ga.: Will Delavoye, 1925.

Lefkon, Wendy, ed. *Birnbaum's Walt Disney World*. New York: Hyperion and Hearst, 1985.

Levine, Lawrence W. *Highbrow/Lowbrow: The Emergence of Cultural Hierarchy in America*. Cambridge: Harvard University Press, 1988.                    **185**

———. "William Shakespeare and the American People." In *Rethinking Popular Culture*, edited by Chandra Mukerji and Michael Schudson, 157–97. Berkeley: University of California Press, 1991.

"Life-Like but Only in Wax." *New York Saturday News*, 7 January 1891.

MacKay, Patricia. "Theme Parks, USA." *Theatre Crafts*, September 1971.

Mammen, Edward W. "The Old Stock Company: The Boston Museum and Other Nineteenth Century Theaters." *Bulletin of the Boston Public Library* 19, nos. 1–4 (January–April 1944).

Maples, Stace. "Viewpoint." *Piercing Fans International Quarterly*, no. 42 (1995): 3.

Martin, Douglas. "The Rebirth of a Sideshow at Coney Island." *New York Times*, 4 September 1992.

Matlaw, Myron, ed. *American Popular Entertainment*. Westport, Conn.: Greenwood, 1979.

McArthur, Judith N. "Demon Rum on the Boards: Temperance Melodrama and the Tradition of Antebellum Reform." *Journal of the Early Republic* 9 (winter 1989): 518–39.

McCabe, James D., Jr. *Lights and Shadows of New York Life*. New York: Farrar, Straus and Giroux, 1970.

McClung, Robert M., and Gale S. McClung. "Tammany's Remarkable Gardiner Baker." *New-York Historical Society Quarterly* 42 (April 1958): 142–69.

McConachie, Bruce A. "Museum Theatre and the Problem of Respectability for Mid-Century Urban Americans." In *The American Stage*, edited by Ron Engle and Tice L. Miller, 65–80. New York: Cambridge University Press, 1993.

McCullough, Edo. *Good Old Coney Island*. New York: Scribner's, 1957.

McGlinchee, Claire. *The First Decade of the Boston Museum*. Boston: Bruce Humphries, 1940.

McLean, Albert F., Jr. "Genesis of Vaudeville: Two Letters from B. F. Keith." *Theatre Survey* 1 (1960): 82–95.

———. *American Vaudeville as Ritual*. Lexington: University of Kentucky Press, 1965.

McNamara, Brooks. " 'A Congress of Wonders': The Rise and Fall of the Dime Museum." *Emerson Society Quarterly* 20 (3rd Quarter 1974): 216–32.

"Medusa, Child of the Sea, Oddest Human Wonder." *New York Herald*, 9 January 1934.

Middleton, George. *Circus Memoirs*. Los Angeles: George Rice, 1913.

Mink, Randy. "Movie Stars Cast in Wax Entertain Florida Tourists." *New York Post*, 5 August 1980.

Mitchell, Michael. *Monsters of the Gilded Age*. Toronto: Gage Press, 1979.

Moeller, Susan D. "The Cultural Construction of Urban Poverty: Images of Poverty in New York City, 1890–1917." *Journal of American Culture* 18, no. 4 (winter 1995): 1–16.

Musser, Charles. "The Early Cinema of Edwin Porter." *Cinema Journal* 19, no. 1 (winter 1979): 1–39.

———. "The Eden Musée in 1898: The Exhibitor as Creator." *Film and History* 11, no. 4 (December 1981): 73–82.

———. "The American Vitagraph, 1897–1901: Survival and Success in a Competitive Industry." In *Film before Griffith*, edited by John L. Fell, 22–66. Berkeley: University of California Press, 1983.

———. *The Emergence of the Cinema: The American Screen to 1907*. New York: Scribner's, 1990.

———. *Before the Nickelodeon*. Berkeley: University of California Press, 1991.

Nasaw, David. *Going Out*. New York: Basic Books, 1993.

"The National Baby Show." *New York Times*, 27 November 1877.

Norris, John, and Joan Norris. *Amusement Parks*. Jefferson, N.C.: McFarland, 1986.

Northall, William Knoght. *Before and Beyond the Curtain, or Fifty Years' Observation among the Theatres of New York*. New York: W. F. Burgess, 1851.

Odell, George C. D. *Annals of the New York Stage*. 15 vols. New York: Columbia University Press, 1927–49.

Orosz, J. "Curators and Culture: An Interpretive History of the Museum Movement in America, 1773–1870." Ann Arbor, Mich.: UMI Dissertation Information Services, 1986.

Paran, Janice. "Home Is Where Their Art Is." *American Theatre*, October 1992, 34–46.

Peiss, Kathy. *Cheap Amusements*. Philadelphia: Temple University Press, 1986.

Pilat, Oliver, and Jo Ranson. *Sodom by the Sea*. Garden City, N.Y.: Doubleday, Doran, 1941.

Pluchart, François. "Risk as the Practice of Thought." In *The Art of Performance*, edited by Gregory Battick and Robert Nickas, 125–34. New York: Dutton, 1984.

Pollock, Thomas Clark. *The Philadelphia Theatre in the Eighteenth Century*. Philadelphia: University of Pennsylvania Press, 1933.

Powers, Madelon. "Decay from Within: the Inevitable Doom of the American Saloon." In *Drinking*, edited by Susanna Barnes and Robin Room, 112–31. Berkeley: University of California Press, 1991.

Pulley, Brett. "Tussaud's and Movie Chain Join in Disney 42d Street Project." *New York Times*, 16 July 1995.

Quigley, Martin, Jr. *Magic Shadows: The Story of the Origin of Motion Pictures.* New York: Quigley, 1960.

Rahill, Frank. *The World of Melodrama.* University Park: Pennsylvania State University Press, 1967.

Rambusch, Catha Grace. "Museums and Other Collections in New York City, 1790–1870." M.A. thesis, New York University, 1965.

Ramsaye, Terry. *A Million and One Nights.* New York: Simon and Schuster, 1926.

Ripley, Dillon, *The Sacred Grove.* Washington, D.C.: Smithsonian Institution Press, 1969.

Ripley, Robert L. *Believe It or Not!* New York: Simon and Schuster, 1929.

"Ripley Gleans Curious Facts on Every Hand." *New York Times,* 27 December 1934.

"Ripley's Shows Boasts 25 Wonders." *New York Times,* 26 December 1934.

Rosenfeld, Hector. "Barnum's First Freaks." *New York Times Magazine,* 22 May 1904.

Rosenzweig, Roy. *Eight Hours for What We Will.* New York: Cambridge University Press, 1983.

Ryan, Kate. *Old Boston Museum Days.* Boston: Little, Brown, 1915.

Rydell, Robert. *All the World's a Fair.* Chicago: University of Chicago Press, 1984.

Sante, Luc. *Low Life.* New York: Farrar, Straus and Giroux, 1991.

Saxon, A. H. *P. T. Barnum: The Legend and the Man.* New York: Columbia University Press, 1989.

———, ed. *The Autobiography of Mrs. Tom Thumb.* Hamden, Conn.: Archon Books, 1979.

———. *Selective Letters of P. T. Barnum.* New York: Columbia University Press, 1983.

Schechner, Richard. "Restoration of Behavior." In *Between Theatre and Anthropology.* Philadelphia: University of Pennsylvania Press, 1985.

Schwartz, Alvin. *Museums: The Story of America's Treasure Houses.* New York: Dutton, 1967.

Sellers, Charles Coleman. *Patience Wright: American Artist and Spy in George III's London.* Middleton, Conn.: Wesleyan University Press, 1976.

———. *Mr. Peale's Museum: Charles Willson Peale and the First Popular Museum of Natural Science and Art.* New York: Norton, 1979.

Senelick, Laurence. "Variety and Vaudeville: The Process Observed in Two Manuscript Gagbooks." *Theatre Survey* 19, no. 1 (May 1978): 1–5.

———. *The Age and Stage of George L. Fox, 1825–1877.* Hanover, N.H.: University of New England Press, 1988.

Siegal, Fred. "Theatre of Guts: An Exploration of the Sideshow Aesthetic." *Drama Review* 35, no. 4 (winter 1991): 107–24.

Sifton, Paul G. "Pierre Eugène Du Simitière (1737–1784): Collector in Revolutionary America." Ph.D. diss., University of Pennsylvania, 1960.

*Sights and Wonder in New York.* New York: J. S. Redfield, 1849.

Singman, Tom. "Navel Maneuvers." *New York Times Magazine,* 22 January 1995.

Skinner, Otis. *Footlights and Spotlights.* Indianapolis: Bobbs-Merrill, 1924.

Slide, Anthony. *Early American Cinema.* Metuchen, N.J.: Scarecrow Press, 1994.

Snow, Richard. *Coney Island: A Postcard Journey to the City of Fire.* New York: Brightwaters Press, 1984.

Snyder, Robert. *The Voice of the City.* New York: Oxford University Press, 1989.

Southerland, Daniel E. *The Expansion of Everyday Life, 1860–1876.* New York: Harper and Row, 1989.

Spann, Edward K. *The New Metropolis.* New York: Columbia University Press, 1981.

Stansell, Christine. *City of Women: Sex and Class in New York, 1789–1860.* New York: Knopf, 1986.

Staples, Shirley. *Male-Female Comedy Teams in American Vaudeville.* Ann Arbor, Mich.: UMI Research Press, 1984.

Stein, Charles W., ed. *American Vaudeville.* New York: DaCapo Press, 1984.

Stocking, George, ed. *Objects and Others.* Madison: University of Wisconsin Press, 1985.

Stone, Henry Dickinson. *Theatrical Reminiscences.* New York: Benjamin Bloom, 1873.

Stover, Kate F. "Is It *Real* History Yet? An Update on Living History Museums." *Journal of American Culture* 12, no. 2 (summer 1989): 13–17.

Sussman, Warren I. *Culture as History: The Transformation of American Society in the Twentieth Century.* New York: Pantheon, 1984.

Taubman, Howard. *The Making of the American Theatre.* New York: Coward-McCann, 1965.

Taylor, Robert Lewis. "Profiles: Talker-II." *The New Yorker,* 26 April 1958.

Thomas, David. *The Origins of the Motion Picture.* London: Her Majesty's Stationery Office, 1964.

Thompson, C. J. S. *The Mystery and Lore of Monsters, with Accounts of Some Giants, Dwarfs, and Prodigies.* New York: Citadel Press, 1970.

Thomson, Rosemarie Garland, ed. *Freakery: Cultural Spectacles of the Extraordinary Body.* New York: New York University Press, 1996.

Ticknor, Howard Malcolm. "The Passing of the Boston Museum." *The New England Magazine* 27, no. 4 ( June 1903): 379–96.

Toll, Robert C. *Blacking Up.* New York: Oxford University Press, 1974.

———. *On with the Show.* New York: Oxford University Press, 1976.

Trollope, Francis. *Domestic Manners of America.* London, 1832. Reprint, New York: Knopf, 1949.

Tucker, Louis Leonard. " 'Ohio Show Shop': The Western Museum of Cincinnati, 1820–1867." In *A Cabinet of Curiosities: Five Episodes in the Evolution of American Museums,* edited by Whitfield J. Bell Jr., 73–105. Charlottesville: University Press of Virginia, 1967.

Twitchell, James B. *Carnival Culture.* New York: Columbia University Press, 1992.

Vardac, A. Nicholas. *From Stage to Screen.* Cambridge: Harvard University Press, 1949.

"A Visit to the Eden Musée." 28–30 September 1899. Museum of the City of New York.

"Visit Raven Chanticleer's Wax Museum." *New York Amsterdam News,* 4 December 1993.

Wall, A. J. "Wax Portraiture." *New York Historical Society Quarterly* 9, no. 1 (April 1925): 3–26.

Wallace, Irving. *The Fabulous Showman.* New York: Knopf, 1959.

Wallace, Michael. "Mickey Mouse History: Portraying the Past at Disney World." *Radical History Review* 32 (1985): 33–58.

———. "The Politics of Public History." In *Past Meets Present,* edited by Jo Blatti, 37–53. Washington, D.C.: Smithsonian Institution Press, 1987.

Wells, Helen. *Barnum, Showman of America.* New York: David McKay, 1957.

Werner, M. R. *Barnum.* New York: Harcourt, Brace, 1923.

Wilmeth, Don. *American and English Popular Entertainments.* Detroit: Book Tower, 1980.

———. *Variety Entertainment and Outdoor Amusements.* Westport, Conn.: Greenwood, 1982.

Wilson, Gahan. "Freaks." 25 April 1966. Clipping file, New York Public Library for the Performing Arts.

Wittenberg, Ernest. "Échec!" *American Heritage* 11, no. 2 (February 1960): 33–84.

Wittlin, Alma S. *The Museum: Its History and Its Task in Education.* London: Routledge and Kegan Paul, 1949.

Wood, J. G. "Dime Museums." *Atlantic Monthly* 55 (January–June 1855): 759–65.

Wright, Richardson. *Hawkers and Walkers in Early America.* Philadelphia: Lippincott, 1927.

*Selected Programs, Broadsides, and Guidebooks*

Sources: Billy Rose Theatre Collection, New York Public Library for the Performing Arts (NYPL); New-York Historical Society (NYHS); Museum of the City of New York (MCNY); Players Collection (PC); Adelphi University (AU);

Philadelphia Free Library (PFL); Chicago Historical Society (CHS); San Diego Historical Society (SDHA).

Barnum's "American Museum Illustrated," guidebook, 1850. NYHS; n.d., NYPL, AU.

**190**

Bill, Meade's Midget Hall, n.d. NYPL.

Bill, Travelling Museum, n.d. NYHS.

Broadside, American Museum, 1 June 1791, 25 November 1773. NYHS.

Broadside, Barnum's New Museum, 2 September 1865. NYHS.

Broadside, Boston Museum. In *Hawkers and Walkers in Early America*. Philadelphia: J. B. Lippincott, 1927.

Broadside, Egyptian Museum, 1855. NYHS.

Broadside, Mrs. Jarley's Wax-Works Show, 10 May 1870. NYHS.

Broadside, "Museum and Wax-works," 25 November 1793, NYHS.

Broadside, Peale's New York Museum, c. 1840. NYHS.

Broadside, Scudder's American Museum, 1 July 1819. NYHS.

Broadside, Star Museum, 11 March 1889. NYPL.

Broadside, Tammany Museum, 29 September 1794. NYHS.

Guidebook, [Boston] Eden Musée and chamber of horrors, n.d. Collection of Brooks McNamara.

Guidebook, Eden Musée, 1884, 1885, 1886, 1887, 1890, 1897, 1898, 1899, 1905, 1906, 1907, 1909. NYHS, NYPL.

Guidebook, Egyptian Musée, n.d. PC.

Guidebook, Guinness World of Records. Author's collection.

Guidebook, Madame Tussaud's, 1897, 1986. NYPL, author's collection.

Guidebook, New York Museum of Anatomy, 1863, 1870. NYPL, NYHS.

Guidebook, Ripley's Believe It or Not! Author's collection.

*Life of the Living Aztec Children*, 1860. NYPL.

"Museum and Wax-Works," broadside, 25 November 1793. NYHS.

Program, American Museum, 1 June 1791. NYHS.

Program, Austin and Stone's Dime Museum, 28 November 1891. NYPL.

Program, Boston Museum, 1852, 1872. NYPL.

Program, Bunnell's Museum, 28 November 1891. NYPL.

Program, Colonel Wood's Museum, Chicago, n.d. CHS

Program, Colonel Wood's Museum, Philadelphia, n.d. PFL.

Program, Egyptian Museum, 1886. PFL.

Program, European Museum, n.d. PFL.

Program, Hagar and Campbell's New Dime Museum, 1883. PFL.

Program, Hope Chapel, 1860. NYPL.

Program, Ninth and Arch Museum, 1889, 1892. PFL.

Program, Zoro Gardens Home of the Nudists, 1935. SDHA.

Prospectus, Barnum's Museum Company, n.d. NYHS.

Scudder, John. *A Companion to the American Museum.* New York: G. F. Hopkins, 1823. NYHS

*Sketch of the Life of Miss Millie-Christine; or, Christine-Millie,* n.d. NYPL.

*Sketch of the Life, Personal Appearance, Character and Manners of Charles S. Stratton, the Man in Miniature Known as General Tom Thumb.* New York: Van Norden and Amerman, 1847. NYPL, NYHS.

**191**

# Index

# About the Author

A teacher, actor, and director, Andrea Stulman Dennett received her Ph.D. in Performance Studies from New York University. She has written on many aspects of popular entertainment from television talk shows to disaster spectacles at the turn of the century.